An Augustinian Essay on Toleration

An Augustinian Essay on Toleration

MANFRED SVENSSON

OXFORD
UNIVERSITY PRESS

OXFORD
UNIVERSITY PRESS

Great Clarendon Street, Oxford, OX2 6DP,
United Kingdom

Oxford University Press is a department of the University of Oxford.
It furthers the University's objective of excellence in research, scholarship,
and education by publishing worldwide. Oxford is a registered trade mark of
Oxford University Press in the UK and in certain other countries.

Published in the United States of America by Oxford University Press
546 Fifth Avenue, New York, NY 10036, United States of America.

British Library Cataloguing in Publication Data
Data available

Library of Congress Control Number: 2026942268

ISBN 9780197912720

DOI: 10.1093/9780197912737.001.0001

The manufacturer's authorized representative in the EU for product safety is
Oxford University Press España S.A. of Parque Empresarial San Fernando de Henares,
Avenida de Castilla, 2 – 28830 Madrid (www.oup.es/en or product.safety@oup.com).
OUP España S.A. also acts as importer into Spain of products made by the manufacturer.

Contents

Acknowledgments

I have been interested in the history of toleration for almost as long as my memory of things academic reaches back. Sadly, my memory is less precise when it comes to recalling all those who, through their conversation, have kept this interest alive and to whom I owe thanks. Many of these are former students. I first taught a course on toleration in 2010 and have regularly returned to this topic and to the philosophers whose work informs this book. I have learned much from my students at the University of the Andes, and they are the first I want to thank.

The first concrete step toward this book was an essay on tolerance that won the 2011 Prize for Essays in Contemporary Humanities, organized by the Humanities Department of Diego Portales University, the Arts and Letters supplement of the newspaper *El Mercurio*, and the Chilean Goethe-Institute. I am grateful to all involved at these institutions; the idea of a longer book on tolerance took shape thanks to their generosity. Jeffrey Stevenson translated a revised version of that essay into English, though this proved premature: I would continue working on this project for many years, and little remains of the sections Jeff liked most. Special thanks go to Luis Placencia, whose critical discussion convinced me to set aside Spinoza and focus on authors I could better understand. At a slightly later stage, I had the opportunity to collaborate with Holger Zaborowski on a special issue on Locke's *Letter* and with Vyacheslav Karpov on a collective volume on toleration and secularization. Both projects significantly broadened my concerns and my readings. Over the years, I have presented on the various themes addressed in this book at Westminster Seminary California, the University of Magallanes, and the L'Abri Fellowship in Belo Horizonte. I am grateful to the participants at these events for their thoughtful engagement.

If the final version of this book took so long, this is partly because competing interests often pushed it to the background. But it is also because I was convinced only gradually to give Augustine the prominent place he now holds. I had been thinking about Augustine's potential contribution to this topic for a long time—Martín Cuevas will probably recall our discussions dating back to 2008—but the decision to make this connection central to this book grew out of conversations with my colleagues Joaquín García-Huidobro and Daniel

Mansuy. I am grateful to work in an intellectual milieu in which proper attention to Augustine has always been the norm. I have also long benefited from collaborating with Patricio Domínguez. We have both repeatedly taught on the *City of God*, and for several years we worked together on translating Augustine's philosophical letters into Spanish. This has been essential to the understanding of Augustine that readers will find in this book.

The essay evolved from a long-term interest in both toleration and Augustine that matured in recent years. The final stages of the work were made possible in part by funding from the National Fund for Scientific and Technological Development (Fondecyt, Chile, Project No. 1240636). Among other things, this grant enabled my research stays at the de Nicola Center for Culture and Ethics at the University of Notre Dame. Special thanks to Jennifer Newsome Martin and Margaret Cabaniss at the de Nicola Center. The final draft benefited from the careful reading of Gabriela Caviedes and Eduardo Fuentes, and subsequently of two anonymous reviewers at Oxford University Press. I owe them all deep gratitude for investing their time and for their helpful feedback. Any remaining faults are my own. At Oxford University Press, I am grateful for the encouragement and guidance of Tom Perridge and Sofia Belimova. As has often been the case in recent years, I must thank Rebecca West for her careful revision of my English. My greatest debt, as always, is to Carolina, Félix, Tobías, and Linnéa.

Abbreviations

In what follows, I have used the abbreviations of the *Augustinus-Lexikon* (Basel: Schwabe, 1986–2024) and the Latin critical editions listed below. Unless otherwise stated, translations of Augustine's works are my own.

bapt.	*De baptismo libri septem*	CSEL 51
beata v.	*De beata vita*	CCSL 29
cat. rud.	*De cathecizandis rudibus*	CCSL 46
c. ep. Parm.	*Contra epistulam Parmeniani*	CSEL 51
c. Faust.	*Contra Faustum Manicheum*	CSEL 25, 1
civ.	*De civitate Dei*	CCSL 47–48
c.litt. Pet.	*Contra litteras Petiliani*	CSEL 52
c. mend.	*Contra mendacium*	CSEL 41
conf.	*Confessiones*	CCSL 27
doctr. chr.	*De doctrina christiana*	CCSL 32
ench.	*De fide, spe et caritate*	CCSL 46
en. Ps.	*Enarrationes in Psalmos*	CCSL 38-40
ep.	*Epistulae*	CCSL 31-31B/CSEL 44/57
exp. Gal.	*Expositio epistulae ad Galatas*	CSEL 84
f. et op.	*De fide et operibus liber unus*	CSEL 41
gr. et lib. arb.	*De gratia et libero arbitrio*	PL 44
lib. arb.	*De libero arbitrio*	CCSL 29
ord.	*De ordine*	CCSL 29
pat.	*De patientia liber unus*	CSEL 41
perf. iust.	*De perfectione iustitiae hominis*	CSEL 42
s.	*Sermones*	PL 38/PLS/Dolbeau
s. dom. m.	*De sermone domini in monte*	CCSL 35
spir. et litt.	*De spiritu et littera*	CSEL 60
trin.	*De trinitate*	CCSL 50/50A
vera rel.	*De vera religione*	CCSL 32

Series containing these critical editions

CCSL	Corpus Christianorum. Series Latina. Turnhout, 1959–.
CSEL	Corpus Scriptorum Ecclesiasticorum Latinorum. Vienna, 1866–.
Dolbeau	*Vingt-six sermons au peuple d'Afrique*. Paris, 1996.
PL	Patrologiae cursus completus, Series Latina (ed. J.P. Migne). Paris, 1844–64. Supplementum (ed. Hamman). Paris, 1958–1974.

Introduction

Rooted Toleration

"Each story shows how hatred and intolerance, through all the ages, have battled against love and charity." These are the opening words of *Intolerance: Love's Struggle Through the Ages*, one of the great films of the silent era. Released in 1916, it presented four stories that sought to illustrate this message of opposition between intolerance and love.[1] The four stories are widely separated in time: a contemporary drama of labor disputes, the intrigues surrounding the St Bartholomew's Day Massacre, the crucifixion of Christ, and the fall of Babylon in 539 BC. These stories are not only separated chronologically but arguably disparate in their nature and causes as well. But the film's producer, D.W. Griffith, does not seem to have been of this opinion. He believed that the analogies between these events were strong enough to produce a great epic drama. And there was undoubtedly a thread that connected them. In all four stories, the intrigues of the powerful inflict suffering on ordinary citizens. This is not an arbitrary link between distinct chapters of human history. The question is whether "intolerance" is an appropriate umbrella term under which to present this drama. After all, historians and students of toleration will recognize only one of these stories—the St Bartholomew's Day Massacre—as their typical subject matter.

What kind of mentality includes the fall of an ancient empire, early twentieth-century social dramas, and the crucifixion of Christ under the same heading as that massacre? The answer to this question opens the door to much of the contemporary confusion regarding toleration. In this film, every conceivable vice is understood as a form of intolerance: the exploitative capitalist of the early twentieth century and the hypocritical Pharisee of the first years of our era share the same fundamental vice. Intriguingly, though intolerance is seen as the cause of all human misery, tolerance plays no positive role in this

[1] For the background and reception of the film (most positive in the Soviet Union!) see William Drew, *D.W. Griffith's Intolerance: Its Genesis and Its Vision* (Jefferson, NC: McFarland, 1986).

An Augustinian Essay on Toleration. Manfred Svensson, Oxford University Press. © Manfred Svensson 2026.
DOI: 10.1093/9780197912737.003.0001

film. After summarizing all vices as intolerance, we are to set our hopes on progressively leaving these vices behind until love can ultimately triumph. How to act if love does not win—on this there is silence.

A century later, the approach to toleration we find in Griffith's *Intolerance* remains in good standing. Of course, some things have changed. Toleration was absent from the film, while it is often present in our discourse. But the presence of this word should not deceive us: the flight from intolerance continues to be driven by unclear ideas of what we hope will take its place. We invoke tolerance, but we expect it to play the same role that love played in Griffith's film. We treat it like a weak form of love. Like Griffith's love, this tolerance is treated as an independent virtue in which all goods are summed up. It is an all-encompassing virtue, and it is no wonder that so many prefer to leave the word tolerance behind and describe this project with a different title.

In this book, I rather insist on the value of toleration, while remaining attentive to the larger framework on which it depends. There is a soil in which tolerance can grow; there are other virtues that should accompany it. It depends on a broad web of moral dispositions, but also on a vision of evil and conflict, of history, hope, and personhood. In his *Eclipse of Reason*, published in 1946, Max Horkheimer counted tolerance among the concepts that had lost their roots, including their intellectual roots, noting that though such concepts continue to be posited as goals, "there is no rational agency authorized to appraise and link them to an objective reality."[2] The result is a discourse on tolerance that has reached the point of exhaustion. Our calls for toleration may have become sterile precisely because they first became orphaned. This book seeks to establish what toleration would look like if it were to be rescued from this state of orphanhood. It will do this by sketching some rival understandings of toleration and then explaining its nature, subjects, and limits within a broadly Augustinian framework.

As this initial description suggests, limits are important, but they can demand only a small part of our attention. The concerns about them, however, are instructive. The expanded limits of toleration are seen by some as one of the great problems of our society. This may be more controversial in certain areas than in others, but as a general observation I take this concern to be justified. A permissive society may proudly compare itself to a totalitarian one, but it has its own pathologies. A permissive approach to drug use, to the use of digital technology, or even to vulgarity may show its worst consequences only after significant parts of our social life have already been wrecked. Many of

[2] Max Horkheimer, *Eclipse of Reason* (New York and London: Continuum, 2004), 16.

our problems can be described in terms of such permissiveness. But this concern with the limits of toleration also takes another form, when Christians and members of other traditional faiths start to feel cornered, and the complaint about the limits of toleration begins to point to its narrowness, to the "intolerance of the tolerants." Here the problem is that tolerance is not wide enough, and *we* are outside the limits of the tolerable. These two reactions are not necessarily contradictory. There may be much to be said for both the observation of the loss of traditional limits and the criticism of the boundaries that are put in their place. But if this is all one has to say regarding toleration, it will inevitably be read as opportunistic. Why were arbitrary (or seemingly arbitrary) limits on toleration not so relevant before? This is how such complaints are read, and this reading is partly justified. If there are serious problems in the contemporary approach to toleration, these should be addressed not with simple one-liners about the excesses and the narrowness of toleration, but with careful reflection, not only thinking about the limits of toleration but about its nature as well.

But what is its nature? Here is another instructive complaint. Many today claim that tolerance should be abandoned not as an excessive but rather an insufficient ideal. This kind of criticism comes from various perspectives. Many see the affirmative attitudes that Christians are called to have, the general call to love, or the specific call to "honor everyone" (1 Pet. 2:17) as incompatible with the reticence that is part and parcel of tolerance. New Testament scholar N.T. Wright, for example, equates tolerance with shrugging our shoulders and walking away, leaving others to do their own thing. Who could doubt that this falls short of Christian character? If that is a good description of tolerance, love should certainly take its place.[3] Wright is not alone. In the words of archbishop Charles Chaput, tolerance is "a negative. And it's not a Christian virtue."[4] This is only the Christian version of a critique of toleration that runs across contemporary thought, with recognition, respect, hospitality, and other dispositions continually proposed as replacements for what appears to be the arrogant and condescending nature of modern tolerance. Is this in fact its nature? The idea of toleration seems to come under fire from very different corners of our religious, political, and academic world. But that situation has also invited widely differing voices in its support. I find myself broadly concurring with such positions. Tolerance is often a just and humane answer to our conflicts. It will

[3] N.T. Wright, *After You Believe: Why Christian Character Matters* (New York: HarperOne, 2012), 254.
[4] Charles J. Chaput, "Religious Tolerance and the Common Good," *First Things*, May 23, 2007, https://www.firstthings.com/web-exclusives/2007/05/religious-tolerance-and-the-common-good.

never be replaced by love, hospitality, or recognition. But if voices from multiple quarters acknowledge this fact, we must address the usual question: why *another* book on this virtue?

The Lost Foundations of Toleration

In recent years, defenses of the limited project called toleration have come from a range of positions, including both philosophers who defend various forms of the Enlightenment heritage and believers within robust confessional traditions.[5] How different are these approaches? Let us consider theologian D. A. Carson's *The Intolerance of Tolerance*. As this title indicates, it touches on many of the contemporary concerns we have just summarized. In fact, it is a fairly standard defense of the traditional practice of toleration by an orthodox Calvinist theologian who appreciates something like an "Enlightenment legacy" in this regard. Critical references to postmodernism abound in this work, and the "old tolerance" he sets out to defend is substantively represented by authors such as Voltaire, Lessing, and Mill.[6] This makes sense if our understanding of tolerance has gone astray in recent decades. And this is the predominant view in contemporary apologies of tolerance. When we read about the need for "recovering toleration's lost foundations," this literature means modern foundations.[7] In contrast, in this book I emphasize that many of the trends that are rightly described as problematic—from the calls to leave tolerance behind to the blurring of the distinction between persuasion and intolerance—are not as recent as is often imagined. These are rather confusions that have deep roots in early modern thought. Thus, while it is true that throughout this work I defend a series of practices that are often regarded as typically modern (and I do not dispute the many ways in which this is true), there are "lost foundations" further back that deserve our attention.

But this book is not an essay on the history of toleration. Enormous progress has been made over the past decades in the historical investigation of the idea

[5] For a version of "radical" Enlightenment that defends toleration in opposition to Christian influence see Jonathan Israel, *Radical Enlightenment. Philosophy and the Making of Modernity 1650–1750* (Oxford: Oxford University Press, 2001), 265–70. For a "moderate" alternative—defending a moderate Enlightenment (Israel's terminology) and acknowledging religious roots of tolerance—see Jürgen Habermas, *Between Naturalism and Religion. Philosophical Essays* (Cambridge: Polity, 2008), 251–311.

[6] Donald Carson, *The Intolerance of Tolerance* (Grand Rapids: Eerdmans, 2012).

[7] So, for instance, Adam Wolfson, "What Remains of Toleration," in *The Liberal Tradition in Focus: Problems and New Perspectives*, ed. João Carlos Espada, Marc F. Plattner, and Adam Wolfson (New York and Oxford: Lexington Books, 2000), 37. Another good example is Ingrid Creppell, *Toleration and Identity. Foundations in Early Modern Thought* (New York and London: Routledge, 2003).

and practice of toleration. As a result, the ancient, medieval, and early modern worlds are now more familiar territory for historians of toleration. This historical research may still suffer from many gaps, and several chapters will likely forever be disputed. But there can be no doubt about the 180-degree turn that has taken place.[8] If decades ago F.A. Hayek could write that tolerance is "of course" essentially and inseparably linked to the history of liberalism, today such a statement would reveal only an appalling ignorance of the relevant historical scholarship.[9] Liberalism, to be sure, plays a significant role in the history of toleration, and toleration in the history of liberalism. But wherever there are human beings, conflicts arise—here an "of course" is more apt—and wherever conflicts arise, the possibility for tolerance appears. In other words, we have always had tolerance. Sometimes it emerges only as a pragmatic solution, to be resolved without appeal to great philosophical or theological theories. But often it leads to deeper reflections, some of which truly deserve a place in the history of the idea of toleration.

Our recent turn to this premodern history of toleration has, however, mostly had the effect of making the history of this idea more colorful. Let me illustrate this point with a contribution by Cary Nederman, who has been at the forefront of this historical task. In a survey essay, he rightly criticizes the double prejudice that makes toleration a merely modern and merely Western phenomenon. The four alternative approaches to toleration he traces to medieval and non-Western sources are skepticism, functionalism, nationalism, and mysticism. Now it is true that these approaches differ from the arguments for toleration that we most commonly hear. But it is not in the least clear that they can reshape our discourse on toleration where it is most in need of reform. Take mysticism, for example. Here Nederman follows religious scholar Gustav Mensching in pointing to a mysticism that makes God's omnipresence the starting point for an argument for respect for all that exists. "One good way does not conflict with another," writes Meister Eckart, a statement that is

[8] See, among others, Cary Nederman and John Christian Laursen, eds, *Difference and Dissent: Theories of Toleration in Medieval and Early Modern Europe* (Lanham, MD: Rowman & Littlefield, 1996); Harald Zimmermann and Alexander Patschovsky, eds, *Toleranz im Mittelalter* (Sigmaringen: J. Thorbecke, 1998); Cary Nederman, *Worlds of Difference: European Discourses of Toleration c. 1100–c. 1550* (University Park, PA: The Pennsylvania State University Press, 2000); John Coffey, *Persecution and Toleration in Protestant England 1558–1689* (Essex: Pearson Education, 2000); Andrew R. Murphy, *Conscience and Community: Revisiting Toleration and Religious Dissent in Early Modern England and America* (University Park: Pennsylvania State University Press, 2001); Benjamin Kaplan, *Divided by Faith. Religious Conflict and the Practice of Toleration in Early Modern Europe* (Cambridge, Mass: The Belknap Press of Harvard University Press, 2007). Closest to the argument of this book is Jed W. Atkins, *The Christian Origins of Tolerance* (Oxford: Oxford University Press, 2024).

[9] Friedrich Hayek, "Individual and Collective Aims," in *On Toleration*, ed. Susan Mendus and David Edwards (Oxford: Oxford University Press, 1987), 46.

approvingly quoted by both Mensching and Nederman.[10] But this is quite revealing about the limits of their project.[11] Like Griffith's *Intolerance*, it assumes that love wins and that all the *ways* in question are good. Consequently, it does not give us a single word of advice about how to deal with ways that are in conflict. This is the fundamental flaw of such projects. If some forms of modern progressivism would make us believe that such conflicting ways will disappear, that we are moving towards a consensus we will all be able to celebrate, such an illusion will not be corrected by a premodern mysticism that drifts in the same direction.

I hope that, in contrast, this book will make some modern and premodern insights into the idea of toleration fruitful for a constructive contemporary enterprise that, without being agonistic, recognizes that conflict is not eradicable. Given his view that the contest between the two cities will persist "until the final judgment," it should come as no surprise that Augustine is a key player in this discussion.[12] Augustine is, furthermore, an authority across Christian traditions, a fact that still gives particular weight to his insights. Some other Augustinian voices, such as those of Aquinas or Calvin, will also join us along the road, but this is above all a constructive essay that draws on Augustine himself. As noted by John Bowlin, appeal to authors such as Augustine can help to protect tolerance from the "collateral damage" it can suffer in the midst of passionate contemporary debate about the merits or demerits of modernity and, we should add, the merits and demerits of liberalism.[13]

To be sure, there are serious risks attendant upon such a search for light in the past. We may well end up projecting our own beliefs onto the texts of those who would find contemporary values nearly inconceivable and certainly unacceptable. But there is also a danger that this caution will blind us to the calls for tolerance that are actually there: not wishing to see *laissez-faire* individualism

[10] Cary Nederman, "Toleration in a New Key: Historical and Global Perspectives," *Critical Review of International Social and Political Philosophy* 14, no. 3 (2011): 356. Eckart is, of course, just one example. The more usual late-medieval candidate is Nicholas of Cusa. In the words of Solari, his is a "medieval version of tolerance, with a certain modern air." Enzo Solari, "De pace fidei: de la libertad a la tolerancia," *Teología y vida* 53, no. 4 (2012): 472. For all of its medieval roots, Ratzinger has rightly described this as the standard contemporary view of religious toleration. Joseph Ratzinger, *Truth and Tolerance. Christian Belief and World Religions*, trans. Henry Taylor (San Francisco: Ignatius Press, 2004), 21–23.

[11] I have discussed another contemporary version of this argument (in that case drawing from Cusa and Bodin) in Manfred Svensson, "Beyond Dogmatomachy: Eric Voegelin's Bodinian Understanding of Toleration and Symbolization," *The European Legacy* 26, no. 6 (2021): 587–602. As I argue there, in this matter Bodinian elements overshadow the otherwise Augustinian thought of Voegelin.

[12] *civ.* I, 35.

[13] John Bowlin, "Tolerance Among the Fathers," *Journal of the Society of Christian Ethics* 26, no. 1 (2006): 3–36.

in Paul or Augustine, we may end up not seeing their calls for patience.[14] This is an attempt to see them and to draw out the consequences for contemporary thinking about toleration.

Augustinian Liberalism?

This turn to Augustine will come as no surprise to those familiar with the way Augustine's political thought has been received and interpreted during the past decades. In 1970 Robert Markus' *Saeculum: History and Society in the Theology of St. Augustine* opened the eyes of a generation to the complexity of Augustine's developing social thought.[15] Previously, Augustine had often been characterized as an apologist of a Christianized Rome. Looking at the expansion of Christendom, for example, one medieval author wrote that now there was only "one city," as if the conflicting loves about which Augustine wrote would cease to exist under the conditions of a Christian empire.[16] In contrast, Markus reminded readers of Augustine's deep insight into the ambivalence of all things temporal, empires included. This did not incline Augustine to read the Empire as the Beast of Revelation 13, but rather to seek a middle way between this apocalyptic tradition and the Eusebian celebration of the Empire. How can this distinctive approach be described? At its heart we obviously find the idea of the two cities. In book XV of the *City of God* Augustine writes that it is only "figuratively" (*mystice*) that he had written about two cities.[17] In other words, he wrote about two cities not as two empirically different political realities but as different psychological orientations or types of love. Types of love do of course establish types of communities, but these communities unfold their historical existence intermingled and intertwined. Markus stressed not only their intermingling, but also their invisibility. If the two loves could in no way be identified with the Church or with Pagan Rome, Augustine might more easily become a fruitful conversation partner in the contemporary political discussion. Markus himself would later revise some aspects of his interpretation. Since Augustine rejected both the Eusebian celebration of the Christian Empire and its apocalyptic identification with the Antichrist, Markus had

[14] This justified caution, and the concomitant problems, stand out in Stephen C. Barton, "Paul and the Limits of Tolerance," in *Tolerance and Intolerance in Early Judaism and Christianity*, ed. Guy G. Stroumsa and Graham N. Stanton (Cambridge: Cambridge University Press, 1998), 121–34.

[15] Robert Markus, *Saeculum: History and Society in the Age of St. Augustine* (Cambridge: Cambridge University Press, 1970).

[16] Otto of Freising, quoted in Markus, 164.

[17] *civ.* XV, 1.

interpreted his conception of Rome as "theologically neutral."[18] Augustine's critique of the sacral conception of the Empire, he had written in *Saeculum*, "implies a pluralistic, religiously neutral civic community."[19] As he would later reframe it, neither government nor politics in general is neutral. History, however, is.[20] The intermingling of the two cities is a feature of the whole of historical existence. It will be overcome, but not in history. An Augustine thus emerged whose work could enter contemporary discussion in numerous constructive ways, baffling both conservative and liberal expectations about the orientation of his work.

More recent work has been less inclined to stress the invisibility of the two cities, and it can thus largely be considered "post Markus."[21] But in any case the door had been opened for the extremely rich work of the past several decades, in what pertains both to the actual exposition of Augustine's thought and to creative Augustinian political thinking regarding liberal and secular politics.[22] Among these more systematic efforts we find some who would describe their project as "Augustinian liberalism." This label is sometimes projected back on mid-twentieth-century authors, but it was not in fact coined until 1991, by Paul Weithman. The liberal dimension of Weithman's approach was his Rawlsian restriction of religious argument; the Augustinian element was the grounding of this precept in humility. Unconcerned with deadly sins such as pride, the typical liberal approach rather sets out to curb human cruelty or treachery. As Weithman argues, liberals would gain by also considering extraordinary vices such as pride. Since acts of pride can be characterized as "motivated by an undue desire for preeminence or superiority," those concerned with pride should have "reason to accept the liberal constraint on their political argument."[23] Eric Gregory has given us the most substantive defense

[18] Markus, *Saeculum: History and Society in the Age of St. Augustine*, 55.

[19] Markus, 173.

[20] Robert A. Markus, *Christianity and the Secular* (Notre Dame: University of Notre Dame Press, 2006), 49–70.

[21] For a good synthesis of this shift see James Wetzel, "Introduction," in *Augustine's City of God: A Critical Guide* (Cambridge: Cambridge University Press, 2012), 2–5.

[22] Along with the more recent works I will discuss below, one should at least count Jean Bethke Elshtain, *Augustine and the Limits of Politics* (Notre Dame: University of Notre Dame Press, 1997); John von Heyking, *Augustine and Politics as Longing in the World* (Columbia: University of Missouri Press, 2001); Charles Mathewes, *The Republic of Grace: Augustinian Thoughts for Dark Times* (Grand Rapids: Eerdmans, 2010); Veronica Roberts Ogle, *Politics and the Earthly City in Augustine's City of God* (Cambridge: Cambridge University Press, 2021).

[23] Paul Weithman, "Toward an Augustinian Liberalism," *Faith and Philosophy* 8, no. 4 (1991): 466 and 470. For a critique centered on the different understandings of pride in Augustine and early modern liberalism, see Michael P. Krom, "Modern Liberalism and Pride. An Augustinian Perspective," *Journal of Religious Ethics* 35, no. 3 (2007): 453–77. For a more substantive discussion of the place of humility in Augustine's political thought see Mary M. Keys, *Pride, Politics, and Humility in Augustine's City of God* (Cambridge: Cambridge University Press, 2022).

of the importance of one such extraordinary virtue, namely love. His ambitious *Politics and the Order of Love* has rightly been praised for the way it reintegrates the perfectionist side of Augustine's understanding of love with his non-perfectionist politics. Besides giving us an account of the way Augustinian reflection on love can nourish liberalism, Gregory has offered a good description of the different kinds of Augustinian liberalism. Over against the dominant Augustinian realism of a Niebuhrian kind, which stresses the limits of politics, and over against the association of Augustine with Rawls, presented by Weithman, Gregory calls for a mixture of "Augustinian moral psychology, perfectionist ethics, and liberal politics," an orientation he identifies with Martin Luther King Jr.[24]

Though Gregory in no way is parochial, there is something peculiarly American to each part of his classification of Augustinian liberalisms. And if Martin Luther King Jr is "the great Augustinian liberal of modernity,"[25] he may also be the one most closely linked to the history of a particular nation. Writing from outside that context, I see no pressing need to take issue with each of these liberalisms. It may appear that I am closest to Niebuhr's realism, though changing the focus from the restraining of evil toward an emphasis on its permission (through self-restraining tolerance). But what I am presenting here is not a full-fledged vision of political life. I defend restraint (self-restraint and political restraint), but I do not reduce politics to restraint (nor did Niebuhr, obviously). I am critical of those who would leave tolerance behind in their search for some higher virtue. I believe that toleration as a specific "negative" ideal must be defended, but I concur with those who admonish us to something more than the critique of utopian thinking. I make an Augustinian defense of the specific virtue of tolerance, but one that is compatible with giving prominence to other "extraordinary" or "positive" virtues as well (Michael Lamb's recent discussion of hope being a good example[26]).

Thus, while I obviously rely on much that has been written within the strands of Augustinian liberalism, I do not claim to write on behalf of any of them, nor on behalf of any other type of liberalism (or postliberalism). I write, with the help of Augustine, on a particular virtue, tolerance, that is commonly thought to be rooted in the liberal tradition. Given my doubts about that rooting, it would be strange to label my effort as situated within any kind of liberalism.

[24] Eric Gregory, *Politics and the Order of Love. An Augustinian Ethic of Democratic Citizenship* (Chicago: The University of Chicago Press, 2008), 13.
[25] Gregory, 19.
[26] Michael Lamb, *A Commonwealth of Hope. Augustine's Political Thought* (Princeton: Princeton University Press, 2022). Lamb's, we should note, is more of a "republican" than a "liberal" Augustinianism.

For anyone thinking about toleration, however, there is a rich store of shared concerns with the liberal tradition. Whether one emphasizes the differences between that tradition and Augustinianism or speaks of an Augustinian liberalism, this is a discussion that can only help those involved to clarify their positions, gaining both depth and precision.

It is noteworthy, however, that toleration—regarded by many, friend and foe, as *the* liberal virtue—has been largely absent from this discussion. Augustinians who engage with it are often eager to show that Augustine helps us move beyond it. Both the work of Eric Gregory and that of Kristen Johnson, for instance, share this inclination, though Johnson's somewhat more explicitly. Both, indeed, can be said to move discussions on liberalism in a deeper direction by moving beyond toleration; in the case of Gregory through a robust discussion of love as a political virtue, in that of Johnson through showing how Augustinian theology can help us enrich public conversation in ways that avoid the pitfalls both of liberal toleration and of the agonistic assertion of conflict.[27] These concerns are justified, but it is also possible to go deeper than the garden-variety toleration without going beyond it. The work of Augustine is particularly suited to lead us in such a project, not only because of his fundamental positions on the nature of peace and conflict but also because of his actual observations, manifold and acute, on toleration.

Given the negative role that Augustine's writings have played in the history of coercion, this is obviously a controversial claim.[28] To those who cannot imagine that anything worthwhile about toleration could have come from Augustine's pen, I do not wish to offer any argument in advance. I offer this book as the evidence to be considered, hoping that the discussion will prove useful to Augustinians, liberals, and Augustinian liberals of all stripes. I write, however, especially with those in mind who, whatever their broader intellectual commitments, think about toleration. Thomas Nagel once wrote that "liberalism should provide the devout with a reason for tolerance."[29] One may wonder whether liberalism has succeeded in this regard, but in recent

[27] Kristen Deede Johnson, *Theology, Political Theory, and Pluralism: Beyond Tolerance and Difference* (Cambridge: Cambridge University Press, 2007). This is, however, a very moderate version of the "beyond tolerance" discourse, conscious that it "will not occur in this saeculum" (p.177).

[28] For summaries of the reception see Klaus Schreiner, "'Duldsamkeit' (tolerantia) oder 'Schrecken' (terror).' Reaktionsformen auf Abweichungen von der religiösen Norm, am Beispiel des augustinischen Toleranz- und Gewaltkonzeptes und dessen Rezeption im Mittelalter und in der frühen Neuzeit," in *Religiöse Devianz. Untersuchungen zu sozialen, rechtlichen und theologischen Reaktionen auf religiöse Abweichungen im westlichen und östlichen Mittelalter*, ed. Dieter Simon (Frankfurt: Klostermann, 1990), 159–210; and Daniel Mansuy and Manfred Svensson, "Tolerance," in *The Oxford Guide to the Historical Reception of Augustine*, vol. 3, ed. Karla Pollmann and Willemien Otten (Oxford: Oxford University Press, 2013), 1815–18.

[29] Thomas Nagel, "Moral Conflict and Political Legitimacy," *Philosophy and Public Affairs* 16, no. 3 (1987): 229.

decades the discussion of toleration has certainly been enriched by many new perspectives, some of which have made toleration a more attractive ideal for religious believers. But "the devout" can also look for such reasons among their own, and in doing this they can actually help their fellow citizens to arrive at richer accounts of toleration. After all, if tolerance is the answer to the "Manichean" nature of contemporary debates, the great opponent of that mentality was Augustine rather than John Stuart Mill.

Just Enduring

Toleration is presented in this Augustinian essay as a form of enduring. What is tolerated is put up with, not celebrated; it is endured, not enjoyed. Because of this reticent character of tolerance, it is often referred to as "mere" tolerance. Some call it "mere" toleration in order to disparage it, others to commend it. In the real world, as William Galston has written, there is actually nothing "mere" about it.[30] One can even speak, as Jeremy Webber, of the "generosity of toleration."[31] So I join those who commend this grudging disposition, while noting that this "mere" enduring is also a "just" enduring. "Patience—writes Augustine—is tolerating evils for the sake of justice."[32] We must stress the limited nature of tolerance, but there is clearly more than passive resignation in this view of tolerant bearing of evils. We are often called to a just exercise of tolerance. Besides this relation to justice, this book presents tolerance as embedded in other virtues. As Robert Dodaro has noted, "studies of Augustine's political thought to date have for the most part ignored the role of virtues."[33] Toleration is one of the areas in which that approach can be particularly fruitful. I will offer no detailed account of Augustine's view of virtues, nor will I spend much time with the specific virtues required to develop tolerance. I will, however, highlight the importance of the unity of the virtues, a teaching that becomes particularly visible when Augustine writes concerning toleration. A topic like the unity of the virtues—common to all ancient virtue ethicists, but with some unique Augustinian emphases—may sound awkward to our ears. But there are no solitary virtues, and the idea of their fundamental

[30] William Galston, *Liberal Pluralism: The Implications of Value Pluralism for Political Theory and Practice* (Cambridge: Cambridge University Press, 2002), 120.

[31] Jeremy Webber, "The Generosity of Toleration," in *Recognition versus Self-Determination. Dilemmas of Emancipatory Politics*, ed. Avigail Eisenberg, Andrée Boisselle, and Jeremy Webber (Vancouver and Toronto: UBC Press, 2014), 269–92.

[32] *s.* 283 augm., 7.

[33] Robert Dodaro, "Political and Theological Virtues in Augustine, Letter 155 to Macedonius," *Augustiniana* 54, no. 1 (2004): 474.

unity is essential for the account of tolerance offered in this book. Here I am in substantial agreement with Eric Gregory and John Bowlin.[34] Tolerance, as I have mentioned, is often dealt with like a virtue that can survive as the only virtue to aspire to. Slavoj Zizek's questioning is pertinent: "Why are today so many problems perceived as problems of intolerance, not as problems of inequality, exploitation, injustice?"[35] His question could have served as a good review of the 1916 *Intolerance* film. But instead of leading us to write against toleration (as Zizek chose to do[36]), his question can help us rethink tolerance's place among our political concerns and its place among the virtues. Part of its current fragility can be due to this solitude. Attention to the unity of the virtues is a time-honored Aristotelian and Augustinian way of preventing such isolation.

Beyond the realm of virtue, in our understanding of the practice of toleration, another similar integration is necessary. We often describe a politics of toleration contrasting it with a politics of respect-based equality. Is this contrast justified? It is true that a "permission conception" of toleration tends to keep the other at arm's length.[37] There are many historical examples of tolerating without respecting. No wonder we desire to go beyond that. But there is more to the story of toleration than literal or metaphorical ghettos. As John Owen wrote in 1646, "toleration is the alms of authority; yet men that beg for it, think so much at least their due."[38] A project of mere toleration can be criticized as "alms" that can be arbitrarily withdrawn by those in power, but if toleration sometimes is due to those who ask for it, the situation changes. We sometimes permit because we respect; toleration sometimes is an act of justice. As Edmund Burke once noted, many tolerate because they see "amongst all things of value, a just ground of preference. They favor, therefore, and they tolerate. They tolerate, not because they despise opinions, but because they respect justice."[39] Burke took this combination of favored preference and respect for justice as the ground for a tolerant religious establishment.[40] This is not the position that this book supports. His words remind us, however, that not even

[34] This is the main thrust of Bowlin's book but see especially John Bowlin, *Tolerance Among the Virtues* (Princeton and Oxford: Princeton University Press, 2016), 2 and 34; Gregory, *Politics and the Order of Love. An Augustinian Ethic of Democratic Citizenship*, 149–96.

[35] Slavoj Žižek, "Tolerance as an Ideological Category," *Critical Inquiry* 34, no. 4 (2008): 660.

[36] Slavoj Žižek, "A Plea for Leninist Intolerance," *Critical Inquiry* 28, no. 2 (2002): 542–66.

[37] For the characterization of a "permission conception" of toleration, see Rainer Forst, *Toleration in Conflict: Past and Present* (Cambridge: Cambridge University Press, 2013), 26–31.

[38] John Owen, *A Country Essay for the Practice of Church Government There*, VIII, ed. William H. Goold, The Works of John Owen (Edinburgh: T&T Clark, 1862), 55.

[39] Edmund Burke, *Reflections on the French Revolution* (London: J.M. Dent & Sons, 1955), 147.

[40] Michael W. McConnell, "Edmund Burke's Tolerant Establishment," in *Religious Liberty in Western Thought*, ed. Noel B. Reynolds and W. Cole Durham (Grand Rapids: Eerdmans, 1996), 203–44.

all forms of religious establishment rest on permission without respect. Just enduring takes many forms.

Outline of the Book

This is an Augustinian essay, but not strictly a book about Augustine. Throughout the book, I move flexibly between sections in which I draw directly on Augustine and sections in which I go beyond him (the last chapter mentions him only once). I sometimes bring his voice to bear on problems very different from those he faced, hopefully in a faithful way. It is also a book that interacts with some important voices in the history of modern political thought, though with Locke slightly more than others. No monolithic Lockean origin of liberalism or toleration is thereby presumed. But since Locke is quite explicit regarding his own theological commitments, we will be better equipped to show the ways in which such commitments can be tied to an understanding of toleration and the ways in which they contrast with those of Augustine. Finally, it is a book that interacts with the more specialized contemporary literature on toleration. Only in dialogue with this literature, in and of itself a body of scholarship worthy of attention, can Augustine's thought on toleration be fruitfully brought to bear on contemporary discussions. But this is also a literature in which Augustinian intuitions are sometimes more than hinted at. John Gray, for instance, defends toleration as subverting the "humanist or Pelagian" creeds "for which human evils are problems to be solved rather than sorrows to be coped with or endured."[41] John Horton, similarly, writes of the "surprisingly Manichean perspective" in contemporary discussions of evil.[42] I have come across no comparable allusion to Donatism among contemporary political philosophers, but it is my view that this mention of Augustine's rivals deserves to be fleshed out.

The book is divided into three general parts and eleven more specific chapters. The first part focuses less on the specific features of toleration (though it is here that I offer a first outline of the concept) and more on the rival understandings of toleration as they have developed since the seventeenth century. This discussion is important because our approach to toleration, even in its most mundane forms, is substantially influenced by our view of the history of the concept. While this first part is not a history as such, but

[41] John Gray, *Enlightenment's Wake: Politics and Culture at the Close of the Modern Age* (New York and London: Routledge, 2007), 27.

[42] John Horton, "Why the Traditional Conception of Toleration Still Matters," *Critical Review of International Social and Political Philosophy* 14, no. 3 (2011): 295.

rather an exploration of contrasting conceptions, along the way I hope to clear the ground of several historical misunderstandings. Chapter 1 starts by considering how the diversity of conceptions of toleration tends to render arguments in its favor hollow. Some describe our society as excessively tolerant; others lament its lack of tolerance. I suppose that it fails in different directions on different issues. But the absence of a common understanding of toleration may be an equally great problem. To some extent we may need what Andrew Sabl has called a "toleration of tolerations," an understanding of various different and even incompatible reasons for toleration. But if calls to toleration are going to convey any meaningful message, we must mean by the term the same set of practices or virtues. This means avoiding the pitfalls discussed in the two chapters that follow. Calls for tolerance are sometimes calls for less than tolerance, sometimes calls for more. Some calls for tolerance are simply calls for peace, calls to consensus, calls that treat our differences as indifferent. This way of looking at toleration is the object of Chapter 2. In that process, tolerance also acquired its "wholly blessed status" (as Wendy Brown puts it), and thereby the isolation noted at the outset of this introduction. Chapter 3 considers calls for tolerance that are, instead, calls to go beyond it. There are, of course, various ways to go beyond tolerance. Sometimes toleration is simply replaced by freedom, a freedom that does not entail a negative judgment upon the things allowed, but without any positive judgment upon the behavior of others, either. But sometimes more is meant: toleration is to be replaced by actual celebration of our differences or by diverse kinds of politics of recognition. While most of those who write on these subjects treat these moves beyond toleration as a very recent phenomenon, I seek to show that the two approaches I describe in Chapters 2 and 3 have existed since the beginning of the modern discussion on tolerance. We are used to hearing about the Enlightenment rise of toleration, but the Enlightenment critique of toleration—manifest in these two departures from it—is also central to the history of this concept.[43] In Chapter 4, I turn from the polemical description of rival views to the development of the Augustinian account of toleration that is at the center of this book. I do not spend much time justifying what to many must appear to be an awkward choice of patron saint. After all, that choice would be questionable if my focus were on the limits of toleration, which it is not. Focusing instead on its nature implies thinking about its components, but also about the subjects who tolerate. These components and subjects are the objects of the second and third parts of the book.

[43] For an approach slightly different from the one developed here, but conscious of the Enlightenment's ambivalence in this regard, see Juan Pablo Domínguez, "Introduction: Religious Toleration in the Age of Enlightenment," *History of European Ideas* 43, no. 4 (2017): 273–87.

Chapter 5 will therefore focus broadly on the realities that we tolerate. Can we, for instance, tolerate an identity, or only actions? But the most central aspect of this chapter is the simple fact that while we tolerate things we judge to be evil, we seldom think enough about evil. I thus ask what it would mean to apply the Augustinian understanding of evil—and of the good that underlies it—to the discussion on tolerance. Evil was, of course, one of the great philosophical interests of Augustine, and I seek to show how his reflection on its nature can refresh our thinking on tolerance. But several other issues emerge from a consideration of evil. First, we must ask about the sense in which Augustine is a "pessimist" and to what extent tolerance depends on particular expectations, on a particular anthropology, or even on a particular view of history. This is the subject of Chapter 6. In Chapter 7 I will address the question of limits and judgment. If it is evil that we tolerate, we must acknowledge the centrality of judgment in human experience and leave behind the association between "judgmentalism" and intolerance. Finally, Chapter 8 addresses the relationship between toleration and different conceptions of personhood. The contemporary fixation on identity has brought new challenges to the distinction between persons and actions, a distinction that is crucial for toleration to make some sense. We tolerate actions or ideas, not persons. But what happens with this distinction when the line between person and action is blurred, or when both are subsumed under the idea of an identity?

The third and final part is dedicated to the subjects of tolerance. Tolerance can be a virtue of individuals (Chapter 9), a policy of states (discussed in Chapter 10), and a practice within smaller communities (the focus of Chapter 11). Each actor deserves some specific discussion, and in English even a terminological distinction between toleration and tolerance is often made: toleration typically describes the public policy, tolerance the personal virtue.[44] Among premodern authors, as I will discuss later, similar terminological distinctions were also made: Aquinas, for instance, would use *permissio/tolerantia* for the political practice, and *patientia/tolerantia* for the personal virtue.[45] But though I will devote these sections to the differences between the personal virtue and the political practice, I am not particularly concerned with

[44] For an illuminating use of the distinction see Andrew R. Murphy, "Tolerance, Toleration, and the Liberal Tradition," *Polity* 29, no. 4 (1997): 593–623.

[45] Haefeli wrongly claims that this distinction was not relevant before the modern era. Evan Haefeli, "The Problem with the History of Toleration," in *Politics of Religious Freedom*, ed. Winnifried Fallers Sullivan et al. (Chicago and London: The University of Chicago Press, 2015), 105. The opposite is more likely: that it is a quite traditional distinction that was blundered during much of the modern era and has been aptly recovered by contemporary work on toleration. For the distinction in Aquinas see Manfred Svensson, "A Defensible Conception of Toleration in Aquinas?," *The Thomist* 75, no. 2 (2011): 291–308.

the terminological distinction. After all, it is unavailable in many other languages (in my own Spanish, no less), and it is not even followed, or made in the same sense, by all those who write about toleration/tolerance in English.[46] The two terms will, therefore, be used interchangeably throughout most of the book, except in those few places where a terminological distinction seems particularly helpful.

[46] See the contrast between Preston King, *Toleration*, 2nd edn (London: Frank Cass, 1998), xii and 9–13; Andrew Jason Cohen, *Toleration* (Cambridge: Polity Press, 2014), 12; and Veit Bader, "Moral Minimalism and More Demanding Moralities: Some Reflections on 'Tolerance/Toleration,'" in *Tolerance, Intolerance and Respect. Hard to Accept?*, ed. Jan Dobbernack and Tariq Modood (Basingstoke: Palgrave Macmillan, 2013), 25.

I

RIVAL UNDERSTANDINGS OF TOLERATION

1
The "Traditional" Conception of Toleration

A Plurality of Tolerations

As early as 1646, John Owen observed that "a man may profess to oppose both toleration and non-toleration without any contradiction at all, because in their several senses they do not always intend the same."[1] Theologically Owen was a staunch Augustinian, in an age in which Augustinianism was losing its dominant status, becoming one disputed position among others.[2] But it is the disputed nature of toleration, as he identifies it, that interests us here. For the rampant confusion surrounding the meaning of this fundamental concept remains painfully still with us. Now few openly oppose toleration as they did in the time of Owen. The conceptual confusion remains, but now everyone, sincerely or not, claims to be tolerant. And such a confusion is not a merely theoretical problem. Our society is largely based on expectations of reciprocal toleration, but we lack a shared understanding of what is being expected. Under such conditions, the allegiance to toleration can be extremely fragile, and the rhetoric of toleration can be perceived as blatantly manipulative. What is the origin of this problem? And to what degree is it really a problem?

Let us begin with the question of origins. Even though Owen was writing before the great wave of Enlightenment literature on toleration, something new was already in the air. There is nothing resembling his remark in the earlier tradition of reflection on toleration. Seneca, Augustine, and Aquinas would have assented to the same definition of the concept. By the time of Owen, that definition seemingly had become controversial. The massive discussion of toleration in his generation perhaps helps us explain his observation. When everybody is writing for or against a practice, some state of confusion can be expected. Confessional division also complicated the question. Toleration where? Within the same religious body? Within the nation? A man may profess

[1] Owen, *A Country Essay for the Practice of Church Government There*, 57.

[2] On this, see Paul C.-H. Lim, "Owen the Polemicist," in *T&T Clark Handbook of John Owen*, ed. Crawford Gribben and John W. Tweeddale (London and New York: T&T Clark, 2022), 197–222.

An Augustinian Essay on Toleration. Manfred Svensson, Oxford University Press. © Manfred Svensson 2026.
DOI: 10.1093/9780197912737.003.0003

to oppose toleration in one but not in the other, without any contradiction at all. But if the truth of Owen's words is even more patent today, something more than the quantitative increase in the discussion and the ramification of problems must be added. Perhaps we can explain our situation in the following terms: tolerance makes the coexistence of a plurality of worldviews in our society possible, but the resulting situation entails a plurality of visions about tolerance as well. A world made plural through the practice of toleration has ended up including a plurality of tolerations. This fact is central to the nature of our misunderstandings regarding pluralism and toleration. The mutual accusations of intolerance that are such a common feature of our political and cultural landscape may often be self-serving. But the fact that they can be formulated reflects the existence of effectively divergent understandings of toleration.

In order to take our stand regarding toleration, we need to sort out these different approaches to toleration which, in the words of Owen, "do not always intend the same." We must ask how deep the difference between different conceptions of tolerance is, and to what degree this plurality of understandings of tolerance should be taken as good or bad news. How wide is this diversity of conceptions? Just how much disagreement can there be about the nature of tolerance? Not all virtues give rise to the same kind nor degree of disagreement. Human beings differ in the importance they attach to honesty or punctuality, but there is a reasonable agreement on these being virtuous dispositions. The nature of these virtues is to some extent unproblematic. Concerning tolerance, in contrast, there is not even consensus on it being a virtue. Perhaps it is a pragmatic compromise, a lesser evil. Perhaps it is downright evil. And if it is a good, the confusion about its nature is widely acknowledged. David Heyd writes that "our firm belief in the value of tolerance is not matched by analogous theoretical certitude," and that "there is a deep theoretical doubt concerning the likelihood of providing it with a stable philosophical ground."[3] Robert Paul Churchill, while less skeptical about what we can achieve, has also written about the "extraordinary degree of confusion" surrounding our conception of tolerance.[4] Such confusion only affects some virtues. Politically relevant virtues, in contrast with punctuality, are the subject of constant dispute.

[3] David Heyd, "Introduction," in *Toleration. An Elusive Virtue*, ed. David Heyd (Princeton: Princeton University Press, 1996), 3 and 10.

[4] Paul Robert Churchill, "On the Difference between Non-Moral and Moral Concepts of Tolerance: The Case for Toleration as an Individual Virtue," in *Philosophy, Religion, and the Question of Intolerance*, ed. Mehdi Amin Razavi and David Ambuel (Albany, NY: State University of New York Press, 1997), 190.

One could easily collect laments about the state of confusion in our discussion about justice. We assent to the need for virtues such as responsibility or justice, but we lack a shared understanding of their nature and their extent. Are we responsible for what we intend only, or are we responsible for all the foreseeable effects of our actions? Are we responsible for what happens in our immediate context, or should we rather stress our responsibility toward the most distant human beings? Does justice require that we give each his due or that we secure equitable outcomes for everyone? For everyone except avenging angels (and their human imitators), justice is a concept open to some controversy. We may all long for a just society, but that is a consensus that hardly brings light into our discussions. This is unequivocally true about toleration as well. A good dose of ambiguity and controversy will always be part of the landscape, about toleration no less than about responsibility and justice. If the meaning of any of these concepts is completely controverted, however, there are reasons to be concerned. And that is where we find ourselves. In political as well as in religious and philosophical discourse we come across calls for tolerance, but many rightly wonder what they are being asked to do when they are told to be tolerant.

This is not to say that we need a perfectly shared understanding of this idea. Augustine himself would likely affirm our need both for a reasonably clear concept of toleration and for a certain latitude in the reasons for toleration we consider acceptable, analogous to the conditions underlying the search for peace he describes in the *City of God*: "The things necessary for this mortal life" are used by members of both cities, "though the end they have in view and the use they make differs widely."[5] Some tolerate temporal evils with an eye to earthly goods, while others tolerate them with an eye to purification, heavenly consolation, and the hope of conversion. Augustine expects such differences in motivation and sees them as part of the "concord between the two cities in things pertaining to this life."[6] Although the two cities have different motivations for peace, they at least have some concord regarding peace "in things pertaining to this life." The question, then, is whether our current situation is one of such latitude within a broadly shared understanding of toleration—with room for different motivations for the same practice—or whether we have dramatically, perhaps intolerably, competing visions of this ideal. Let us explore this question further.

[5] *civ.* XIX, 17.
[6] *civ.* XIX, 17.

A Toleration of Tolerations

We need some shared understanding of toleration and, at the same time, some latitude within that understanding. Andrew Sabl has framed this as the need for a "toleration of tolerations."[7] His proposal is worth pondering. One can easily find libertarian or solidaristic, secularist or religious, elitist or skeptical reasons for toleration. The proponents of these different views have good reasons, as Sabl points out, to regard each other as offering not just different reasons for toleration, but rather rival visions—and thus potentially harmful views—that will inevitably undermine toleration. Under such circumstances, each of these views faces a strong temptation not to recognize these rival positions as approaches to toleration at all, but rather to promote or enforce a unified political culture that guarantees what each of them perceives as the right conditions for long-term toleration. If we take libertarian approaches to toleration to be the recipe for such long-term toleration, the fact that some derive toleration from their solidaristic premises may be read as a threat instead of a blessing. The same holds true for the secular or religious conditions that may be thought of as indispensable for true toleration. If we believe that only a fully secular world will be tolerant, the fact that some derive reasons for tolerance from their religious belief will be of little comfort. In response, we resist the apparent compromise and push for the profound transformation of our society that will create the conditions for true and definitive tolerance. But this search for a unified basis for future tolerance can actually destroy the sources of mutual understanding in the present and foreseeable future. Hence Sabl's conviction that we need to learn to put up "not just with other people's false and potentially dangerous world-views, but with other people's false and potentially dangerous ways of thinking about why they should put up with ours."[8] What we need, then, is a "toleration of tolerations."

There is much to be said for this argument. One can reasonably object to apparently inadequate reasons for toleration, while at the same time being grateful for the way in which those reasons work on those who hold them. "We agree on these rights, providing we are not asked why," was Maritain's famous synthesis of the discussion surrounding the United Nations' Declaration of the Rights of Man.[9] This statement may well capture the goal envisioned by Sabl,

[7] Andrew Sabl, "'Virtuous to Himself': Pluralistic Democracy and the Toleration of Tolerations," in *Toleration and Its Limits*, ed. Melissa Williams and Jeremy Waldron, NOMOS, XLVIII (New York and London: New York University Press, 2008), 220–42.

[8] Sabl, 228.

[9] Jacques Maritain, *Man and the State* (Washington, DC: The Catholic University of America Press, 1998), 77.

and Maritain himself could hardly be accused of being indifferent to questions about the ultimate reason for human rights or the ultimate reason for toleration. Again, however, we must ask whether this is our situation. Maritain accepted a certain latitude regarding the "why," not the "what." One can disagree about motivations and foundations and still have a common understanding of peace, rights, or tolerance. But do we have this common understanding? If not, we must ask about the limits of this plurality of tolerations. Should every use of the term be seen as reflecting one of its legitimate expressions?

Sabl himself presents twelve rival frameworks for toleration, and one may wonder whether they all conform to the basic outline of the concept that we find in common usage. In ordinary language, tolerance continues to be associated with things that are perceived as negative. As its contemporary students sometimes label it, there is an "objection-component" to toleration.[10] This is true, first of all, for our extra-moral language, as when we speak of an intolerable cold or about an organism's tolerance of a medicine. But it is also true when we express a moral evaluation, for example when we pass judgments on the intolerability of torture or when we ask ourselves whether this or that lie can be tolerated. Most of the forms of toleration described by Sabl fit this common-sense approach: we can describe them as different views of toleration, as views that support the same practice for different reasons. But Sabl also includes the philosophies that seek an "active and friendly appreciation for all the ways of life," and the ones that doubt the legitimacy of moral judgment and our capacity for well-grounded convictions.[11] Are such philosophies sources of toleration or are they sources of an altogether different approach to our moral and political conflicts? We can say that we tolerate unpunctuality or excessive noise precisely because these are realities to which we object. It would be absurd to confront them by proclaiming our open-mindedness or respect, our friendly appreciation.

To answer our question more fully, however, these different frameworks for toleration need to be confronted not only in our ordinary language but also in its philosophical elaboration. In one of the most important theoretical accounts of toleration in the recent literature, Preston King presents a crossing of dispositions and actions that helps us to capture the specific nature of toleration. When our actions toward something coincide with our dispositions, he argues, we can describe the result as "favouritism": our positive actions align

[10] King, *Toleration*, 44–51.

[11] Sabl, "'Virtuous to Himself': Pluralistic Democracy and the Toleration of Tolerations," 225–27. Sabl acknowledges, I should add, that his list by no means pretends to be comprehensive.

with the state of affairs toward which we have a positive disposition. At the other end of the spectrum, we have our action against that toward which we have a negative disposition. We call this intolerance. This leaves us with two situations in which actions and dispositions do not match. Sometimes our actions move in a direction opposite to that which we favor. King describes sacrifice in such terms, as a refusal to act in ways that concur with our commitments, preferences, or dispositions. Tolerance, on the contrary, is the intersection of favorable action and negative disposition. Even though such favorable action may consist in mere permission, it is a permission that runs against our disposition: we refrain from acting against the things we condemn. As King himself notes, this fourfold description may be incomplete, as it neglects factors such as indifference or ignorance.[12] But it is good enough for the initial clarification we aim at here, for it captures where the confusion often lies. Intolerance and sacrifice are easy enough to distinguish, but tolerance is often confused with what King calls favoritism. This is evident, for example, when we consider an "active and friendly appreciation for all ways of life" a form of tolerance.

If we want to resist this confusion, we might do well to consider how much tolerance and sacrifice have in common. Both imply a certain tension between our disposition and our action. In later chapters, we will see how well this fits with Augustine's deep insight into the tension or restlessness of human existence. For now, let us simply note that there is a simplicity to intolerance and favoritism that we do not encounter in sacrifice and tolerance. Given a negative disposition or judgment, intolerance acts negatively; given a positive disposition or judgment, "favouritism" acts positively. Tolerance and sacrifice, in contrast, involve a certain asymmetry. Given this asymmetry, both dispositions can even call for the same skeptical unmasking. Is there really a positive disposition behind the negative action? Is there a negative disposition behind the positive action? Such are the questions that can be raised by a philosophy of suspicion. Does not all pretended sacrifice merely mask the fact that we do not actually value the things we are sacrificing? Does not pretended tolerance just hide the fact that we have left our negative disposition behind? Another critical question, finally, suggests that this asymmetrical practice itself is misguided. Ought not we leave behind all negative disposition if we want peace and toleration?

This kind of criticism has its classical formulations. According to a famous line of Rousseau, "it is impossible to live in peace with people one believes to be

[12] King, *Toleration*, xiii.

damned."[13] Asymmetry is impossible. In the next chapter, I will return to the theological and philosophical milieu in which such a statement emerged. For now, let us simply note that this is a relatively sophisticated version of a notion that has become rather common. This view suggests that we cannot live in peace with people with whom we disagree or with people we regard as evil in one way or another. One contemporary critic of toleration considers it "odd to think that we can live and work together effectively with people who lead lives that in one way or another we find reprehensible or disgusting."[14] This is not a call to stop living and working together; it is a call to stop finding things reprehensible. Positive action should come from positive disposition. Rousseau basically gives us a *sub specie aeternitatis* version of this view. But does this view adequately reflect human experience? Rousseau himself offers no arguments for his claim beyond simple assertion. Moreover, upon closer inspection it seems to be as implausible in its sophisticated as in its popular forms. We may not always wish to live in peace with those to whom we object, but it is certainly possible. Most of us do indeed live in peace while raising all sorts of objections to the lives, political visions, and moral choices of our fellow citizens.

Humans seem to be capable of withstanding the tension that tolerance implies. We treat alien political ideals not simply as different from our own, but as rival ideals, as deceptive or harmful ideals—and yet coexistence with those who hold them is usually a reasonable expectation and often a reality. This is not a strange contemporary phenomenon. Throughout history, human beings have been able to organize life together between people of opposing beliefs and practices. As Benjamin Kaplan has written, tolerance *as a creed* may be an Enlightenment novelty; tolerance is not.[15] In his own work on early modern Europe, Kaplan has emphasized the multiple arrangements that made such coexistence possible, arrangements designed not to eliminate conflict but to regulate and contain it. Thus, "most Europeans continued to the very end of the early modern era to use the word tolerate in its traditional meaning: to suffer, to endure, or put up with something objectionable."[16] In the words of

[13] Jean-Jacques Rousseau, *The Social Contract and Other Late Political Writings*, ed. Victor Gourevitch (Cambridge: Cambridge University Press, 1997), 151 (IV, 8).

[14] Philip J. Ivanhoe, "Pluralism, Toleration, and Ethical Promiscuity," *Journal of Religious Ethics* 37, no. 2 (2009): 320–21.

[15] Kaplan, *Divided by Faith. Religious Conflict and the Practice of Toleration in Early Modern Europe*, 355. For this sort of pragmatic arrangement between Jews and Christians in the late-Ancient Mediterranean world, see Paula Fredriksen, *Augustine and the Jews. A Christian Defense of Jews and Judaism* (New York: Doubleday, 2008), 79–102.

[16] Kaplan, *Divided by Faith. Religious Conflict and the Practice of Toleration in Early Modern Europe*, 8.

one Puritan vicar, they exercised a "charitable Christian hatred."[17] As long as this traditional meaning is in some form preserved, we can speak of a "traditional conception of toleration," the formula used by John Horton in his exposition and defense of this conception.[18] This conception can draw from diverse motivations, and it can rest on different foundations. In fact, it predates any theory of toleration.

The Traditional Conception and Its Rivals

If this is the "traditional" conception of toleration, the definition admits many variations and has of course developed in different stages. This book focuses on its Augustinian version. But even within the Augustinian tradition there are several phases of development. Aquinas, as mentioned, already distinguishes between the personal virtue of tolerance and the political practice (*permissio*) in terms absent from Augustine. In later Augustinian thinkers such as Owen, we can see the same tradition moving from a tolerant approach to dissension within the Church to a world that was confessionally torn apart and where the toleration between different ecclesial bodies and religious traditions was at stake.[19] These are very different conditions under which one must put up with something objectionable. Such forbearance is, moreover, sometimes integrated with other positive forms of interaction. Teresa Bejan has, for example, described the project of Roger Williams as embodying an "evangelical toleration."[20] In discussing Williams' relationship to the American Indians, she has emphasized the extent to which he joined the duty of civility and the duty to preach, combining toleration with his participation in missionary enterprises. His toleration, Bejan writes, "was an unapologetically negative form of permission without approval; nonetheless, its emphasis on ongoing evangelical converse and conversation among the tolerated demanded an ethic of inclusion and engagement that went well beyond sufferance or forbearance."[21] Williams'

[17] Quoted by Kaplan, 262. This formula was taken up in the title of Alexandra Walsham, *Charitable Hatred. Tolerance and Intolerance in England 1500–1700* (Manchester: Manchester University Press, 2006).

[18] Horton, "Traditional Conception." For an earlier defense of this conception, one can see George P. Fletcher, "The Case for Tolerance," *Social Philosophy and Policy* 13, no. 1 (1996): 229–39.

[19] I have previously addressed these three stages in Manfred Svensson, "A Dirty Word? The Christian Development of the Traditional Conception of Toleration in Augustine, Aquinas, and John Owen," in *Secularization, Desecularization, and Toleration. Cross-Disciplinary Challenges to a Modern Myth*, ed. Manfred Svensson and Vyacheslav Karpov (Basingstoke: Palgrave Macmillan, 2020), 43–60.

[20] Teresa Bejan, "Evangelical Toleration," *The Journal of Politics* 77, no. 4 (2015): 1103–14.

[21] Teresa Bejan, *Mere Civility. Disagreement and the Limits of Toleration* (Cambridge, Mass: The Belknap Press of Harvard University Press, 2017), 69.

case puts us slightly beyond the Augustinian tradition, but its lesson for contemporary reflection seems clear: the traditional conception can take the limited form of mere toleration, but it can also take this more ambitious form highlighted by Bejan.

But how far can this expansion go? What should we say about the forms of toleration mentioned by Sabl, the "appreciation for all the ways of life" and skepticism of moral judgment? Some argue that these approaches to difference can be reasonably portrayed as forms of toleration. After all, our ordinary language often describes non-judgmental cultures as tolerant. Drawing on this everyday language, Peter Balint has stated that "A tolerant society usually involves significantly more indifference than it does forbearance."[22] But if this is a form of tolerance, it is, as it were, a tolerance without an object.[23] And, in that case, it is not a further version of the traditional conception. Our everyday language may in fact not be entirely coherent, sometimes including the ingredient of rejection and sometimes equating tolerance with indifference. A reflective approach, however, must move beyond that incoherence. While it starts from this everyday language, our reflection on toleration should not aim at simply replicating it at a theoretical level. We want to know not only how people speak about toleration, but on the basis of what understanding of toleration meaningful questions can be raised about it. What does it mean, for instance, to educate our children in toleration? What does it mean for the State to both tolerate and create conditions for tolerance? What does it mean for a religion to be tolerant? Such questions cannot be aptly discussed within accounts of toleration that leave out every element of judgment. They cannot be satisfactorily answered under conditions in which "a man may profess to oppose both toleration and non-toleration without any contradiction at all."[24] We need a "toleration of tolerations," but an appreciation for all ways of life is a form of moving beyond any form of this practice. A tolerant society may include a significant dose of indifference, but complete skepticism of moral judgment removes toleration's objection-component altogether.

For this reason, this book does not move directly to the "judgmental" and "evangelical" tolerationism of Augustine. We first need to contrast rival understandings of toleration or rival visions of human coexistence that pose as toleration. This means addressing the many forms in which we are called

[22] Peter Balint, *Respecting Toleration: Traditional Liberalism and Contemporary Diversity* (Oxford: Oxford University Press, 2017), 6.

[23] Glen Newey describes it as an intransitive form of toleration. Glen Newey, *Toleration in Political Conflict* (Cambridge: Cambridge University Press, 2013), 7.

[24] Owen, *A Country Essay for the Practice of Church Government There*, 57.

to leave toleration behind in the pursuit of a higher virtue, as we will do in Chapter 3. But it first calls for a revision of the ways in which we moved in the first place to *less* than toleration, or to a toleration with a radically weakened place for objections. The widespread unawareness of rival conceptions suggests precisely the success of this view: a toleration based on turning disputed claims into indifferent differences will also treat the difference between conceptions of toleration as secondary. If we need to make the difference between the different conceptions of toleration explicit it is, in fact, because minimizing disagreement (or weakening toleration's objection component) has been central to one of them.

2

Toleration Above All, Toleration Alone

The Chief Distinguishing Mark

"The design seems to have been, that what is wanting in them singly in *reason* may jointly be made up in *noise*."[1] This is how John Owen characterized the large number of writings on toleration published around 1667. By that time, he himself was one of the many Nonconformist theologians that had been expelled from the Church of England in 1662. The author of the Clarendon Code, the legal instrument for this ejection, had fallen from power in 1667, prompting new pleas for toleration from Congregationalists like Owen. His comments, then, were obviously directed to the literature against toleration that was published in this context. But centuries later we might well apply the same judgment to a significant portion of the literature in its favor. Here, too, noise can prevail over reason. To attempt to compensate the lack of reason by sheer numbers of books, letters, and petitions is as possible for toleration as it is against it.

But perhaps this is too harsh a judgment. For if a change has taken place, it is not only a change of direction, from writings against to writings in favor of toleration. It is also a change in the kind of literature that has been published over the past centuries. Owen was describing a literature against toleration that was primarily produced by the advertising agents of Court and Church. Today, in contrast, we are talking about a philosophical literature. For it was only after Owen's generation that philosophy made toleration a significant object of study. John Locke, no less, was a student at Christ Church, Oxford, when Owen was head of the college. Is it true that after centuries of *philosophical* discussion we remain confused about toleration? Should we think of this vast literature as philosophical noise? Even if our answer to this question may be in the affirmative (as to some extent I will be arguing), its achievement is quite impressive. At the beginning of the seventeenth century, the majority of Europeans regarded

[1] John Owen, *Indulgence and Toleration Considered*, XIII, ed. William H. Goold, The Works of John Owen (Edinburgh: T&T Clark, 1862), 519. Italics in the original.

An Augustinian Essay on Toleration. Manfred Svensson, Oxford University Press. © Manfred Svensson 2026.
DOI: 10.1093/9780197912737.003.0004

as patently false the idea that a political community should (or even could) tolerate the peaceful coexistence of significant religious differences. A century and a half later, this was no longer the case, and in part (though perhaps only in part), this literature paved the way. If this was noise, it was politically effective noise. Appreciating the good of peaceful coexistence between those who strongly differ, however, one can still raise questions about the intellectual tradition in which our discourse on tolerance is rooted.

Locke's *Letter Concerning Toleration* is likely the most influential text in the history of the concept. In its pages readers find the benevolent liberalism that many today believe they inhabit (or fear they are losing), combined with a somewhat surprising exclusion of Catholics and atheists. As a result, the *Letter* appears to be an important work for its historical moment, but quite trivial for ours. For in such a reading, Locke basically seems to say that faith is a voluntary matter, that God does not want us to be hypocrites, that State and Church have different and separate functions, and that by making these necessary points and distinctions tolerance will increase. Locke seems to say all this in a tone so completely inoffensive to us, which has to such an extent become the *lingua franca* of our day, that we can hardly find his text moving or intellectually challenging. It is this text that for many has come to represent the "traditional conception" of toleration. At most we react against what seem to be his limitations. "It was a great thing to go so far," we may be tempted to say with Thomas Jefferson, "but where he stopped, we must go on."[2] Alex Tuckness has described this as the "dominant view" on Locke and toleration today.[3] But it is not only debatable whether these are the main points of the *Letter*. The way in which Locke arrives at its conclusions is widely debated as well.

For quite a while Locke was thought to reach toleration thanks to the triumph of a secular rationality, even though this need not be one antagonistic to Christianity. One can still come across that interpretation; it may remain even still the most common one. Today, however, the theological nature of the arguments of Locke and his contemporaries is increasingly understood. We have come to recognize his *Letter Concerning Toleration* as Locke's *Theologico-Political Treatise*, to borrow Spinoza's title. Those who agree on the role played by religious arguments in the *Letter* may of course remain divided regarding the nature of the theology in question. Some consider Locke's argumentation to be the mature fruit of a Christianity intent on freeing itself from its Constantinian

[2] Thomas Jefferson, "Notes on Locke and Shaftesbury," in *The Papers of Thomas Jefferson. Volume 1, 1760–1776*, ed. Julian P. Boyd (Princeton: Princeton University Press, 1950), 548.

[3] Alex Tuckness, "Rethinking the Intolerant Locke," *American Journal of Political Science* 46, no. 2 (2002): 289.

past.[4] Defending the roughly orthodox character of his thought, some authors portray Locke as a reasonable Christian advocating a reasonable liberalism.[5] When John Dunn played the first card in this "religious turn" in Locke studies, he even placed Locke in the Calvinist camp—and thus within a broadly Augustinian tradition—something few students of Locke would do today.[6] Others in fact think that his political philosophy is tied to a contractualist vision of the Church and to his anti-Trinitarian theology.[7] A close reading of the first paragraph of the *Letter* will suffice to understand why these questions arise and why they are worth pondering. The letter, dedicated to the Erasmian theologian Philip van Limborch, begins with the following lines:

> Since you ask my opinion about mutual toleration among Christians, I reply briefly that I regard it as the chief distinguishing mark of a true church. For however much some people boast of the antiquity of places and names, or of the splendor of their ritual; others of the reformation of their teaching, and all of the orthodoxy of their faith (for everyone is orthodox to himself): these claims, and others of this kind, are more likely to be signs of men striving for power and empire than signs of the church of Christ. If a man possesses all these things, but lacks charity, meekness, and good will in general towards all mankind, even towards those who do not profess the Christian faith, he falls short of being a Christian himself.[8]

This is, of course, primarily an exhortation, more an attempt to move than to persuade. As Mark Lilla has written, in the *Letter* Locke raises many powerful questions that he does not always care to answer.[9] It is easy to see that this first paragraph does not represent an argument with demonstrative intent. After all,

[4] Thus, for instance, Jennifer A. Herdt, "Locke, Martyrdom, and the Disciplinary Power of the Church," *Journal of the Society of Christian Ethics* 23, no. 2 (2003): 19–35.

[5] For two different versions see Jeremy Waldron, *God, Locke, and Equality: Christian Foundations in Locke's Political Thought* (Cambridge: Cambridge University Press, 2002) and Greg Forster, *John Locke's Politics of Moral Consensus* (Cambridge: Cambridge University Press, 2005).

[6] See John Dunn, *The Political Thought of John Locke: An Historical Account of the Argument of the "Two Treatises of Government"* (Cambridge: Cambridge University Press, 1969). For a more precise account of Locke's theological convictions see John Marshall, "Locke, Socinianism, 'Socinianism', Unitarianism," in *English Philosophy in the Age of Locke*, ed. M.A. Stewart (Oxford: Clarendon Press, 2000), 111–82.

[7] I offer my version of this reading in Manfred Svensson, "John Locke, Liberal Theology, and Toleration," in *Liberale Theologie Heute—Liberal Theology Today*, ed. Jörg Lauster, Ulrich Schmiedel, and Peter Schüz (Tübingen: Mohr Siebeck, 2019), 99–109.

[8] I quote Locke's Letter according to the translation provided in John Locke, *Epistola de Tolerantia/ A Letter on Toleration*, ed. Raymond Klibansky, trans. J.W. Gough (Oxford: Oxford University Press, 1968), 59.

[9] Mark Lilla, *The Stillborn God: Religion, Politics, and the Modern West* (New York: Knopf, 2008), 97.

who would respond by trying to defend the positions Locke ridicules? Who would affirm that the heart of Christianity, or of any other religion, consists in the "antiquity of its places and names" or in "the pomp of its external praise"? But even though this is an exhortation, the paragraph reveals some of the conceptual changes that the understanding of tolerance is undergoing. If we examine this paragraph closely, we find first that tolerance is presented not as a very important virtue, but rather pointedly as *the* cardinal virtue. The language that Locke uses to affirm this primacy of tolerance, however, is specifically theological vocabulary: tolerance is the principal sign or mark (*criterium*, *nota*) of the true Church, thus replacing the classical four marks of oneness, holiness, catholicity, and apostolicity. This is, to say the least, a bold move, and it should be clear at this point that Locke is not simply backing his position theologically but rather developing a specific theological program. And it is not "anti-Catholicism" that is at stake, as if just that specific prejudice had to be removed in order to broaden his Christianity and his toleration.[10] Locke is just as far removed from classic Protestant theology. His theology is rooted in a peculiar form of anticonfessional (and anti-Augustinian) "Christian humanism," to the main "marks" of which we will soon return.

But let us first consider Locke's success in establishing the primacy of tolerance. Despite several promises to the contrary, Locke never wrote a work on ethics.[11] The closest to a moral treatise among his mature works is a treatise on a single virtue, which is not *amicitia* but *tolerantia*. The initial movement of the *Letter* is not a change in the nature of the concept in question but rather a change in the hierarchy of virtues, in the incomparable value assigned to tolerance. Any observer can see that this "transvaluation of values" proved to be very influential. Visiting the United States in 1939, Dietrich Bonhoeffer was surprised to find that for some, "the notion of tolerance becomes the fundamental notion of everything Christian."[12] But early on, this Lockean legacy had also made its way to authors who stood apart from Christianity. Voltaire, for instance, begins the article on toleration in his *Philosophical Dictionary* by referring to it as "the first law of nature."[13] If we want to be aware of the

[10] Jeremy Waldron has even cast reasonable doubt on the idea that Locke did exclude Catholics from toleration. Waldron, *God, Locke, and Equality: Christian Foundations in Locke's Political Thought*, 218–23.

[11] For this promise see John Marshall, *John Locke: Resistance, Religion and Responsibility* (Cambridge: Cambridge University Press, 1994), 263.

[12] Dietrich Bonhoeffer, "Essay about Protestantism in the United States of America, August 1939," in *Theological Education Underground, 1937–1940*, Dietrich Bonhoeffer Works (Minneapolis: Fortress Press, 2012), 15:448.

[13] M. de Voltaire, "Toleration," in *A Philosophical Dictionary* (London: John and Henry L. Hunt, 1824), 6:272.

unusual novelty inherent in the words of Locke and Voltaire, we simply have to ask what would have been described as the "first law of nature" or as "main mark of the Church" before Locke. One could think, for example, of traditional classifications of the cardinal virtues. It is sometimes argued that "tolerance never surfaces in pre-modern accounts of the virtues."[14] In his famous account of the origins of Enlightenment, Paul Hazard wrote that up to then tolerance "had not been a virtue at all, but, on the contrary, a sign of weakness, not to say of cowardice."[15] As we shall see, Augustine's work is as good a correction of such overstatements as one can get. Tolerance was not a "dirty word."[16] But it is true that if we turn our eyes to the classical philosophers and their teaching on the virtues, it is justice, prudence, or friendship, long before tolerance, that are counted as the principal marks of the virtuous citizen. If one wishes to find tolerance among these virtues, one will find it as a component of the virtue of fortitude.[17] It was far from occupying the first place among human excellences. If we turn to the Bible instead of the philosophers, we will find a similar discrepancy with our culture's hierarchy of values. There "the weightier matters of the law" are justice, mercy, and faithfulness, not tolerance (Matt. 23:23). Were it not for other reasons, this change alone would be enough to make the *Letter* a critical turning point.

But a change in the hierarchy of virtues is also a change in the relationship of tolerance to other virtues and thus in the very nature of toleration. The transition to becoming the principal virtue may, for example, be accompanied by a transition to the independence of tolerance, to the idea that we can be tolerant without having other virtues. Tolerance is frequently spoken of in this way. As a Universalist newsletter put it in 1834, "tolerance alone can make us happy, tolerance alone enables us to enjoy life, tolerance alone shall therefore be the ruler of [our] actions."[18] Here we are not called to be tolerant as part of a general call to be just, merciful, or faithful, but rather as a pillar sufficient in itself for human coexistence. But this is not the kind of transition that we find in Locke. In his work, there is no attempt to make tolerance independent, nor to

[14] Thus, for instance, Trudy D. Conway, *Cross-Cultural Dialogue on the Virtues: The Contribution of Fethullah Gülen* (Dordrecht: Springer, 2014), 21.

[15] Paul Hazard, *The Crisis of the European Mind 1680–1715* (New York: New York Review Books, 2013), 300.

[16] As it was described by Blair Worden, "Toleration and the Cromwellian Protectorate," in *Persecution and Toleration*, ed. W.J. Sheils, Studies in Church History 21 (Oxford: Blackwell, 1984), 200. Worden is right that "more often than not" the term was used disparagingly in Puritan England (as, one might add, in some corners of the contemporary discussion). But there is no reason to accept this as a description of the larger Western trajectory.

[17] See István Bejczy, ed., *Virtue Ethics in the Middle Ages. Commentaries on Aristotle's Nicomachean Ethics, 1200–1500* (Leiden and Boston: Brill, 2008), 291–95.

[18] G.I.G., "Tolerance," *Herald of Truth* (Geneva, NY), August 30, 1834, 43.

separate it from other virtues, but rather to merge it with some of them: charity, meekness, benevolence. This change is a second important feature of the first paragraph of the *Letter*. In part due to its dependence on the Christian virtue of charity, Derrida has written with skepticism regarding tolerance.[19] However, the question is more complex than Derrida makes it out to be. In the initial paragraph of the *Letter*, tolerance is not merely associated with love (*caritas*), but rather identified with it. It is not a consequence of love, nor does it merely depend on it. And if it is the same thing as kindness or love, it is not a virtue specifically needed in order to resist or put up with evil, as in the traditional conception. In fact, the steps we have followed so far can be seen as two sides of the same coin: the consolidation of tolerance as the principal virtue requires that it be identified with love. Such an identification diminishes its specificity. It hides the dependent nature of tolerance. But in return it gives tolerance an unquestionably binding nature, which was a fundamental objective for Locke. We must be tolerant, since there is no quarrel about the fact that we must love.

A Philosophy and Theology of Conflict Avoidance

But along with this shift of meaning in the concept of toleration, early modern thinkers undertook a transformation of religion, a transformation that sought to domesticate what was seen as its potential for conflict. Let us return for a moment to Griffith's film *Intolerance*. Moving through the ages, the movie attempts to portray the injustice that has prevailed from the earliest times. In the Judean story, this injustice is embodied in the religious establishment. The birth of Jesus, in contrast, is heralded as the arrival of the "Man of Man, the greatest enemy of intolerance." A version of the Christian religion is thus accepted as an antidote to intolerance. The question is how to describe this version of Christianity. Griffith will not help us much here, but exploring the understanding of religion that became common among modern political philosophers may shed some light on the question. From Locke's *Letter* onward, writings on toleration have in fact been a typical vehicle for new understandings of religion, belief, and the Church. Rousseau's belief, as we have seen, was that "it is impossible to live in peace with people one believes to be damned."[20] If faced with this disjunction we choose to live in peace, there

[19] Giovanna Borradori, *Philosophy in a Time of Terror: Dialogues with Jürgen Habermas and Jacques Derrida* (Chicago: University of Chicago Press, 2003), 127.

[20] Rousseau, *The Social Contract and Other Late Political Writings*, 151 (IV, 8).

cannot be a place for future damnation. The call to reject all intolerance will be interpreted as implying that one must positively affirm that salvation can be arrived at through any religion.[21] Coexistence will then require a civil religion that radically cuts off all sharp edges from religion. And this is exactly what Rousseau pleads for: a civil religion with few and simple dogmas, teachings in no need of commentary. Belief in the powerful, beneficent, and provident Divinity, together with the sanctity of the Laws, are its positive dogmas. As in Griffith's film, intolerance alone is the negative dogma of Rousseau's civil religion.[22] With multiple variations, this minimalist religion lies at the heart of much of modern political philosophy.[23] And Locke did develop this understanding of Christianity precisely with toleration in view. The transformation of religion that we find in the *Letter* is, in fact, even more visible than its changes in the understanding of toleration. Historians of liberalism, and above all its contemporary critics, have often emphasized one aspect of this transformation, the liberal privatization of religion. While there is some merit to this critique, Locke is not a straightforward apologist for such a privatization. If anything, he is rather emphatic regarding the importance of freedom of public worship.[24] We might rather say that he seeks to transform religion so that it can remain public but rendered harmless. The two ways through which this transformation takes place are Locke's construction of boundaries and his doctrinal minimalism. Taken together, these two features can be described as his philosophy and theology of conflict avoidance.

Let us first consider briefly the construction of boundaries. The fact that Locke establishes a separation between Church and State is by no means the central issue here, as Christianity has always been characterized by some version of such a duality. But Locke's precise wording is not trivial in the least. He regards it above all "necessary to distinguish between civil and religious matters (*res civitatis et religionis*), and to mark the true bounds between the Church and the commonwealth (*inter ecclesiam et rempublicam*)."[25] He considers "their origin, their end, and their whole substance" as "utterly and completely different."[26] He aims not only at distinguishing, but at a strict

[21] For a fine discussion see Douglas Kries, "Rousseau and the Problem of Religious Toleration," in *Piety and Humanity. Essays on Religion and Early Modern Political Philosophy*, ed. Douglas Kries (Lanham, MD: Rowman & Littlefield Publishers, 1997), 259–86.

[22] Rousseau, *The Social Contract and Other Late Political Writings*, 151 (IV, 8).

[23] For a survey of civil religion in modern political philosophy see Steven Frankel and Martin D. Yaffe, eds., *Civil Religion in Modern Political Philosophy. Machiavelli to Tocqueville* (University Park, PA: The Pennsylvania State University Press, 2020).

[24] Locke, *Epistola de Tolerantia/A Letter on Toleration*, 91.

[25] Locke, 65.

[26] Locke, 87.

drawing of limits (*limitesque... rite definiendos*).[27] This same language of strict boundaries separating different "provinces" can also be found in his discussion of faith and reason in the *Essay Concerning Human Understanding*. The absence of such "measures and boundaries" is the source of "great disputes."[28] Unsurprisingly, he described religion as "those actions which [please or displease] God without any concerning at all my neighbor, civil society, or my own preservation in this life."[29] Fearing the intolerant consequences of religion's overarching nature, it is reduced to a relationship with God alone, with no effects on other relationships or on the orientation of our lives. Ingrid Creppell has described this as a construction of boundaries not only between groups but also between spheres of life and authority, even within each individual mind.[30] This "compartmentalizing of the world" forces us to think twice about the way we act when we cross a given boundary; the mere act of crossing it can be interpreted as intolerant.[31] If Church and State are not only separated by their means but also by their aims, if one is devoted to the salvation of souls and the other to civil and external goods, then every incursion into the muddy territory in between—education, the family, public morality—will be subject to this charge of intolerance.

Such a logic of separations is indeed a central feature of modern intellectual life. But this again confirms that it is not the traditional concept of toleration that we find in Locke. Throughout the *Letter* toleration is often spoken of in its classical sense, as a disposition of endurance or as a practice of non-interference with regard to disapproved-of things. Locke writes, for instance, that it is "not the magistrate's business to censure with laws or check with his sword everything he believes to be a sin against God."[32] So far so good. Simultaneously, however, the structural aspects of the *Letter* that we are considering lead to a vision that makes such endurance and non-interference superfluous. If compartmentalization is a significant aspect of Locke's approach to toleration, the objection-component of toleration is inevitably softened. When tolerating becomes identical with staying within certain boundaries, it

[27] Locke, 65.

[28] John Locke, *An Essay Concerning Human Understanding*, ed. P.H. Nidditch (Oxford: Clarendon Press, 1975), IV, xviii, 1–2.

[29] John Locke, "Critical Notes upon Edward Stillingfleet's Mischief and Unreasonableness of Separation," in *John Locke: Writings on Religion*, ed. Victor Nuovo (Oxford: Oxford University Press, 2002), 74. For the analysis of this passage see John Perry, "Locke's Accidental Church: The Letter Concerning Toleration and the Christian Witness to the State," *Journal of Church and State* 47, no. 2 (2005): 278–79.

[30] Creppell, *Toleration and Identity. Foundations in Early Modern Thought*, 92.

[31] Creppell, 118.

[32] Locke, *Epistola de Tolerantia/A Letter on Toleration*, 115.

becomes a way of avoiding "great disputes" rather than a way of living justly within those disputes.

This is even more evident in his discussion of substantive doctrinal claims. Since "all are orthodox unto themselves," Locke rejects claims to orthodoxy as a mark of the true Church. But the strategy he adopts is neither that of basing toleration on skepticism, nor that of inviting orthodox Christians or any others who hold to robust systems of belief to retreat into the private sphere. Rather, the call is for them to reinterpret their faith as centered on a minimal, non-conflictive doctrine. Edwin Curley has given this strategy the historically apt name of "Erasmian liberalism."[33] Erasmus' *philosophia Christi* was in fact a plea for a simple Christianity, consisting mainly of a good life, and certainly not in detailed theological disputation. This is often presented as a return from "speculation" to Biblical simplicity. In the letter to Paul Volz that prefaces the second edition of his *Enchiridion*, however, Erasmus affirms that also the Bible is too complex and demanding, even for scholars like himself. What is required is for pious and learned men to read the Scriptures and its best interpreters and extract a brief summary, simple and learned, in which the "things pertaining to the faith should be resolved in very few articles."[34] Early modern political philosophers almost unanimously took up the task. Hobbes' description of "Jesus is the Christ" as the *unum necessarium* well summarizes that effort,[35] and Locke himself never tires of complaining about the "bundles of articles" of the churches and about the fact that believers accept these "bundles" of articles without separating fundamental articles from those that are unnecessary.[36] Also the exclusion of Catholics—typically explained in terms of their loyalty to a foreign ruler—can be seen in this light. In *An Essay Concerning Toleration,* Locke had presented fidelity to the pope, a foreign monarch, simply as an example of this more generalized problem: the tendency of people to receive the doctrines of their "party" "all at once in a bundle," mixing together that which is necessary and that which is unimportant.[37] That things sometimes "do come in bundles," as John Perry writes, seems to be utterly unknown to Locke.[38]

[33] Edwin Curley, "Sebastian Castellio's Erasmian Liberalism," *Philosophical Topics* 31, nos 1–2 (2003): 47–73.

[34] Erasmus von Rotterdam, "Epistola Ad Paulum Volzium," in *Ausgewählte Schriften* (Darmstadt: Wissenschaftliche Buchgesellschaft, 1968), 1: 12–14.

[35] Thomas Hobbes, *Leviathan*, ed. Noel Malcolm (Oxford: Clarendon Press, 2014), 938 (III, 43).

[36] John Locke, *Political Essays*, ed. Mark Goldie (Cambridge: Cambridge University Press, 1997), 146.

[37] John Locke, *An Essay Concerning Toleration: And Other Writings on Law and Politics, 1667-1683*, ed. J.R. Milton and Philip Milton (Oxford: Oxford University Press, 2006), 284.

[38] John Perry, *The Pretenses of Loyalty: Locke, Liberal Theory, and American Political Theology* (Oxford: Oxford University Press, 2011), 129.

From Softened Objection to Indifference

How does this assault on the "contrivers of symbols, systems and confessions" relate to toleration?[39] The implicit claim—that doctrinal minimalists are more tolerant than persons with more comprehensive views—only makes sense in the light of a specific account of what toleration is, an understanding of toleration in which toleration's objection-component is removed or at least softened. Teresa Bejan has called attention to the ways in which this approach to toleration lives on in contemporary liberalism. Both in Jeremy Waldron and John Rawls she finds the understanding of the tolerant society as the harmonious society, a society in which the potentially conflictive edges have been shrugged off, and men's tongues have been tamed.[40] Indeed, seventeenth-century strategies are often deployed in contemporary debates. Toleration emerged from the so-called wars of religion, and it is now needed in the so-called culture wars.[41] People no longer talk about tolerance as the main mark of the true church, but its primacy is still asserted as the main virtue of civilized or reasonable people. The isolation of toleration is maintained, as if it were possible to cultivate a climate of tolerance without simultaneously cultivating a culture of justice or of compassion. The ranks of doctrinal minimalists have been followed by moral philosophies that have at their core the distinction between disputable comprehensive views of life and a minimal morality that is taken to be less controversial. This is the reason Michael Sandel has written about a "minimalist liberalism."[42] Even the language of things indifferent (*adiaphora*), which in the sixteenth and seventeenth centuries was often used in reference to rites or conflicting doctrines, is now used in ethical controversies—or rather, to avoid these controversies. We had a religion organized around fundamental articles and now an ethics reduced to fundamental rights, from Erasmian liberalism to Kantian liberalism. Not everyone adhered to the fundamental articles of religion in the past, as not everyone now respects fundamental rights; but the hope is cherished that if we maintain the reduction to these *minima*, at some point everybody will acknowledge the reasonableness of this core. Tolerance can be articulated in different ways with this understanding of religion and

[39] Locke, *Epistola de Tolerantia/A Letter on Toleration*, 155.

[40] Bejan, *Mere Civility. Disagreement and the Limits of Toleration*, 20–22.

[41] Rightly so called? That is of course disputable in both cases. See William T. Cavanaugh, *The Myth of Religious Violence: Secular Ideology and the Roots of Modern Conflict* (Oxford: Oxford University Press, 2009); and James Davison Hunter, *Culture Wars. The Struggle to Define America* (New York: Basic Books, 1991).

[42] Michael J. Sandel, *Democracy's Discontent: America in Search of a Public Philosophy* (Cambridge, Mass: Harvard University Press, 1996), 100–03.

morality. It can, for example, be reduced to those who subscribe to the same list of rights considered obvious; or it can be understood as the very virtue of subscribing to these fundamental rights, such that tolerance itself becomes a creed. But whichever way one goes, in this context appeals to tolerance are calls for consensus rather than calls for complex forms of coexistence.

But if, following Preston King, we characterize toleration as involving some tension between our dispositions and our actions, we must ask to what extent the result of this process should count as a version of toleration at all. As we have seen, there are elements of genuine toleration in Locke. But every tension would seem to disappear if the traits we have discussed in this chapter were to prevail. When Tocqueville came across this mentality, he in fact concluded that the "alleged tolerance" he met in America—and which he now would find everywhere—actually "amounts to good old indifference."[43] Is there a legitimate place for this indifference within our "toleration of tolerations"? A certain type of indifference is indeed compatible with real toleration. In the words of Aquinas, "we can also call those acts indifferent, which are barely good or barely evil (*parum boni vel parum mali*)."[44] As these words suggest, objections are not always absent from our indifference: we do have objections, but we permit things that we consider *indifferent enough* to let them be. But the process that we have seen unfold in Locke's work is something different. Permitting actions of others, whether we consider them extremely or barely evil, is a way of relating to *their* actions. But tolerance can also be reinterpreted as a way of relating to *our own* beliefs. And this is partly what we find in Locke's *Letter*, an indifference to the actions or beliefs of others that requires a prior transformation of our own convictions. These must be revised, compartmentalized, shortened, or separated from our practical lives if we are to be counted as tolerant.

But if this is the main form in which toleration has spread in the contemporary world, it could hardly be expected to last too long. Writing in 1983, Milan Kundera wondered what would take the place of a common culture in Europe. Just as God had given way to culture, he believed, culture would now give way. To what? "Will it be the principle of tolerance?" he asked. "But won't this tolerance become empty and useless if it no longer protects a rich creativity or a strong set of ideas?"[45] Toleration is always costly, but it can become

[43] Alexis de Tocqueville, *Letters from America*, trans. Frederick Brown (New York and London: Yale University Press, 2010), 89.

[44] *S. Th.* I-II, q. 92, a.2. My translation. For all subsequent translations of Aquinas, I follow the work of the Fathers of the English Dominican Province.

[45] Milan Kundera, *A Kidnapped West. The Tragedy of Central Europe*, trans. Linda Asher and Edmund White (London: Faber, 2023), 47–48.

too costly. If tolerance means giving up our concern for the things that matter most to us, many who consider tolerance a noble ideal will nevertheless find the price paid for it too high. Many who might be inclined to tolerate fear that this is the risk: if the tension between disposition and action is resolved by weakening our dispositions, toleration means giving up both our core beliefs and our character. If this is toleration, then higher commitments may require a revolt against it. This is a big "if," however. As we have seen, this understanding of toleration is the result of a deep transformation of the concept. Since this transformation still clashes with our ordinary language, a return to and even an Augustinian deepening of the traditional conception of toleration is possible. But before we attempt this, we need to consider another transformation of toleration. The tension of tolerance can be undermined not only in the weak forms explored in this chapter but also in the seemingly more robust moves beyond toleration that have been at the center of more recent discourse.

3

Moving Beyond Tolerance

Hospitality, Recognition, and Agonistic Respect

The Enlightenment Critique of Toleration

In the previous chapter, I considered a twofold transformation of toleration: on the one hand, its introduction and establishment as the preeminent virtue; on the other hand, its identification with a peaceful coexistence in which conflict disappears. The first of these steps required identifying toleration with love; the second was linked to phenomena such as the compartmentalization of human life and doctrinal minimalism. If this program of conflict avoidance were entirely successful, toleration would arguably become superfluous. Given the problematic nature of human persons, however, this is a logic that never fully unfolds. It may advance considerably, but we are stuck in a world where tolerance in the traditional sense will always be needed. But what do we mean by "the problematic nature of human persons?" We do not need to dwell on Augustine's views yet. Suffice it to say that human beings often interpret the world in essentially opposite ways. This does not turn conflict into the central fact of human existence.[1] But there are many differences that cannot be treated indifferently. Instead of treating differences as legitimate objects of contestation and tolerance, however, the pendulum has swung toward their positive affirmation. If the early modern world approached toleration in the terms outlined in our previous chapter—moving below or behind toleration—the move is now beyond it. In recent decades, this shift has been particularly notorious. Authors as diverse as Jacques Derrida, Zygmunt Bauman, and Martha Nussbaum—and, as we shall see, many others—consistently or occasionally describe toleration as "parsimonious," "ego-centered and contemplative," "grudging and weak," proclaiming that it can only be saved if it is transformed

[1] For a broadly Augustinian defense of this point, see Johnson, *Theology, Political Theory, and Pluralism: Beyond Tolerance and Difference.*

An Augustinian Essay on Toleration. Manfred Svensson, Oxford University Press. © Manfred Svensson 2026.
DOI: 10.1093/9780197912737.003.0005

into respect, solidarity, or recognition.[2] Instead of erasing differences, these must be affirmed. It is a radical shift. The rejection of toleration in the name of some deeper value or in the name of openness to all values can sometimes be as blunt as its rejection in the name of intolerance.[3]

In the face of such critiques, other voices urge us to defend an early modern, classical liberal, or Enlightenment understanding of this virtue. Today, writes Frank Furedi, the "term finds itself used in ways that would shock the philosophers and thinkers who developed this concept."[4] But this ignores how deeply rooted this call to move beyond toleration is in modern intellectual life. Sometimes the same works that gave rise to a neutralizing or minimalist understanding of toleration also called for a move beyond tolerance, toward love or benevolence. In the case of Locke's *Letter*, we have seen that this move can be explained in terms of the rhetorical nature of the text. Locke seeks to make tolerance binding, and for this purpose he identifies it with the duty to love, which Christians should know to be binding. However, Locke's terminology in *An Essay Concerning Toleration*—written two decades earlier but never published—suggests that there is more to these words than rhetoric. Locke begins this *Essay* saying that he will deal with "the question of freedom of conscience," but this phrase replaces that of an earlier draft that presented its topic as "the question of tolerance."[5] If such a change does not seem relevant to us, it is precisely because we have been brought up to believe that the two concepts, tolerance and freedom of conscience, may not be all that different. To treat them as almost identical, however, is a novelty of Locke's generation (also to be found in thinkers very different from him, such as William Penn).[6] This freedom of conscience is less demanding than the more positive attitude of love. Like tolerance, it can be understood as a way of regulating conflicting visions: freedom of conscience regulates our beliefs by allowing them to be

[2] Borradori, *Philosophy in a Time of Terror: Dialogues with Jürgen Habermas and Jacques Derrida*, 161; Zygmunt Bauman, *Modernity and Ambivalence* (Cambridge: Polity Press, 1991), 256; Martha Nussbaum, *Liberty of Conscience: In Defense of America's Tradition of Religious Equality* (New York: Basic Books, 2008), 24. For another variation on this theme, see Apel Karl-Otto, "Plurality of the Good? The Problem of Affirmative Tolerance in a Multicultural Society from an Ethical Point of View," *Ratio Juris* 10, no. 2 (2008): 199–212.

[3] Not all cases are equally blunt, of course, but the shared tendency of so various schools and scholars is worth noting. While introducing a rather nuanced collection, Modood and Dobbernack push for a "space beyond toleration" that can "accommodate any position that tips the balance of toleration as it is conventionally understood." Jan Dobbernack and Tariq Modood, "The Acceptance of Cultural Diversity in Europe: Theoretical Perspectives and Contemporary Developments," in *Tolerance, Intolerance and Respect*, ed. Jan Dobbernack and Tariq Modood (Basingstoke: Palgrave Macmillan, 2013), 9.

[4] Frank Furedi, *On Tolerance: A Defence of Moral Independence* (London: Bloomsbury, 2011), 2.

[5] Locke, *An Essay Concerning Toleration: And Other Writings on Law and Politics, 1667–1683*, 269 and 303.

[6] With regard to Penn see Murphy, *Conscience and Community*, xii.

expressed. But it can also be conceived in terms that render toleration superfluous, as an enlightened replacement for a premodern burden-bearing. Both of Locke's works, thus, place us at the beginning of an effort to overcome tolerance, an effort in which quite disparate streams of thought have converged.

Once our gaze falls on this fact, the careful reader of the history of toleration will indeed be surprised at how long and explicit this process of overcoming tolerance is. This is especially clear in programmatic texts such as Immanuel Kant's 1784 essay "What is Enlightenment?," George Washington's 1790 letter on religious freedom, or Thomas Paine's *Rights of Man*. The enlightened ruler, Kant wrote, "even declines the arrogant name of *tolerance*."[7] Washington, for his part, wrote "Henceforth one will no longer speak of tolerance."[8] Thomas Paine, finally, affirmed that both tolerance and intolerance are forms of despotism.[9] And beyond such programmatic texts we continue to find this orientation. Condorcet's influential outline of human progress, published in 1795, condemned the "insolence of the ruling sect called by the name of toleration."[10] A half-century later, Goethe would concur with his now well-known dictum: "Tolerance should be a passing disposition. It should lead to recognition. To tolerate is to insult."[11] These are calls not simply to go beyond tolerance but rather to leave it behind as something of which it will no longer be spoken. As Alexander Vinet wrote shortly after Goethe, tolerance is an "insufficient palliative" for "times of fanaticism and oppression," and ultimately an "insult to the rights of humanity."[12] This passing disposition is necessary in a kind of intermediate phase between the age that did not know of tolerance and the age that will not need it. One recent article thus speaks of the "purgatory of tolerance."[13] Such tolerance would be useful for the plural but not yet pluralistic world.[14] To be sure, there is a "postmodern" ingredient in the contemporary ambivalence about tolerance. But if we are to understand the force of this tide, the Enlightenment critique of toleration must be brought into the picture.

[7] Immanuel Kant, *Practical Philosophy* (Cambridge: Cambridge University Press, 1999), 21. Italics in the original.

[8] George Washington, "Letter to Moses Seixas," in *Sourcebook and Index: Documents That Shaped the American Nation*, ed. Joy Hakim (Oxford: Oxford University Press, 2002), 92.

[9] Thomas Paine, *Rights of Man, Common Sense, and Other Political Writings* (Oxford: Oxford University Press, 2008), 137.

[10] Marquis de Condorcet, *Outlines of an Historical View of the Progress of the Human Mind* (London: J. Johnson, 1795), 199.

[11] Wolfgang Goethe, *Maximen und Reflexionen*, VI, Werke (Frankfurt: Insel, 1981), 507.

[12] Alexander Vinet, *Outlines of Philosophy and Literature* (London: Daldy, Isbister & Co., 1877), 276.

[13] Dan Rather, "America Is Stuck in the Purgatory of Tolerance," *Time*, November 7, 2017.

[14] For an example of this pervasive language in the discussion about religious pluralism see Gustav Niebuhr, *Beyond Tolerance. How People Across America Are Building Bridges Between Faiths* (New York: Penguin Books, 2008). For its impact in the discussion of same-sex marriage see Darel E. Paul, *From Tolerance to Equality. How Elites Brought America to Same-Sex Marriage* (Waco: Baylor University Press, 2018), 67–88.

The Replacements and the Return

We must go beyond toleration. So we are told already by key Enlightenment thinkers. But when we go back to their late-modern heirs, we find that the attitudes and practices that are proposed as a replacement for toleration differ considerably. It is one thing to move from toleration to freedom of expression or conscience; it is another thing to move from toleration to recognition or approval. The reasons for leaving tolerance behind also vary. Some of the reasons given namely point to the very nature of toleration. Others point to peculiarities of the Enlightenment that may or may not be present in our world as well. Is it Kant's enlightened monarch alone who should decline the "arrogant" name of toleration, or is a critique of the idea of State toleration itself implied in Kant's words? There are countless variations of these arguments, as we can see if we turn from toleration by the State to toleration between individual persons or groups. In a contemporary rendering of Goethe's *dictum*, some would argue that tolerance is always offensive, that if we respect each other, this respect will prove incompatible with mere toleration. Most of these arguments will include, in one form or the other, a reference to the pervasive pluralism of contemporary societies as a reason for transforming toleration into more affirmative dispositions. But is it true that this step is required? Or is a more plural world a circumstance that actually calls for a return to toleration as traditionally conceived? We may find out the answer by calmly considering some of the substitutes that are often proposed: hospitality, recognition, and agonistic respect.

We can begin to address these proposals by first noting the relative absence of postmodern work on toleration. There is a popular association between postmodernity and toleration: our times are reviled or celebrated for their "postmodern tolerance." But in fact, such a characterization often comes from opponents of either tolerance or postmodernism (or both). It is actually a rather rare experience to find a plea for toleration, even as a passing virtue, among the philosophers who are usually labeled postmodern. We seek in vain among them for a work that includes the word "tolerance" in its title, as the works of Locke and Voltaire did among the moderns.[15] It is not, of course, that the concern for our mutual understanding is unknown to postmodern philosophers: anyone who wishes to read on exclusion, marginalization, invisibilization, and so on will find a wealth of reflections on these topics in

[15] A short review is, for instance, all we find in the case of Foucault. Michel Foucault, "The Gray Mornings of Tolerance," in *Aesthetics, Method, and Epistemology*, ed. James D. Faubion (New York: New Press, 1998), 229–31.

the works of Vattimo, Foucault, or other thinkers lumped together under that label. Their silence on toleration is precisely a way to deal with what they perceive as the shortcomings of this practice in dealing with these problems. As in many other matters, taking a look at Derrida can be particularly fruitful. In Derrida we do not find silence, but rather a conscious distancing from the concept of tolerance. He is obviously not calling for a return to intolerance. His is a stance that, while preferring "shows of tolerance to shows of intolerance," nonetheless continues to have "reservations about the word tolerance."[16]

Derrida's rejection of tolerance as an ideal is based on two grounds. First, there is the religious origin of the concept. Although he sees the language of toleration as appropriated by Jews and Muslims as well, he describes it as "a form of charity[,] a Christian charity."[17] On the other hand, for Derrida tolerance is little more than "the good face of sovereignty"[18] because it always speaks from a position of superiority. Those in power tolerate as a concession. Both criticisms are, of course, related: this is a condescending charity that could be withdrawn. Tolerance understood in this way is a poor or small-minded form of coexistence. It is crucial to note that this critique is not aimed at perfecting our understanding of tolerance. It is not that we should strive for an adequate notion of tolerance, one that is freed from this potential withdrawal of arbitrary toleration. The concept itself is seen as a dead weight that should be abandoned and replaced by hospitality.[19] There are many questions one could raise at this point, since hospitality is even more rooted in the Abrahamic tradition than tolerance. Derrida, one might counter, is trying to offer an account of hospitality different than the one developed in the Jewish and Christian traditions. But this arguably makes his unwillingness to develop an alternative account of toleration all the more striking.

A similar turn from tolerance to hospitality can also be found in Christian moral theology. A good account of hospitality from this quarter, one that does not share the "postmodern" elements, is that offered by Luke Bretherton. In his *Hospitality as Holiness*, he examines and accepts several of the objections to toleration that we have rehearsed above. He recognizes that toleration is not a purely modern phenomenon, that questions of tolerance have been constant in the Christian tradition; but he treats the contemporary objections to toleration as valid for such older accounts as well. Hospitality, in his view, stands out as having more antecedents in Christian social practice and as

[16] Borradori, *Philosophy in a Time of Terror: Dialogues with Jürgen Habermas and Jacques Derrida*, 127.
[17] Borradori, 127.
[18] Borradori, 127.
[19] Borradori, 128–29.

being more explicitly grounded in the theological tradition. And these more substantively Christian roots of hospitality lead to the conclusion that tolerance "is inadequate when addressing the question of how Christians should relate to those with whom they disagree."[20] So far Bretherton's judgment in this work. In more recent writing, however, he has moved from the opposition between tolerance and hospitality to a vision that reasonably integrates them. He aims now at "toleration with hospitality," a formula that makes room for the many objectionable differences we still encounter in communities characterized by hospitality.[21] This is an altogether different project, one of integration instead of replacement, one that finds a legitimate place for the traditional conception of toleration. This, as we shall see, is also the conclusion tortuously arrived at in some contemporary reflection on recognition and "agonistic respect."

While hospitality may sound rather idiosyncratic to some ears, recognition is perhaps the attitude that most frequently has been proposed as a replacement for toleration. But a variety of philosophies of recognition have been developed in recent decades, some with a more uneasy relationship to the liberal tradition than others. A common starting point for many of these philosophies of recognition is the fact that we are not constituted in an autonomous way. Our development depends at least in part on the response that we receive from others. Those who are the object of no recognition—those who are seen by others in a one-sidedly negative light, for instance, or those who are not seen at all—are in a peculiarly difficult situation. Not only is their interaction with others damaged, but they are also prevented from developing a healthy relationship with themselves. If we care about the good of others, then, recognition will be a crucial aspect of the way we treat them. This does not imply that toleration should be left behind, and not all philosophies of recognition imply this. But it is often implied, and again we should stress that this is not only a "postmodern" argument.[22] Nor is it found only among

[20] Luke Bretherton, *Hospitality as Holiness: Christian Witness Amid Moral Diversity* (Farnham: Ashgate, 2006), 125.

[21] For his more recent discussion see Luke Bretherton, "Toleration with Hospitality," in *Christ and the Common Life. Political Theology and the Case for Democracy* (Grand Rapids: Eerdmans, 2019), 258–88.

[22] This tendency, Siep has argued, has been present among philosophers of recognition since this kind of concern began to be formally developed in German idealism. Ludwig Siep, "Toleranz und Anerkennung bei Kant und im Deutschen Idealismus," in *Toleranz als Ordnungsprinzip? Die moderne Bürgergesellschaft zwischen Offenheit und Selbstaufgabe*, ed. Michael Kahlo and Christoph Enders (Paderborn: Mentis, 2007), 177–93. For an attempt at affirming the place of tolerance in these authors, but in my view confirming the tendency I criticize, see Enzo Solari, "Contra la ilusión religiosa fanática y la furia de la destrucción: tolerancia, respeto y reconocimiento en Kant y Hegel," *Tópicos, Revista de Filosofía* 62, no. 1 (2022): 121–64.

philosophers. It can be found, to begin with, in much of popular discourse and activism, where recognition hardly means anything less than approval (as slogans such as "acceptance without exception" show). A similar approach retains the word toleration but emphatically tells us to understand it as a form of approval. The UNESCO Declaration of Principles on Tolerance, for example, calls us to move beyond one understanding of tolerance, namely tolerance as "concession, condescension or indulgence," inviting us to understand it as "respect, acceptance and appreciation of the rich diversity of our world's cultures, our forms of expression and ways of being human."[23] This is a significant departure from the 1945 Charter of the United Nations, which in its preamble soberly called "to practice tolerance and live together in peace with one another as good neighbours."[24] As we will discuss in later chapters, the understanding of recognition or tolerance of the UNESCO Declaration obviously depends on the way in which our differences are being understood. If the different "ways of being human" are understood in terms of merely cultural differences, it is difficult to find a legitimate response other than acceptance and appreciation. Preserving tolerance requires that we take account of forms of difference that are not cultural.

The UNESCO statement, as we have seen, does not call us to move beyond toleration but rather reinterprets toleration *as* recognition. This is also the title of one influential academic approach to these issues, Anna Elisabetta Galeotti's *Toleration as Recognition*. But she offers something more than the UNESCO statement, because she pretends that her theory is one that still makes room for toleration. It is, however, a very peculiar adaptation of the concept that survives. Galeotti argues that the classical approach to toleration was only suited to the kind of conflicts that people faced in the early modern period. People argued about elective aspects of their lives, and it was obvious that toleration was an appropriate response to such problems. A belief is, in her view, as elective as an action. The politically salient debates today, however, are not about elective but rather about ascriptive identities, such as race or gender. Because they cannot be changed, they are presented as more central to personal identity. Is tolerance or recognition the adequate response to such traits? The first impression one gains from Galeotti's work is that she pleads for a weak kind of recognition: not the affirmation of the intrinsic value of all forms

[23] UNESCO, *Declaration of Principles on Tolerance*, November 16, 1995, arts 1.1 and 1.2, available at: https://unesdoc.unesco.org/ark:/48223/pf0000151830 [accessed 2 January 2023].

[24] United Nations, *Charter of the United Nations*, October 24, 1945, Preamble, available at: https://www.un.org/en/about-us/un-charter/preamble [accessed 2 January 2023].

of life but the affirmation of the differences as important for their bearers.[25] But this does not mean that such identities should be treated with the tools of equality before the law; toleration as recognition must be pursued for its symbolic meaning. Same-sex marriage, for example, thus becomes "a direct consequence of the toleration of homosexual identity."[26] In what sense does toleration with its objection-component then survive? Galeotti contends that her proposal is still one of toleration, since she accepts that private objections to a given way of life may still be legitimate. However, these objections should not only remain private; they must be publicly ignored. The objectors themselves are not being asked to change their minds or to value the objected difference positively, but society is. Traditional toleration is thus backed into a corner. It subsists, but never in a way that is publicly relevant for the questions that, in Galeotti's own estimation, are more decisive today.

But not all discussions of recognition lead us in this direction. Concern for recognition does not necessarily lead to the banishment of toleration. The work of Charles Taylor is a good example of how a philosophy of recognition can simultaneously make room for toleration.[27] In examining his case, Jean Bethke Elshtain rightly notes that it is "by no means simple" to set out Taylor's position.[28] She describes his view as one of a "deep toleration" that is not grudging or instrumental at its core. In other words, both elements of recognition and of toleration are present. But what is the source of this capacity to integrate recognition and toleration? The key reason is arguably Taylor's awareness of two different aspects of the human condition. On the one hand, there is the element that is shared with other philosophies of recognition, a conviction about the place of the response and judgment of others in our development. On the other hand is his understanding of persons as "strong evaluators." As human beings we not only desire things like a new job or a new house, but we also desire to have different desires from the ones we actually have. Some of our desires are not desirable, and we desire to change them. In Augustine's own words, "there is a love by which we love what we ought not to love, and this love is hated by him who loves that by which he loves what ought to be loved."[29]

[25] Anna Elisabetta Galeotti, *Toleration as Recognition* (Cambridge: Cambridge University Press, 2002), 103–04.

[26] Galeotti, 170.

[27] For the main statement of his theory see Charles Taylor, "The Politics of Recognition," in *Multiculturalism: Examining the Politics of Recognition*, ed. Amy Gutmann (Princeton: Princeton University Press, 1992), 25–73.

[28] Jean Bethke Elshtain, "Toleration, Proselytizing, and the Politics of Recognition," in *Religious Pluralism, Globalization, and World Politics*, ed. Thomas Banchoff (Oxford: Oxford University Press, 2008), 97.

[29] *civ.* XI, 28.

Hence the distinction between weak and strong evaluation. Human beings, as Taylor writes, are not only "simple weighers of alternatives," but also "strong evaluators."[30] Not only do we ask whether we will eat now or later, plan this or that vacation, but we also make evaluations of ways of life that we recognize as incompatible with each other, ways of being that are in non-contingent conflict with each other. We furthermore develop a language of worth and baseness to describe such contrasts.[31] Strong evaluation is hence not compatible with the idea of leaving toleration behind. If the need for recognition and our condition as strong evaluators are adequately integrated, one can arrive at a "recognition with toleration" similar to the "hospitality with toleration" we just discussed. Its affirmative side distinguishes such a proposal from "mere" toleration, without therefore capitulating to unreasonable demands for approval. In the reception of Taylor's work, however, the emphasis on recognition has been more central than the description of human beings as strong evaluators, and the relationship between recognition and toleration hence tends to be conceived in terms of opposition rather than integration.

Finally, if we turn to the agonistic political philosophers, we find a similar trajectory, even though they are further removed from the pacifying inclinations of so much modern thought. Agonistic political philosophers are anxious about the emphasis on harmony and consensus that is characteristic of much contemporary liberal theory. If we are to deal honestly with difference, they tell us, we must acknowledge the pervasive nature of conflict. Such a diagnosis could lead to a revitalization of toleration, a virtue that is obviously needed when engaging in conflict. But since toleration has often been characterized as *the* liberal virtue, agonists tend to view it with suspicion. Toleration is often harshly rejected, as we have seen with Žižek.[32] But as we shall see, after this initial rejection it is often reclaimed. Chantal Mouffe, for instance, describes the main forms of liberal pluralism as deficient because they relegate pluralism to the private sphere as something that "we must bear grudgingly or try to reduce." Instead, she argues, pluralism should be seen as an "axiological principle," as something that we should "celebrate and enhance."[33] This might sound like Galeotti. But as her discussion moves on and the full consequences of her political philosophy unfold, Mouffe is forced to describe tolerance in traditional terms. Its true meaning, she tells us, "does not entail condoning ideas we

[30] Charles Taylor, "What Is Human Agency?" in *Philosophical Papers: Volume 1, Human Agency and Language* (Cambridge: Cambridge University Press, 1985), 23.
[31] Taylor, 19–24.
[32] Above I have already referred to Žižek, "A Plea for Leninist Intolerance."
[33] Chantal Mouffe, *The Democratic Paradox* (London and New York: Verso, 2000), 19.

oppose or being indifferent to standpoints that we disagree with, but treating those who defend them as legitimate opponents."[34] Not indifference, not celebration and enhancement, but just enduring. The same movement of rejection and reclaiming can be found in Wendy Brown's *Regulating Aversion*, one of the most complete analyses of toleration from this agonistic perspective. Above all, Brown tells us, she "seeks to track the complex involvement of tolerance with power."[35] This disguised power, she argues, does not lose any of its force when it tolerates: it marks the objects of tolerance as undesirable, marginalizes them, and thus creates a breeding ground for resentment. In other words, her question is not simply what has become of tolerance, but what kind of political discourse is circulating under the guise of current tolerance talk. "What retreat from stronger ideals of justice is conveyed by giving tolerance pride of place in a moral-political vision of the good"?[36] But while this critique of liberal tolerance is the dominant tone of her book, Brown concedes that "tolerance as such is not the problem," that "tolerance as a public value [does] have its place."[37] This is, of course, a welcome clarification, though one must ask why some thinkers put themselves in the position of having to make it.

Let us finally turn to William Connolly. Although his main concern is not tolerance itself but pluralism, Connolly has written in a way that is roughly congenial to Mouffe and Brown. In the context of this concern, he writes of tolerance as "an underdeveloped form of critical responsiveness grounded in misrecognition."[38] This is by now familiar language: it is good to have tolerance, but with the advent of a more developed attitude or virtue toward difference, it should be left behind. The cardinal virtues to which Connolly invites us are critical responsiveness (toward oppressed or invisibilized constituencies) and agonistic respect (toward those who "have already attained a place on the register of cultural recognition").[39] The distinction between these virtues is crucial. Insofar as critical responsiveness is directed towards those who are below the level of recognition, it is a "careful listening and presumptive generosity."[40] In a setting where such careful listening takes precedence, there will not be much judgment and hence not much place for tolerance either. But this does not hold for agonistic respect. Connolly introduces it as a "kissing cousin

[34] Mouffe, 102.
[35] Wendy Brown, *Regulating Aversion: Tolerance in the Age of Identity and Empire* (Princeton: Princeton University Press, 2009), 9.
[36] Brown, 5–6.
[37] Brown, 14.
[38] William E. Connolly, *The Ethos of Pluralization* (Minneapolis: University of Minnesota Press, 1995), xvii.
[39] William E. Connolly, *Pluralism* (Durham and London: Duke University Press, 2005), 123.
[40] Connolly, 126.

of liberal tolerance."[41] So, as with the other authors we have considered, we see something very similar to the traditional ideal of toleration emerging after the critique of liberal tolerance. The difference between these "kissing cousins" would be that tolerance is granted to private minorities by the majorities that have the power equally to refrain from tolerating, while agonistic respect works among equals. Connolly also wants to highlight the contrast between agonistic interdependence and the "passive letting the other be" that presumably characterizes tolerance.[42] But to what extent are these essential ingredients of toleration? And, if they are, is there not a legitimate place for this passive letting be, often granted by majorities? And is it the case that toleration can only be acceptable among equals, that it has no legitimate place when it comes to those who are "struggling to move from an obscure or degraded subsistence below the field of recognition"?[43] Several such questions can be raised after rehearsing this argument. But the most important question is the one that has emerged throughout this section. As Connolly acknowledges, his perspective "remains close enough to liberal tolerance to invite comparison and critical negotiation."[44] Why do so many contemporary thinkers put themselves at odds with a concept of toleration that they subsequently set out to rehabilitate? This must be given some further thought.

Unconditional Affirmation and Conditional Tolerance

Why does a substantial portion of contemporary political thought pass through the rejection of tolerance only to reclaim it later? Part of the answer to this question lies in their concern about tacit liberal exclusions and in their acute perception of what is lost in a depoliticized world. They may be right to see toleration as one of the concepts that often serves as an umbrella and rationalization for these phenomena. The emphasis on unconditional hospitality at the expense of tolerance can thus be understood as a response to an earlier condition of marginalization, a marginalization that took place precisely as a policy of tolerance. One should certainly be more hesitant to synthesize modern or Western history along these lines. But to the extent that it is summarized in such terms, the call for unconditional hospitality will not seem out of place: not

[41] Connolly, 123.
[42] William E. Connolly, *The Augustinian Imperative: A Reflection on the Politics of Morality* (Lanham, MD: Rowman & Littlefield Publishers, 2002), 156.
[43] Connolly, *Pluralism*, 126.
[44] Connolly, *The Augustinian Imperative*, 156.

conditional toleration but rather unconditional recognition will bridge the gap between fellow human beings. The mere mention of tolerance would, in contrast, seem to introduce into our relationships a conditional nature that continues to keep the other at arm's length—a form of misrecognition. The rhetoric against toleration can then be read as a correction of the liberal tradition as it was discussed in our previous chapter: recognition, hospitality, and agonistic respect bring back precisely the robust identities that neutralist or minimalist approaches to toleration exclude. But as politics is rehabilitated, as tacit exclusions are removed and robust identities become public, we will have more, not less, need for toleration. As Connolly puts it, we should strive for relations of interdependence and contestation in which those involved understand "self-restriction amidst conflict."[45] This approaches a definition of tolerance, and hence again our question. Why is there a widespread tendency to leave toleration behind, and then to reclaim it, albeit somewhat reluctantly? Why is the concern for recognition or hospitality not framed as a corrective to flawed versions of toleration, rather than conceiving of these dispositions as its replacements?

Indeed, it is intriguing how seldom one encounters the idea that a disposition of recognition and a disposition of tolerance can be cultivated simultaneously as we respond to reality. For if the realities we face are multidimensional, as most of them are, they require multidimensional responses as well. If we can read a book in awe of its greatness while rejecting the theories it channels, something analogous is possible in the relationship between fellow citizens. As Peter Jones has noted, "it is not difficult for people simultaneously to recognise and to disapprove."[46] Both dispositions can be cultivated together, without attempting to overcome toleration. As Jeremy Webber has argued, there is no need to press for a "single master concept" in the field.[47] Moreover, the line of demarcation between toleration and recognition does not leave toleration on the side of mere abstention and condescending distance from that which is tolerated. As Webber argues, any tolerating accommodation of a practice "requires that one determine the existence and scope of that practice."[48] Toleration thus conceived implies a restraint that "is itself informed by knowledge of the belief" to which one objects, a knowledge that includes at least "its scope and its importance to the people who hold it."[49] Sometimes recognition

[45] Connolly, 29.
[46] Peter Jones, "Toleration, Recognition and Identity," *The Journal of Political Philosophy* 14, no. 2 (2006): 131.
[47] Webber, "The Generosity of Toleration," 270.
[48] Webber, 283.
[49] Webber, 285.

is also described in such terms. This does not imply recognizing in the sense of approving but rather in the sense of acknowledging the value of a belief or a culture to those who hold it or belong to it.[50] When treated in such terms, the compatibility and proximity of toleration and recognition is worth emphasizing.

But theoretical discussions of recognition often ignore how emphatically their popular reception runs in the direction of simple approval. In positing its incompatibility with toleration, such discussions in fact themselves push in that direction. That project, however, must be resisted. It must be resisted, first, because it clashes with human nature. Many arguments against toleration are arguments against the very phenomena of judgment, strong evaluation, and deep disagreement. As Horton writes, "the kind of negative attitudes associated with the traditional conception of toleration are often no more than a familiar and unexceptional concomitant of what it is to believe that actions, practices or ways of life are wrong."[51] To demand strong forms of recognition between groups that judge each other's ways of life to be wrong is to ignore how essential that judgment of wrongness often is to the nature of each side. Strong forms of recognition place impossible demands and thus illustrate what Webber has called the "intolerant sting" of recognition.[52] But rejecting toleration in the name of recognition is also pragmatically misguided for other reasons. Clarity about the limited nature of toleration will, after all, help us to respond to those who refuse to tolerate with the excuse that they are being asked to approve. This is a common temptation. There are some who think they must persecute error, John Owen wrote, because "what is forborne they suppose must needs be approved."[53] This may sometimes be a cynical excuse. But a culture that is confused about the nature of toleration will be a fertile soil for such excuses. If the alternatives that are left standing are those of recognition and intolerance, it is unrealistic to imagine us all turning to recognition.

Avoiding a turn to intolerance, then, requires offering an account of our relationships that preserves toleration's moment of negativity. But while preserving that moment of negativity, we can also preserve some crucial emphases of the turn to recognition, which has been inspired by legitimate concerns. To bear, in the words of Glenn Tinder, "is not only to suffer but also

[50] For one such discussion of the meanings of recognition see Sune Laegaard, "State Toleration, Religious Recognition and Equality," in *Tolerance, Intolerance and Respect. Hard to Accept?* ed. Tariq Modood and Jan Dobbernack (Basingstoke: Palgrave Macmillan, 2013), 65–67. For the ways in which this can be combined with direct and indirect recognition see Jones, "Toleration, Recognition and Identity," 134.

[51] Horton, "Traditional Conception," 300.

[52] Webber, "The Generosity of Toleration," 272.

[53] Owen, *Indulgence and Toleration Considered*, XIII, 538.

to support or uphold."[54] A rich and just political life requires recognition of the other as an equal, the willingness to listen to his or her arguments with a generous spirit. It requires that we question our own prejudices, and it depends on an openness to the enrichment that those of whom we know little or nothing can bring into our lives. These standards might equally sum up the philosophy of hospitality. Within this context, tolerance is not only eminently humane but also a fundamental necessity. As the rest of this book will show, however, this integrated vision can come not only from the contemporary philosophical scene, but also from a distant past. And if the critiques we have surveyed are not only "postmodern" but also depend on a recurrent Enlightenment critique of toleration, then the new beginning we need may be found, at least in part, much further back. Let us turn, then, to the case for an Augustinian approach.

[54] Glenn Tinder, *Tolerance: Toward a New Civility* (Amherst: University of Massachusetts Press, 1976), 139. As Peter Königs has more recently noted, the acceptance component of toleration has received far less attention than its objection component. Peter Königs, "The Simplicity of Toleration," *Critical Review of International Social and Political Philosophy* 24, no. 1 (2021): 7.

4

Thinking about Tolerance with Augustine

Beyond *Compelle intrare*

Toleration is often treated as a central achievement of modernity. There is certainly a grain of truth, and perhaps more than a grain, to this view. Times of conflict, both within and between different communities, naturally call for this practice in a particularly intense way. But toleration, we should also recall, is as old as humanity. Human flourishing requires cooperation, but the grouping together necessary for such cooperation also brings with it the realities of discord and conflict. Toleration, then, is one of the requirements for maintaining the health of any community. Reflection on toleration can, of course, come later, after the actual practice, but by the time of Augustine it was already present. And as this book argues, the guiding thread of his reflection still has much to offer. For many, however, this will be an outlandish idea. Although Augustine remains a significant participant in the contemporary theological and philosophical discussion in other respects—about the nature of time and eternity, about the Trinity and the self, about memory and illumination, and so on—few Augustinians expect him to shed light on this precise question. For not only did he not write a work commending toleration; he is rather known for the opposing stance, for explicitly abandoning his early commitment to toleration. At least a brief look at his trajectory is thus in order.

In his early Letter 23, written around the year 392, Augustine had committed himself to avoiding any form of coercion, so that by persuasion "the truth might be made conspicuous to those who search for it in peace."[1] This early defense of freedom was soon to be abandoned, and Augustine would go on to develop carefully crafted arguments in support of the imperial coercion of the Donatists. Why? It is sometimes claimed that the Christian turn from advocacy of tolerance to intolerance simply reflects a change in the social position of Christianity, from persecuted to the dominant religion. Against this superficial impression, it is useful to remember that both these tendencies

[1] *ep.* 23, 7.

An Augustinian Essay on Toleration. Manfred Svensson, Oxford University Press. © Manfred Svensson 2026.
DOI: 10.1093/9780197912737.003.0006

could be present in a single author, even before this change in the Church's social position took place.[2] But the change of course plays some role. Donatists themselves had been the first to bring these issues before the emperor, but this they could only do because there was in fact a Christian emperor.[3] Before Constantine's conversion, Augustine writes, men could serve God by living faithfully, but no one could serve God as a ruler. After this conversion, we can ask how rulers are to serve him.[4] Other arguments were likewise historically contingent. Augustine judged that truly anarchical conditions had developed under the Catholic-Donatist controversy, and this anomia impacted both the rich and the weakest members of society.[5] But most crucial to his change of heart was the testimony of former Donatists who were grateful for the salutary pressure that helped break their stubbornness—the "force of custom"—and thus set them free.[6] Augustine was as far as Locke from believing in forced conversions, but he did believe that certain forms of "terror" (*stimulus terroris*) could break irrational fears. He believed that force—in the form, for example, of confiscation of property—could in this *indirect* sense contribute to an honest inward turning of the heart.[7] And he also believed that the illegitimate violence of the Donatists could be distinguished from the correction engaged in by their rivals. They looked the same, but they could be differentiated by their motive.[8]

Since Augustine himself tells us that not every action is good by virtue of its good motive or intention, one can question some of these arguments even on Augustinian grounds.[9] One might also note that he found coercion justifiable by relying on experience (or the testimony of former Donatists) instead of theological argument.[10] Whatever our estimation of them, however, it is undeniable

[2] See Guy S. Strousma's observations regarding the tensions in the work of Tertullian. Guy G. Stroumsa, "Tertullian on Idolatry and the Limits of Tolerance," in *Tolerance and Intolerance in Early Judaism and Christianity*, ed. Guy G. Stroumsa (Cambridge: Cambridge University Press, 1998), 173–84. For Lactancius' notable defence of toleration between Tertullian and Augustine see Elizabeth D. Digeser, *The Making of a Christian Empire. Lactancius and Rome* (Ithaca, NY: Cornell University Press, 2000).

[3] *ep*. 185, 2, 6.

[4] *ep*. 185, 5, 19.

[5] *ep*. 185, 4, 15.

[6] *ep*. 93, 1, 1 and 185, 2, 7.

[7] Most clearly in *ep*. 93, 5, 18; see also *ep*. 93, 1, 1 and 185, 3, 13.

[8] On this see Geoffrey D. Dunn, "Discipline, Coercion, and Correction. Augustine against the Violence of the Donatists in Epistula 185," *Scrinium* 13 (2017): 114–30.

[9] For the rejection of mere good motives as standard of moral evaluation see *c. mend*. 8, 17, a passage that John Finnis has described as "foundational for Catholic moral theology from the thirteenth to the twentieth century." John Finnis, *Moral Absolutes. Tradition, Revision, and Truth* (Washington, DC: The Catholic University of America Press, 1991), 65.

[10] Though extremely critical of Augustine, Schreiner makes this partially exonerating point. Schreiner, "'Duldsamkeit' (tolerantia) oder 'Schrecken' (terror).' Reaktionsformen auf Abweichungen von der religiösen Norm, am Beispiel des augustinischen Toleranz- und Gewaltkonzeptes und dessen Rezeption im Mittelalter und in der frühen Neuzeit," 167.

that Augustine's arguments for coercion nourish virtually the entire later tradition of justifying persecution.[11] These were arguments specifically designed to deal with the problem of the Donatist schism, not with any other heresy, nor with Paganism. As for Jews and Judaism, Augustine's arguments in support of their toleration left an important mark on the centuries that followed.[12] But the anti-Donatist arguments also took on a life of their own that wound up being applied to cases far removed from their original target. Since the dawn of the modern era, Augustine has thus been identified as a source of obfuscation rather than wisdom regarding the duty of toleration. As Jed W. Atkins has noted, he "receives far more attention as a theorist of coercion than as one of tolerance."[13] When Pierre Bayle published his great *Commentaire Philosophique* in favor of toleration (1686), he did so by directly addressing Augustine.[14] Bayle's work, as the subtitle reads, dwells "on these words of the Gospel, Luke 14.23, 'Compel Them to Come in, that My House May be Full.'" It was in these very words, *compelle intrare*, that the Augustinian tradition of coercion had found scriptural support for the use of force as an external and indirect aid to religious persuasion.[15] Locke was not as vocal as Bayle in writing against an authority extolled by all Christian confessions, but his friend Philip van Limborch gives a good summary of what nearly every apologist for toleration thought in their generation: that "everyone who has defended persecution after Augustine ... has done so relying solely on his authority." Persecutors, argued van Limborch, always make use of Augustine's arguments as "the strongest, even though in themselves they are absurd and demonstrably contrary to Scripture."[16] We can now add that everyone who today defends toleration feels the need to say something negative concerning Augustine's place in its history. "Within the context of the Augustinian inheritance," as one historian puts it, "there was no virtue or

[11] For a general survey of this reception see Mansuy and Svensson, "Tolerance". For a consideration of its more specific pre-Lockean forms see Mark Goldie, "The Theory of Religious Intolerance in Restoration England," in *From Persecution to Toleration. The Glorious Revolution and Religion in England*, ed. Ole Peter Grell, Jonathan Israel, and Nicholas Tyacke (Oxford: Clarendon Press, 1991), 331–68.

[12] On this see Fredriksen, *Augustine and the Jews. A Christian Defense of Jews and Judaism.*

[13] Atkins, *The Christian Origins of Tolerance*, 219.

[14] Pierre Bayle, *A Philosophical Commentary on These Words of the Gospel, Luke 14:23, "Compel Them to Come In, That My House May Be Full"* (Indianapolis: Liberty Fund, 2000).

[15] Whether this Biblical text played such an important role for Augustine himself, or whether his theory was rather forced into this text which he otherwise could comment differently, is discussed by Emilien Lamirande, *Church, State and Toleration. An Intriguing Change of Mind in Augustine*, The Saint Augustine Lecture 1974 (Villanova: Villanova University Press, 1975), 51–57.

[16] Philip van Limborch, *History of the Inquisition* (London: Simpkin and Marshall, 1816), 78. We can safely assume Locke's agreement with this statement, since he can almost count as Limborch's co-author in this work. John Locke, *The Correspondence of John Locke*, ed. E.S. de Beer (Oxford: Oxford University Press, 1976), III, Letters 1033, 1034, 1058.

truth to be found in the idea of tolerance."[17] For Rainer Forst, Augustine is the chief example of the "Janus face" of Christian toleration.[18] For three centuries, a broad consensus has thus prevailed.

Augustinians themselves have spilled much ink either apologizing for this aspect of Augustine's work or explaining why a more nuanced judgment is possible.[19] This book does not enter into that discussion. Its argument is not based in any kind of revisionism. In an age that believes that everything must be purged and cancelled to start anew, it may even be healthy to begin with a tainted author. My point is simply that, even if one accepts the harshest and most undifferentiated judgments about Augustine, it is still possible to think constructively with him about toleration. A further look at the nature of the Donatist controversy may help us understand why. The Donatists themselves had a peculiar position concerning tolerance. It is not just that they called for an imperial intervention before the Catholics did or that they were unable to draw a sharper line excluding the violent faction of the Circumcellions (though both of these things are true). More important is the fact that Donatism was, in a way, a schism over the very notion of schism. Technically, it came down to the specific point that those tainted by their failures during times of persecution could not administer the sacraments validly. A strong expectation of corporate purity obviously underlies this vision, often accompanied by a peculiar psychology as well (such as a sense of superior holiness deriving from separation and smaller numbers).[20] This strict conception of their internal life is the flipside of their later rejection of imperial coercion. It can be said that they pleaded for tolerance in the world and discipline in the Church. And it is here that we must return to Augustine. For in his work this internal "intolerance" and the external tolerance of the Donatists are turned upside down. He defends the use of coercion to bring the Donatists back to the Church, but his writings are interspersed with abundant pleas for the tolerance that should

[17] C. Scott Dixon, *Contesting the Reformation* (Oxford: Wiley-Blackwell, 2012), 147. For a similar approach see Alexandra Walsham on the "Augustinian assumptions" that made toleration anathema. Walsham, *Charitable Hatred*, 2.

[18] Forst, *Toleration in Conflict: Past and Present*, 47–69. For an earlier critique see Robert Joly, "L'intolérance de saint Augustin, doctrine ou attitude?," in *Hommage à Marcel Renard, I*, Collection Latomus (Brussels: Latomus, 1969), 101: 493–500.

[19] For a rather naïve defense see Daniel X. Burt, "Friendly Persuasion: Augustine on Religious Toleration," *American Catholic Philosophical Quarterly* 74, no. 1 (1990): 63–76. For more sophisticated accounts see John Bowlin, "Augustine on Justifying Coercion," *The Annual of the Society of Christian Ethics* 17 (1997): 49–70; von Heyking, *Augustine and Politics as Longing in the World*, 222–57; and, above all, Atkins, *The Christian Origins of Tolerance*, 219–53.

[20] For a recent overview of the controversy see Peter Iver Kaufman, *Incorrectly Political. Augustine and Thomas More* (Notre Dame: University of Notre Dame Press, 2007), 71–98. For detailed discussion of its many aspects, see the studies collected in Richard Miles, ed., *The Donatist Schism: Controversy and Contexts* (Liverpool: Liverpool University Press, 2016).

be practiced within the ecclesial community, which he saw as a mixed body of the good and the evil. These will be separated, but only on the seashore, at the end of the *saeculum*. In the meantime, the Church "corrects as many as she can and bears with those she cannot correct."[21] If the Donatists were obsessed with the risk of contamination and rushed to discriminate between nominal and real Christians, Augustine would rather see that rashness excluded. This Augustinian reversal of the Donatist position became the dominant doctrine in the West for centuries. Its imprint can be found in an almost identical form in Augustinians as diverse as Thomas Aquinas and Martin Luther.[22] But what should we think about this reversal? We can consider some of its consequences disastrous and still ask ourselves whether we have something to learn from what Augustine wrote about tolerance within the Church. And there is no reason why we should not extend some of the insights into the nature of tolerance found there to the rest of our social life.

Augustine's Reasons for Toleration

But where is the novelty of Augustine's view? As in other aspects of his thought, Augustine obviously draws on both Christian insights and a broad ancient philosophical tradition. Alan Kreider has reminded us that the first Christian treatise on any particular virtue was on patience. As he points out, the early Church gave us three treatises on patience, often extolling it as the highest virtue, and as the one most peculiar to Christians. Kreider was fond of Tertullian and Cyprian. He was not as fond of Augustine, whose *De patientia* was the third of these treatises.[23] He is also critical of the ancient philosophers, whom he describes as "unwilling to recognize patience as a virtue."[24] This is hardly a fair assessment, and our consideration of Augustine's reasons for toleration should start here. As contemporary scholarship has shown, there are relevant insights into toleration and patience among the ancient philosophers, though not all

[21] See, for instance, *ep*. 93, 9, 34.

[22] Aquinas' commentary on Matthew 13 in his *Lectura Super Mattheum* and Luther's sermon on the same chapter in WA 52: 130–35, for instance, quote the same selection of anti-Donatist texts.

[23] Kreider is highly critical of Augustine's account of patience, which in his view devalues the exterior patient act. He not only suspects "additional motives" (283, alluding to the coercion of the Donatists), but also describes Augustine's ethics as "situational" and "elastic" (285). Alan Kreider, *The Patient Ferment of the Early Church. The Improbable Rise of Christianity in the Roman Empire* (Grand Rapids: Baker Academic, 2016). Augustine is notably absent from the discussion in Michel Spanneut, "Le stoïcisme dans l'histoire de la patience chrétienne," *Mélanges de science religieuse* 39, no. 3 (1982): 101–30.

[24] Kreider, *Patient Ferment*, 20.

schools approached it in explicit terms. One recent study, for instance, has persuasively argued that tolerance is a good candidate for the third of Aristotle's "unnamed virtues." These nameless virtues, which Aristotle discusses in book IV of his *Nicomachean Ethics*, all relate to our social relationships (they are not equal to friendship, but they are like it). The possessor of the third of these virtues is characterized by Aristotle as someone who can both agree and disagree in the right way, seeking a golden mean between flattery and quarrelsomeness.[25] This sounds like a "kissing cousin" of toleration. But if this attribution is correct, it draws out the main features of a rather implicit view of toleration, one that remains unnamed in its source. The case of Stoicism is very different. It has often been suggested that here we find the first explicit Western discussion of tolerance.

There is much in the Stoic tradition that seems to address the contemporary weaknesses that we have discussed so far. Although the political practice of tolerance has been favorably viewed in the modern West, Andrew Fiala notes how the ancient virtue of tolerance has been forgotten. Drawing on Marcus Aurelius, Epictetus, and Seneca, he shows how their praise of tolerance describes it as rooted in justice, control of our own emotions, a general notion of impartiality, and the training in proper judgment. Tolerance thus conceived avoids the "disruptive emotion of anger" while preserving the "proper concern and moral outrage that follow from a concern for justice."[26] Fiala invites us not only to reconsider tolerance as virtue but also to see its relations to other virtues, grounding it in "wonder and self-restraint" and showing its alliance with "modesty, generosity, and hospitality."[27] This is precisely an "alliance," not a substitute for toleration. Building on the insights of Fiala and others, John Lombardini has suggested a more fine-grained approach to tolerance among the Stoics. Among early Roman Stoics such as Seneca, he finds a different view than that to be found later in the work of Epictetus and Marcus Aurelius. While in both stages *tolerantia* is tied to central Stoic concerns, Lombardini has argued that in the early stage it is more closely tied to the endurance of physical pain. Knowing how to endure it is part of our dealing with externals. In Marcus Aurelius, in contrast, it is firmly tied to justice, which is not concerned with indifferent externals but with things we object to in our dealings with other persons. It is only here that Lombardini sees a proper concept of toleration

[25] Richard Avramenko and Michael Promisel, "When Toleration Becomes a Vice: Naming Aristotle's Third Unnamed Virtue," *American Journal of Political Science* 62, no. 4 (2018): 849–60.

[26] Andrew Fiala, *Tolerance and the Ethical Life* (London and New York: Continuum, 2005), 59–81, 72.

[27] Fiala, 1.

emerging.[28] But there is no consensus on how appropriate it is. Atkins is more cautious about attributing to the Stoics a proper conception of tolerance. In his thorough interpretation, "the idea of objection that attends the notion of tolerance is constantly destabilized based on key components of the Stoic system."[29] Considering, for example, the cosmological and theological ingredients of Stoicism, he notes how its notion of providence tends to dissolve the very notion of evil, thus rendering tolerance *stricto sensu* superfluous.[30]

How does Augustine relate to this ancient philosophical tradition? How should we describe his Christian corrections of the tradition? One explicitly Christian correction concerns the passions, for which he seeks a sound teaching in the Scriptures. There he finds a wise man who lacks neither anger nor sadness. The critical question, he writes, is what makes us angry or sad. In light of this, he rejects the Stoic critique of compassion and argues instead for passions that are subject to the mind.[31] But although this begins as a Biblical critique of the Stoics, Augustine himself points out that his teaching is that of the Platonists and the Peripatetics and that once some misunderstandings are corrected the Stoics too adhere to something along these lines. His critique of the Stoic approach to suicide follows a similar path, with both a polemical and a harmonizing side in his relation to Paganism. Addressing the suicides of Lucretia and Cato, he measures them against the example of the Christian virgins who had been raped, but also against the thought of Virgil and Plato.[32]

His Christian corrections of the Stoics, in other words, are those of a philosopher. Indeed, he rests on a solid philosophical tradition when he speaks of a strength that "is resolved to tolerate any evil rather than consenting to evil."[33] Though Augustine was not familiar with Plato's *Gorgias*, this is very much in line with Socrates' teaching that it is worse to commit injustice or do wrong than to suffer it.[34] This may, in fact, be the core moral–philosophical foundation of tolerance. But while Socratic–Stoic tolerance is a virtue of the uniquely wise, Augustine sees it as part of the wisdom we all should share. "In this life toleration is necessary for the poor and the rich, the healthy and the sick, the captive and the free, the strangers and those at home; toleration is necessary,

[28] John Lombardini, "Stoicism and the Virtue of Toleration," *History of Political Thought* 36, no. 4 (2015): 643–69.

[29] Atkins, *The Christian Origins of Tolerance*, 66.

[30] Atkins, 59.

[31] *civ.* IX, 5.

[32] For his use of these sources see Richard J. Dougherty, "St. Augustine and the Problem of Political Ethics in The City of God," in *Augustine's Political Thought*, ed. Richard J. Dougherty (Rochester, NY: University of Rochester Press, 2019), 13–35.

[33] *civ.* I, 18.

[34] Plato, *Gorgias*, trans. Robin Waterfield (Oxford: Oxford University Press, 1994), 475e.

since we are all pilgrims in the world," he writes in one sermon.[35] Nietzsche famously criticized Christianity as Platonism for the masses, and here Augustine could well agree. Tolerance is part of the shared wisdom of pilgrimage. In the *City of God*, the duty of toleration is underscored for all members of the pilgrim city, "whether they be kings, princes, judges, soldiers, or provincial magistrates, whether they be rich or poor, free or slave, of either sex."[36]

In considering this universal need for toleration, however, we should return to the question Lombardini raised about the Stoics: is this a call for the captive and the free to endure physical evil—poverty and pain—or is a broader view of tolerance suggested? Although all sorts of evils may be everyday objects of tolerance, the evil that drives Augustine's thinking about tolerance is the disruption of human community. What sort of disruption? The early Christians, we should note at the outset, were faced with a challenge quite different from our own. Rather than being confronted, as we often are, with claims about the value of different world religions or about accommodation between rival worldviews, they were confronted with the pious call to preserve the customs of the ancestors. And they rejected that call. With their theological critique of this ancient piety, they helped to give birth to the conflict between visions of the good that is now a common feature of political life.[37] When Augustine writes the *City of God*, he can already take for granted that such a conflict between opposing ultimate loyalties—and the ability to live out such a conflict peacefully—stands at the center of our concern for history and our common life. The novelty of this kind of pluralism is seldom recognized. It is not a clash of interests, civilizations, parties, or classes (which were already theorized by Plato, Aristotle, and Cicero). It is a conflict between ultimate loves, citizenships, or commitments. This is, in fact, a crucial moment in the history of pluralism. All our contemporary theorizing about how different "visions of the good" can coexist ultimately derives from here, from the idea that the most relevant plurality in human society is one of ultimate orientations. Augustine's is not a celebration of these different visions of the good. It is a defense of one of the two cities. But he takes for granted the intermingling of the two societies as a constant of future history, and he acknowledges a search for earthly peace in both cities.

But Augustine's vision of toleration is not formed purely on this view of history and society, nor only on the Stoic and Christian discussions of patience.

[35] *s.* 359a, 5.

[36] *civ.* II, 19.

[37] For this development see Robert L. Wilken, "Religious Pluralism and Early Christian Theology," *Interpretation: A Journal of Bible and Theology* 40, no. 4 (1986): 379–91.

His understanding of some biblical texts is also crucial. Let us close this section considering this source of his thought. While he inaugurated a tradition of interpretation of Luke 14 in support of coercion, Augustine also inaugurated a tradition of interpretation of Matthew 13 in support of toleration. In this chapter, which is central to Augustine's struggle with the Donatists, we find the parable of the wheat and the tares. In this parable, Jesus illustrates the kingdom of God with the image of a field in which, after good seed has been sown, an enemy sows bad seed, and the two seeds grow up together. Seeing this mixture, the owner's servants suggest to their master that they pull up the tares. But the master warns them of the danger of pulling up the wheat at the same time. The task, he tells them, should be left to the reapers, who will separate the wheat from the tares when time is due (Mt. 13:24–30). Augustine often comments on the parable, both in polemical and upbuilding contexts. "You see tares among the wheat. You see evil Christians among the good, and you wish to root up the evil ones. Be quiet. It is not yet time for the harvest," he writes in his sermon 73.[38] There is for Augustine a meaningful distinction between wheat and tares, but discerning between them is a more than risky task. Only the final harvest will release us from our ongoing obligation to tolerate. Augustine's was not, of course, the only possible reading of the text. While Augustine read the field as encompassing both the Church and the world, the Donatists claimed that the parable allowed for mixing only in the world, not in the Church. But however it is read, the parable has helped to raise questions throughout the history of Christian reflection on toleration, from the controversies of the Reformation to the contemporary discussion on identity politics and its claims to purity.[39] As the parable's enduring vitality suggests, its principal ancient commentator can still speak to our debates.

Tolerance and its Inseparable Companions

In the previous section we have considered Augustine's philosophical and biblical sources. But how does he understand the nature of the toleration he prescribes? And how does this understanding help us respond to the problems raised in the first chapters of this book? Perhaps the first thing to emphasize is

[38] *s.* 73, 1.

[39] For the premodern discussion see Roland Bainton, "The Parable of the Tares as the Proof Text for Religious Liberty to the End of the Sixteenth Century," *Church History* 1, no. 2 (1932): 67–89. For contemporary application, see Joshua Mitchell, *American Awakening: Identity Politics and Other Afflictions of Our Time* (New York and London: Encounter Books, 2020), 60–62.

Augustine's integration of tolerance into a broader web of virtues. This is a recurring theme in his sermons and letters: in the "alternation of adversity and prosperity" we are called to "vigilantly exercise patience and temperance."[40] It is the "precepts of patience" along with benevolence that keep us from repaying evil for evil.[41] In practicing toleration, he further writes, we simultaneously exercise the other virtues of those who follow the good path.[42] This integration is especially important for distinguishing between the virtue of tolerance and its vicious lookalike. In Letter 167 to Jerome, we find an extended discussion of this problem. There Augustine writes that Catiline could endure cold, thirst, and hunger, that he stood out for his patience and courage. But, he continues, Catiline's courage was not really prudent, because he chose evil over good; it was not just, because he conspired against his own country. This courage, then, was not truly courageous, but rather a deceptive resemblance of courage.[43] Patience and tolerance are true virtues when the other virtues are also present. There is nothing unique about Augustine's position, which consciously draws on a common classical teaching about the unity of the virtues.[44] But there are some specifically Augustinian twists on this idea of the virtues as "inseparable companions."[45] In Aristotle, for example, it is practical wisdom (*phronêsis*) that accounts for their unity: each moral virtue depends on practical wisdom, and practical wisdom in turn depends on the possession of these virtues —none of them can thus exist without the others. For Augustine, in contrast, it is love that plays this unifying role. Where love is absent, then, only the resemblance of virtue remains. "Many things can be done that have a good appearance, but do not proceed from the root of charity."[46] There is a "terrible" or "inhuman" toleration (*immanis tolerantia*),[47] as well as an innocent or a persevering toleration (*innocentissima tolerantia, perseverantissima tolerantia*).[48] The latter is only to be met when love holds the virtues together.[49] Even if tolerance alone cannot serve as an answer to all the problems of human coexistence, it plays

[40] *ep.* 137, 4, 16.
[41] *ep.* 138, 2, 14.
[42] *cat. rud.* 25, 48.
[43] *ep.* 167, 2, 7.
[44] Joseph Clair's otherwise excellent study errs in separating Augustine from this tradition. What Augustine rejects in Letter 167 is the Stoic teaching about the equality of vices, not the unity of the virtues. Joseph Clair, *Discerning the Good in the Letters and Sermons of Augustine* (Oxford: Oxford University Press, 2016), 70.
[45] *ep.* 167, 2, 7.
[46] *ep. Io. tr.* 7, 8.
[47] *pat.* 4, 4.
[48] *c. ep. Parm.* II, 3, 6; *bapt.* II, 5, 6.
[49] For Augustine's successive ways of explaining their distinctiveness while affirming this unity see John Bowlin, "Augustine Counting Virtues," *Augustinian Studies* 41, no. 1 (2010): 277–300.

a crucial role within this wider web of virtues. Moreover, if tolerance always goes hand in hand with other virtues, it is not as merely grudging as is often suggested. According to Augustine, we can tolerate "not only equitably, but even exultantly."[50]

The unity of the virtues naturally leads us to the question of their hierarchy. How would Augustine approach our discussions of the primacy of tolerance? Locke, as we have seen, describes toleration as the first mark of the true Church. It is still very often thought of in this way. For Andrew Jason Cohen, "What should be tolerated?" is "the most important question of political morality."[51] For Chandran Kukathas, a society that upholds freedom of association and liberty of conscience "is a society for which the first virtue is toleration."[52] Augustinians are perhaps expected rather to side with Wendy Brown, who seeks to strip toleration of its "wholly blessed status."[53] Given Augustine's insight into the ambivalent nature of the practice of toleration, which may in fact only resemble a true virtue, there is some truth to this suggestion. But we should also note how emphatically he puts tolerance at the center of Christian character. After all, he names "the tolerance of those who are patient" in a same approving line alongside "the faith of those who believe."[54] The two things that make the Christian's way narrow, he writes in one sermon, are rejection of pleasure and tolerating suffering (*voluptatis abiectio, et tolerantia passionis*).[55] None of this suggests that these are exclusively Christian virtues. The compatibility between Christianity and the *res publica* is in fact defended by Augustine pointing out that such virtues were already exhibited by the Romans themselves.[56] But it is Christians whom he calls to live rightly and be willing to suffer for it. "Christian firmness, he writes, includes not only doing what is good, but also tolerating what is evil."[57] Toleration, then, is a form of firmness. Weakness lies in those who are enthusiastic about doing good works, but "cannot or will not tolerate suffering."[58] All of this is crucial in determining the place of tolerance. As Robert Spaemann has written, tolerance is self-defeating unless we see it as "a secondary virtue."[59] Here "secondary" does not mean "unimportant,"

[50] *s. dom. m.* I, 5, 13.
[51] Cohen, *Toleration*, 49.
[52] Chandran Kukathas, *The Liberal Archipelago. A Theory of Diversity and Freedom* (Oxford: Oxford University Press, 2003), 119.
[53] Brown, *Regulating Aversion*, 10.
[54] *gr. et lib. arb.* 14, 28.
[55] *s.* 313a 1, the same two are repeated in n. 2.
[56] *ep.* 138, 2, 9–10.
[57] *s.* 46, 6, 13.
[58] *s.* 46, 6, 13.
[59] Robert Spaemann, "Postsekuläre Gesellschaft," in *Postsekuläre Gesellschaft. Perspektiven Interdisziplinärer Forschung*, ed. Walter Schweidler (Freiburg/München: Verlag Karl Alber, 2007), 73.

and Augustine sometimes counts toleration among the primary virtues. Christians appear to be poor, he writes, "but the chapel of their hearts is full of the precious stones of the virtues: justice, truthfulness, love, faith, patience and tolerance."[60] While it depends on some other primary or fundamental virtue such as charity, it follows immediately after it.

Not surprisingly, Augustine speaks less directly to the other pole of our discussion, the call for recognition. But while the terminology of recognition is obviously absent from his work, the concerns it addresses are not. Few thinkers of antiquity were as aware as Augustine of the place of language and human interaction in the formation of the self. He was attentive both to its centrality and to the pathological desire "to love and be loved," "to be feared and loved by men."[61] But concern for this pathology does not make him indifferent to an adequate notion of respect or recognition. In Letter 153, as Joseph Clair has pointed out, Augustine appeals to the humanity of Macedonius and also calls him to respond with piety in the face of the humanity of criminals. "It comes easily and effortlessly to hate the bad because they are bad. It is an uncommon mark of piety [*pietas*] to love the same people because they are human beings, so that at one and the same time you disapprove of their guilt while approving of their nature."[62] Macedonius' disapproval of guilt may lead to punishment, forgiveness, or toleration, but all of these responses must depend on a prior respect for humanity. This perspective on piety is not unlike the Kantian way of relating respect and toleration. This is not recognition of particularities, as in much of contemporary discourse on recognition, but an inclusion in a universal category—humanity—that already enjoys respect.[63] "Take away all boasting and what are human beings but human beings?"[64] This is how Augustine comments on the concession of Roman citizenship to all the inhabitants of the Empire. It is a policy he judges could have come earlier, but it is in any case a gracious and humane measure.[65] A prejudice must be dismantled ("take away all boasting") for this inclusion to take place, and a specific institutional arrangement (formal citizenship) may be necessary in

[60] *en Ps.* 33, 2, 15.

[61] *conf.* II, 2, 2 and X, 36, 59.

[62] *ep.* 153, 3. Clair, *Discerning the Good in the Letters and Sermons of Augustine*, 95 (Clair's translation).

[63] On this distinction see Jones, "Toleration, Recognition and Identity," 131–35.

[64] *civ.* V, 17.

[65] See the fine discussion of *civ.* V, 17 in Mary M. Keys and Colleen E. Mitchell, "Patristic Era. Augustine's Constitutionalism: Citizenship, Common Good, and Consent," in *Christianity and Constitutionalism*, ed. Nicholas Aroney and Ian Leigh (Oxford: Oxford University Press, 2022), 91–107.

order to express our shared humanity. But this is not recognition of a particular form of life, nor does it rule out disapproving judgments.

Augustine is furthermore aware that some might imagine a slippery slope leading from toleration to approval, but he does not endorse any simplistic construal of this process. He had himself written along such lines in his early *Commentary on Galatians*. Only extraordinary vices scandalize us, he observed around the year 394, while we easily accommodate ordinary sins. These ordinary sins "we feel compelled to tolerate, and in tolerating them we often also commit some of them."[66] But this is a text he revises in his *Enchiridion* (written sometime between 421 and 423). After quoting his own *Commentary on Galatians*, he wonders whether it was not an "immoderate indignation" that made him "speak rashly" in this earlier work.[67] Though this is not a complete recantation of his earlier position, he does look at it with some distance, thus implying that there is no necessary slippery slope from tolerating to endorsing or committing evil. The idea of such a slippery slope is also resisted in his exposition of Psalm 128 (written in 412). "First they try to persuade us to consent to their evil deeds; if we do not consent, they ask us to tolerate them." This looks like the obvious place to suggest that toleration will indeed lead to consent. But instead, Augustine writes that toleration may actually create the conditions for a reconsideration: "I don't correct you, I tolerate you; but maybe you will correct yourself while I tolerate you."[68] Finally, in the epilogue to his treatise *On Faith and Works* (413), he also considers misunderstandings that may arise from his call to accept the mixed nature of the Church. Allowing wheat and tares to grow together in the field, allowing clean and unclean animals to live together in Noah's Ark, does not mean relaxing discipline, he notes.[69] His concern, then, is to make clear under what logic someone is being included; that it is "for reasons of toleration, not because of corruption of our doctrine or dissolution of our discipline."[70] As these texts (all quite late in his production) make clear, Augustine is well aware that slippery slopes, or confusions between toleration, indifference, and acceptance, are possible. But he denies any necessary connection between toleration and such consequences. He repeatedly insists on the fact that the duty of toleration is a never-ending one, while at the same time showing that this duty does not override concerns about discipline or correction. As these scattered remarks sufficiently suggest, if we wish to

[66] *exp. Gal.* 35.
[67] *ench.* 21, 80.
[68] *en. Ps.* 128, 7.
[69] *f. et op.* 2, 3 and 27, 49.
[70] *f. et op.* 27, 49.

begin to disentangle toleration from the risks described in previous chapters, Augustine's work is a fruitful starting point. That is the task set for the rest of this book. We need to understand how Augustine's view of history coheres with toleration, how the rejection of the Donatists' rashness can still leave room for the judgment that is part of toleration. But we must also consider how Augustine's sustained reflection on the nature of evil serves our discussion. Arguably, the more we are aware of the reality of evil, the more important we will find tolerance. And no ancient philosopher addressed the problem of evil with such insistence and depth as Augustine. The heightened sensitivity of the Augustinian tradition to the problem of evil can make it a tradition of reflection that is still productive for one of the possible responses to evil, namely, that of tolerance. It is to this understanding of evil that we will next turn.

II
THE OBJECT AND CONDITIONS OF TOLERATION

5

Toleration and Evil as Privation

In rebus adversis

What is an appropriate object of toleration? We can, for example, tolerate noisy neighbors and lazy students, Holocaust deniers and gender activists, Muslim immigrants and Christian heretics. But are these equally legitimate objects of tolerance? And more fundamentally, what do these groups have in common that can make them potential objects of tolerance? To what does tolerance respond? One possible answer is to think of tolerance simply as a response to intolerance. It has no other typical object; rather, it is an attitude that arises as response to intolerance. This is how Gabriel Marcel, for example, described it.[1] But this would fit only some, not all, of the examples just mentioned. It would perhaps fit a majority of the Holocaust deniers and a minority of the Muslim immigrants, but hardly any of the lazy students. The noise of our neighbors may indicate that they are disrespectful, but it is not a sign of their intolerance. Intolerance, in other words, is only one of the many evils that the tolerant must endure. More often, difference is posited as its object. But if tolerance, as we have seen, is something distinct from recognition, if its object is not the diverse, the other, or ways of life that are merely different from our own, then the traditional conception's focus on evil makes sense. Yes, Holocaust deniers are in some sense "different," but this is hardly a reasonable way to single them out. "Difference" is not specific enough when we are talking about toleration. There must be some evil involved in their denial for toleration to be our response. Augustine, like any contemporary of ours, can speak of the importance of "tolerating those who have different opinions" (*diversa sentientes tolerare*),[2] but these "*diversa*" that are held by our fellow citizens are not being singled out as *merely different* ideas: the focus is on sentiments, ideas, and actions that require an attitude of endurance, of patience. If we describe difference as the object of tolerance, it must be objectionable (or at least *de facto* objected) difference.

[1] Gabriel Marcel, "The Phenomenology and Dialectic of Tolerance," in *Creative Fidelity* (New York: Fordham University Press, 2002), 211.

[2] *bapt.* VII, 54, 103.

DOI: 10.1093/9780197912737.003.0008

But evil—or objected difference—has many faces. Our opening examples remind us, first, that evil is present in varying degrees. They also remind us that it is contested. Such a list will elicit no consensus, and many will ask whether the Muslim immigrant, for example, should be listed as an object of toleration rather than inclusion or hospitality. And should the Christian heretic be on the list? This is a different kind of issue, evoked not by his possible customs, actions, or belonging but by his beliefs. Can beliefs be evil? Our thinking about toleration is obviously more oriented toward evil actions. An unspoken thought may be evil, but no one must bear it. Some forms of speech—beliefs and thoughts that are publicly uttered—may however be evil, and to call them so is far from suggesting that they should be silenced. The heretic is obviously to be tolerated in the political community; perhaps not, or only qualifiedly so, in the Church. Once these clarifications are made, our initial list gains in plausibility.

But some further explanation may be necessary. If some of these examples make us uncomfortable, the reason may be that an inappropriate object of tolerance seems to suggest itself. In "lazy student," we know that it is the laziness, not the student, that is objected to; when we hear about the Muslim immigrant as an object of toleration, we may wonder whether this is the sense intended by all who speak this way. And this doubt points to the fact that persons cannot be the object of toleration. We can object to actions; we can object to certain forms of speech, and to the inaction rooted in laziness; but we cannot object to persons. Can we object to identities? Our list of examples includes more than loosely collected actions and beliefs. It includes ways of life, and these may be said to involve a sense of a certain identity as well. Is tolerance the right attitude toward an identity that one perceives as problematic, as grounded in a wrong account of our humanity? Persons as such are not evil, and so they are no appropriate object of toleration, but perhaps our self-understanding can be one of those thoughts that are appropriate objects of tolerance. Self-understanding is one of the things that can go wrong. In any case, it is only insofar as it represents something gone wrong—not as the core of personhood—that an identity or a self-understanding can be the object of tolerance. We can tolerate actions, including speech, or beliefs or ideas, including another person's self-understanding. Inasmuch as we see some evil in them, these seem to be appropriate objects of toleration.

Students of toleration, however, rarely raise questions about the nature of evil.[3] There may be good reasons for this. Those who conflate toleration and

[3] While his work is not particularly profound on this point, Glenn Tinder's work stands out as an exception to this rule. Tinder, *Tolerance: Toward a New Civility*, 116–31.

recognition obviously see no need for much discussion of evil (except, perhaps, for the evil of misrecognition). Those who see evil as the object of toleration, on the other hand, see it as more urgent to inquire into the limits of toleration: for how long, or to what extent, must this evil be tolerated? But we should avoid making hasty assumptions about the nature of evil, as if there were only one conception of what it is. As clearly as there are rival conceptions of tolerance, there are rival conceptions of evil. This is a fact that might have been avoided in discussions of toleration of other times. Today, however, it seems inescapable if we seek a full understanding of our situation. We are at a point where thinking about tolerance forces us to consider the classic question regarding the nature of evil.

This may be justification enough for Augustine to join us in this exploration. If we were asking about the limits of tolerance, there would be good reason to seek another guide. But if understanding its nature implies thinking about evil, one can hardly think of a guide that has made such a lasting contribution.[4] The understanding of evil is, moreover, a subject in which his philosophy still has deep and vigorous defenders. We are also dealing with a subject that Augustine himself often links with his discussion of tolerance. "Nobody is ordered to tolerate something good,"[5] he writes while commenting on Psalm 90. His exposition of Psalm 31 is equally emphatic: "What we call toleration, what we call patience, what we call endurance, what we call forbearance, all this does only exist in the face of evil."[6] Let us consider his even more eloquent words in his sermon 359a:

> Whether it is called patience (*patientia*), or endurance (*sustinentia*), or tolerance (*tolerantia*), the same thing is meant by these several names. . . . Patience seems to be needed not when things are going well, but in adversity (*in rebus adversis*). No one patiently tolerates what is enjoyable. But everything we tolerate, everything we patiently endure, is harsh and bitter; and thus, patience is not needed in happiness, but in unhappiness.[7]

I have stressed this connection between tolerance and evil at earlier points in our discussion. The way in which this connection has been obscured can easily be grasped if we compare these lines from Augustine's sermon with the

[4] For a balanced general survey Gillian R. Evans, *Augustine on Evil* (Cambridge: Cambridge University Press, 1990).
[5] *en Ps.* 52, 1.
[6] *en Ps.* 31, 2.
[7] *s.* 359a, 2.

beginning of Locke's *Letter*, which we discussed in Chapter 2. Like Locke, Augustine places tolerance at the center of the Christian life, and one might even be tempted to say that he too sees toleration as a "mark" of the Church. But if in Locke tolerance is identified with charity, gentleness, and good-will, in Augustine it is identified with patience, with enduring, with putting up with someone or something. From the list given by Locke, Augustine might have considered gentleness or meekness as possible synonyms for tolerance. Love and benevolence, on the other hand, he might have counted as necessary conditions for tolerance, but not as its synonyms. Love and benevolence are not directed exclusively toward things we perceive as evil. Indeed, the connection between evil and toleration has become blurred, as much of our political and moral discussion shows. But it may be impossible and futile to restore it without first thinking more calmly about the nature of evil. In the next two sections, I will first go through the way in which Augustine's understanding of evil evolved in the light of his successive doctrinal controversies and then explore contemporary problems in our relation to evil that shape our approach to tolerance.

Evil and Augustine's Doctrinal Controversies

What, then, is evil for Augustine? According to his widely known yet less widely understood doctrine, evil is the absence or privation of good. What difference can such an understanding of evil make in the contemporary approach to toleration? We can begin by recalling an expectation fundamental to modern political thought: the idea that we can reach consensus regarding evil while affirming the impossibility of knowing the good. In the words of Stanley Hauerwas, "modern accounts of morality are determined by agreements about what constitutes inhumanity."[8] We cannot, it is claimed, agree on what is good for human beings, but we can nonetheless determine which things are evil. We cannot know the good, but we can understand and reject evil. At least since Hobbes, political thought has taken this avoidance of evil as its organizing principle. "Desire is always moved by evil, to fly it," writes Locke.[9] In the words of William Galston, "we speak with confidence of the *summum malum*—the great evils of the human condition—even though we cannot specify a

[8] Stanley Hauerwas, "Seeing Darkness, Hearing Silence. Augustine's Account of Evil," in *Naming Evil, Judging Evil*, ed. Ruth W. Grant (Chicago and London: The University of Chicago Press, 2006), 36.
[9] Locke, *An Essay Concerning Human Understanding*, II, xxi, 71.

universally binding *summum bonum*."[10] For Augustine, all this could only sound absurd. We cannot hope to know about evil without knowing something about the good.

Since this Augustinian thesis underlies the understanding of toleration that I argue for in this book, we should pause to consider it more deeply. One way to approach it is to consider the successive controversies in which Augustine's understanding of evil—of obviously Platonic provenance—was refined. After his conversion, his literary life can be organized around his disputes with the Manicheans, Donatists, and Pelagians. Let us begin, then, with the Manicheans, among whom Augustine had been an *auditor* for nine years. During those nine years, the external link with the Manichean community was constant, although early on it must have seemed difficult for him to be persuaded by their conception of evil. As he wrote in retrospect, even as a Manichean, "I did not give them my assent."[11] But how exactly should we characterize the view to which he did not give his assent? For the Manicheans, as it is often summarized, the world is a war zone between good and evil. But there is nothing specifically Manichean about this conviction.[12] You can see the world as such a battlefield between good and evil, you can divide people into polar opposites, and nonetheless stay clear of Manicheanism. The specifically Manichean approach is to understand this great battle between good and evil in ontological rather than moral terms. Good realities struggle with evil realities, and this cosmic battle is replicated at the divine level: just as there is something substantially good and something substantially evil in the world, good and evil exist at the level of ultimate reality. It was this vision that Augustine spent the first years after his conversion combatting. He opposed those who affirm an evil "with its own proper principle."[13] Evil, he counters, can never be ultimate. Evil is parasitic. "Corruption harms, but it could not harm if it were not a lessening of good."[14] There is no nature of evil, for it is the perversion of a nature. It has no existence of its own but needs something good in which to live. This was the conclusion of Augustine's first decisive controversy, and it leaves traces in his thought beyond the writings against the Manicheans. One might well say that his later

[10] William Galston, "Moral Pluralism and Liberal Democracy: Isaiah Berlin's Heterodox Liberalism," in *Political Philosophy in the Twentieth Century. Authors and Arguments*, ed. Catherine H. Zuckert (Cambridge: Cambridge University Press, 2011), 166. This describes the view of Isaiah Berlin, but it can be taken as a good summary of a great deal of liberal thought.

[11] *beata v.* 1, 4.

[12] Against this common misunderstanding, see Daniel Strand, "Augustine's Privation, Arendt's Banality," in *Augustine in a Time of Crisis*, ed. Boeslaw Z. Kabala, Ashleen Menchaca-Bagnulo, and Nathan Pinkoski (Palgrave Macmillan, 2021), 420–23.

[13] *ep.* 166, 3, 7.

[14] *conf.* VII, 12, 18.

City of God is in fact a monumental effort to conceive of history as a struggle between good and evil, without this entailing a Manichean discourse (the usual subtext when history is conceived as such a struggle). Among the many ways in which this can be shown is the simple fact of his engagement in the task of persuasion. As Mary M. Keys shows in detail, "Augustine does not consider all pagans to be fettered by pride, thus calling into question a rigid, 'humble Christians versus proud pagans' binary interpretation of *The City of God*."[15]

His understanding of evil was further refined in his dispute with the Donatists. It was Donatism that made Augustine aware of the mixed nature of historical existence, and the mixed nature of the Church itself first of all. As a rigorist faction, Donatism rejected such mixture, claiming that sacraments administered by *traditores* were invalid. Augustine, as we have seen, replied with his exposition of Matthew 13. If anyone believes their own group is already purified wheat, they are thereby revealed to be tares.[16] The lessons of the controversy with the Donatists are crucial for the project developed in the *City of God*. If wheat and tares grow together in the Church, such mixture is all the more to be expected when we look at humanity as a whole. Augustine has a rich vocabulary for describing this mixture: the cities are described as *permixta, perplexa, commixta*. But this language of mixture actually covers some slightly different phenomena that we should not conflate. In the initial expansion of the human race, Augustine writes, there "arose a mixture and confusion of both cities by their participation in the same iniquity."[17] Here he is clearly describing a condition in which the two cities become indistinguishable because the city of God has been assimilated to the earthly city. This is a type of mixture one must strive to avoid. When he, in contrast, describes the two cities as passing through history "interwoven and mixed,"[18] this need not involve a corruption of the city of God. There is a type of mixture that preserves the distinctiveness of each city, although this distinctiveness is not equally visible at all times. It is to this second type of mixture that his work is mainly dedicated.

Augustine may not always be up to the task of describing this intermingling concretely, and important examples of truly plural societies do not appear very explicitly in his work. The example of pre-Constantinian Rome, as John Rist has noted, is one that he fails to consider for such purposes.[19] But the

[15] Keys, *Pride, Politics, and Humility in Augustine's City of God*, 48.
[16] *c. litt. Pet.* III, 3, 19.
[17] *civ.* XV, 22.
[18] *civ.* I, 35.
[19] John Rist, "Can the City of God Help Us Deconstruct Multiculturalism?" in *Kampf oder Dialog? Begegnung von Kulturen im Horizont von Agustins De ciuitate Dei*, ed. Christof Müller (Würzburg: Echter, 2015), 30.

discussion with the Donatists is full of lessons that are relevant to such plural contexts. Notions of purity and contamination, for example, were central to the Donatists.[20] They perceived themselves as the Church of martyrs, untainted by contact with the *traditores*. Then as now, such fear of pollution or contagion often inhibits the practice of toleration. Augustine, without neglecting the role of discipline, is attentive to the pathological form such fears can take. Was heaven contaminated by the angels who fell from it? Was Eden infected by Adam? Were the apostles polluted by Judas? Such are the questions he raises in his sermons.[21] There is obviously room in Augustine for our responsibility for the acts of others—for holding parents, for instance, responsible for the actions of their children or for seeing himself as burdened with responsibility for his flock—but not for seeing the evil we tolerate as evil that taints us. One Puritan preacher would write that "by toleration we adopt other men's sins and make them our own."[22] Augustine, in contrast, repeatedly insists that alien wrongs cannot contaminate us, that one can live among the wicked without consenting to their deeds.[23]

But if the anti-Donatist discourse leaves us with the idea that there are some good people who tolerate others who are evil, this would be a very half-hearted Augustinianism. If the clash with the Donatists leads Augustine to emphasize that every human community is mixed, then the later controversy with the Pelagians leads him to assert this mixed nature as a reality in each of us. It is within us that there are occupied territories and liberated zones.[24] Only here do we arrive at a fully Augustinian understanding of evil: this parasitic disorder that can damage any kind of good, that turns every human endeavor into something morally gray, has its roots within us. This is the reason Augustine has so often been described as a realist. In the words of Reinhold Niebuhr, he was "the first great 'realist' in Western history,"[25] because "he takes account of the power and persistence of egoism, both individual and collective, and seeks to establish the most tolerable form of peace and justice under conditions set

[20] Paul Beddoe, "Contagio in the Donatists and St. Augustine," *Studia Patristica* 27 (1993): 231–36. For Augustine's relation to Cyprian in his development of this point, see Atkins, *The Christian Origins of Tolerance*, 242–50.

[21] *s.* 73A, 3.

[22] Thomas Watson, "Christ's Loveliness," in *Discourses on Important and Interesting Subjects, Being the Select Works of the Rev. Thomas Watson. Vol. 1* (Glasgow: Blackie, Fullarton, & Co., 1829), 321.

[23] See, for instance, *s.* 73a, 3; *civ.* I, 28; *c. ep. Parm.* II, 21, 40–41.

[24] Antipelagian concerns are latent throughout the *City of God*. See Robert Dodaro, "Note sulla presenza della questione pelagiana nel De civitate Dei," in *Il De civitate Dei. L'opera, le interpretazioni, l'influsso*, ed. Elena Cavalcanti (Rome: Herder, 1996).

[25] Reinhold Niebuhr, "The Relevance of Christian Realism: An Orientation," in *Reinhold Niebuhr on Politics*, ed. Harry Davis and Robert Good (New York: Scribner's, 1960), 66.

by human sin."[26] But "realism" comes in many forms, and we must be careful not to conflate them. Augustine's anthropology is not that of Machiavelli or Hobbes. Toleration does not require a political anthropology centered on self-preservation. But it does require some form of anti-Pelagianism. An anti-Pelagian bent turns our gaze inward, toward the evil that is in ourselves. In doing so, it tempers expectations and fosters the conditions of humility that are fundamental to tolerance. It also renews our awareness of the impossibility of eradicating evil. As quoted in our introduction, John Gray writes of toleration as "subversive of the shallow optimistic creeds of our age, humanist or Pelagian, for which human evils are problems to be solved rather than sorrows to be coped with or endured."[27] To this one should only add that the view of evil that makes this toleration possible for Augustine is not merely anti-Pelagian. Each of the controversies builds on the previous ones.

Only recently have we become aware of the continuity between these three controversies, and it is crucial for getting all the nuances of Augustine's position right.[28] Augustine affirms the insubstantial nature of evil, but no one who sees the three controversies together could read this anti-Manichean thesis as a minimizing of the reality of evil. There is no dissolving the reality of evil, as Atkins finds the Stoics doing.[29] In the *City of God*, Augustine distances himself from the Stoic belief that the wise man can be happy even in misery; he rejects the minimization of these evils and instead praises Peripatetics and Platonists for offering a truer account of evil than the Stoics. Fortitude is a "witness to the human evils that patience is forced to tolerate," he writes in this context.[30] Augustine denies that evil is a thing; he does not deny that there is moral evil in the world, that evil arises from a distorted will that introduces disorder and rebellion into the world. In fact, Augustine asserts the existence and ineradicable nature of evil as few in history have done. But evil is not substantial, and it is not ultimate. So this is not just a vision of evil, but more fundamentally a vision of goodness, a fact that has obvious consequences for the way in which we confront evil. This approach sees evil for what it is without being overwhelmed by it. Evil is what we tolerate, but it is hard to see how we can be consistently

[26] Niebuhr, 68.

[27] Gray, *Enlightenment's Wake*, 27.

[28] Some studies that have shaped this growing awareness are Jaroslav Pelikan, "An Augustinian Dilemma: Augustine's Doctrine of Grace versus Augustine's Doctrine of the Church?," *Augustinian Studies* 18 (1987): 1–29; Frederick Russell, "'Only Something Good Can Be Evil': The Genesis of Augustine's Secular Ambivalence," *Theological Studies* 51, no. 4 (1990): 698–716; and Peter Iver Kaufman, "Augustine, Evil and Donatism: Sin and Sanctity before the Pelagian Controversy," *Theological Studies* 51, no. 1 (1990): 115–26.

[29] Atkins, *The Christian Origins of Tolerance*, 59.

[30] *civ*. XIX, 4, 4.

tolerant if we are simply saturated by evil and thus blind to the ultimate goodness of reality.

There are serious problems with our loves, but the fundamental goodness of reality makes a calmer approach to evil possible. Gillian Evans has written of the "magnificent calm" that emerges in Augustine's final elaboration of the problem of evil.[31] We can see this as an initial anti-Manichean condition for tolerance: tolerance is possible if what we judge to be evil is part of a reality that is ultimately good, if the world is something that we can love. Just as tolerance is a virtue that depends on other virtues, so the evil that it endures depends on the reality of the good. As we will see in later chapters, sometimes it is a future good that makes our toleration possible, and in this sense tolerance depends on hope; but even if there were no good in the future to hope for, there is a good underlying the evil we face, and it may be enough to impose a duty of toleration on us.

Judging Evil, Suffering Evil

This excursion through these three doctrinal controversies already suggests that Augustine can illuminate our understanding of evil and tolerance in more ways than one. This will become clearer as we now turn to some influential contemporary approaches to evil.[32] If tolerance has the relation to evil that we have emphasized, it is a peculiar kind of virtue. To recognize tolerance as a virtue implies that it can be virtuous to allow evil to exist. This is a conclusion that may provoke revulsion for very different reasons. One of Thomas Mann's characters famously says that "tolerance becomes a crime when applied to evil."[33] This phrasing actually undermines the very meaning of tolerance, but it rightly reminds us that it is often not virtuous to leave evil in peace. Hence the pertinent question of limits, to which we will return below. But we may also hear an objection coming from the opposite direction. There are those who think it is a crime to call anything evil. For some, daring to call something evil is itself a trait of intolerant people. Two or three

[31] Evans, *Augustine on Evil*, xi. See also Charles Mathewes, *Evil and the Augustinian Tradition* (Cambridge: Cambridge University Press, 2001), 1–36.

[32] Beyond the position I discuss below, a further challenge must be considered—the rejection of privation theory as not only incapable of explaining the evils of the twentieth centuty, but also as responsible for that outcome. For an Augustinian evaluation of that critique see John Milbank, "Darkness and Silence: Evil and the Western Legacy," in *Evil in Contemporary Political Theory*, ed. Peter Sutch, Peri Roberts, and Bruce Haddock (Edinburgh: Edinburgh University Press, 2011), 10–43.

[33] Thomas Mann, *Der Zauberberg* (Stockholm: S. Fischer Verlag, 1954), 731.

decades ago, this was a widespread view, and it still prevails in many circles. Indeed, abstaining from making any kind of moral judgment has become one of the core virtues of contemporary society. But the experience of evil does not disappear from the world for that reason. Only our tools for dealing with it do.

I will return to the subject of non-judgmentalism in Chapter 7. For now, let us note that it has a Manichean flipside. In *The Closing of the American Mind*, Allan Bloom mentions that when he asked his students "Who is evil?," the only answer that they could come up with was "Hitler."[34] The reverse side of our culture's non-judgmentalism is its tendency to concentrate evil in a few individual persons or institutions that are the source of all suffering, abuse, or oppression. As John Horton has written, we have a "surprisingly Manichean perspective" on evil.[35] It might be argued that Bloom's 1987 anecdote is outdated, that a non-judgmental culture has given way to the renewed moralism of a "callout culture." But this development is perfectly understandable in terms of the view of evil described here. Callout culture is not a return to old-fashioned judgment, but an expansion of the number of people and institutions that are described as embodying evil. This is the moral imagination of "the age of Hitler," as Alec Ryrie has described it.[36] By rejecting the graduality of evil, it is the tolerable evil that disappears. The evils that our non-judgmental culture can identify as such are embodiments of an ultimate evil, an evil that therefore tends to be seen as unbearable.

There is also a softer version of this vision, one which is not properly Manichean, but rather sees evil as "systemic." This view, ultimately derived from Rousseau, combines the idea of the goodness of human persons with the existence of a radically evil society. This society may corrupt individuals, but it is not human wickedness that is the driving force in this process. But whatever their differences, as Ruth W. Grant has noted, the Rousseauan perspective can become "effectively indistinguishable from Manicheanism."[37] The Rousseauan and the Manichean views of evil generate similar dichotomies, and they rely on the same illusion about the eradicability of evil. Under the influence of these views, the various kinds and degrees of evil that we would otherwise have before us disappear; the evils that remain, on the other hand, we perceive to be intolerable. Bernard Williams writes that toleration's "basic problem" is that it

[34] Allan Bloom, *The Closing of the American Mind* (New York: Simon & Schuster, 1987), 67.
[35] Horton, "Traditional Conception," 295.
[36] Ryrie, Alec, *The Age of Hitler and How We Will Survive It* (London: Reaktion Books, 2025).
[37] Ruth W. Grant, "The Rosseauan Revolution and the Problem of Evil," in *Naming Evil, Judging Evil*, ed. Ruth W. Grant (Chicago and London: The University of Chicago Press, 2006), 66.

is "required only for the intolerable."[38] But this is toleration's "basic problem" only because of the pervasive influence of a certain view of evil. This life has many tolerable evils. We need tolerance to endure them, but we also need a proper conception of evil in order to see them.

This form of Manichaeanism, however, is not the only contemporary approach to evil that makes tolerance difficult or impossible. There are evils we minimize and others we magnify, but above all we are attuned to the good and evil that can *occur* to the human self. Like any other culture, ours is scandalized by the existence of evil; but it is especially in its passive form that it concerns us: suffering upsets us more than moral evil, tragedy more than guilt. According to Augustine, we are all guilty and prone to evil; according to those who would correct him—and here, too, Rousseau lurks in the background—we are all victims. The resulting victimhood culture has its own peculiar relationship to toleration. Before closing this chapter, this deserves some further attention. "We are victims; everything we do is justified" runs counter to the idea of self-limitation that lies at the heart of toleration. In *The Rise of Victimhood Culture*, Bradley Campbell and Jason Manning present this culture as a combination of ingredients of honor and dignity cultures. In honor cultures there is great sensitivity to slight, with even minor affronts leading to conflict. Low tolerance is a hallmark of such cultures; attacks on someone's reputation end in violent retaliation. Cultures of dignity, in contrast, promote the development of a thick skin: insults and disagreements do not challenge our equal dignity, guarded by quiet self-assurance. Only serious harm should be addressed, and then through the intervention of authorities. Victimhood cultures, in contrast, combine the high sensitivity of honor cultures with the appeal to authorities found in dignity cultures. Thus, low tolerance for slight, discomfort, or other difficulties is what we should expect in victimhood cultures.[39] Inasmuch as it combines elements of both honor and dignity cultures, a new intolerance seems to be one of the inevitable features of our society.

But although these recent cultural developments exacerbate our difficulty with suffering evil, we must acknowledge that this difficulty is perennial, and it reveals where we locate our good. According to Augustine's own description of his work, book II of the *City of God* deals with moral evil, and book III with physical evils, "the only evils abhorred by the foolish."[40] Some goods and some

[38] Bernard Williams, "Toleration: An Impossible Virtue?" in *Toleration: An Elusive Virtue*, ed. David Heyd (Princeton: Princeton University Press, 1998), 18.

[39] Jason Manning and Bradley Campbell, *The Rise of Victimhood Culture: Microaggressions, Safe Spaces, and the New Culture Wars* (New York: Palgrave Macmillan, 2018), 14–15; 64–65, 74.

[40] *civ.* IV, 2. This observation is part of Augustine's recurring classification of goods and evils. For other instances of this argument see *spir. et litt.* 11, 18 and *s.* 61, 1–3.

evils—material blessings and sufferings—are common to good and bad people. But this commonality reveals precisely that these are not the evils that make us good or evil, that these are therefore not the goods we should primarily strive for, nor the evils we should primarily flee from. Augustine's view of patience is explicitly tied to this argument. The evils that are shared by the good and the evil do not make us evil, and therefore such evils should be easier to endure. Indeed, God himself permits such evils so that this learning can take place.[41] Those who are evil, however, "not only patiently, but gladly bear the evils that make them evil."[42] This is clearly a moral disorder of considerable proportions. It reveals that we lament a bad house more than a bad soul.[43] The evils that we are willing to tolerate, in other words, are for Augustine a significant measure of the order of our souls.

Whether we focus on this permanent tendency or on the aggravating contemporary forms of Manicheanism or victimhood culture, the result is the magnification of evil and the consequent inability to bear it. All of this suggests that a return to the "magnificent calm" of Augustine's vision of evil may be productive for our thinking about tolerance. In that vision, evil is no longer concentrated in a single figure; there is no longer a specific reality that represents evil. In one sense this makes the range of evil wider, since the range of possible evils is as broad as reality itself. In another sense it makes evil less overwhelming, removing its ultimate condition. As we will see in the next chapter, some of the questions that remain to be resolved are deeply connected to this question of evil. How do we understand evil when we imagine that history can leave it behind? How does our understanding of evil shape our political realism? And does it leave room for hope? Toleration depends in a very fundamental way on our moral and political expectations, and these in turn are influenced by our basic assumptions about human fallenness and by the philosophies of history that populate our world.

41 *civ.* I, 8.
42 *civ.* IV, 2.
43 *civ.* III, 1. See also *s.* 297, 8.

6

Hope, Progress, and Liberating Intolerance

From Hope to Progress

Augustine, as we have noted, has often been described as a political realist. Anticipating Kant's "unsocial sociability," he wrote that nothing is as social as man, and nothing as unsocial as fallen man.[1] His is a realism about human nature, but also about the nature of history. Against the historical optimism of other Christians (which he had shared for a time), Augustine developed what might be called an anti-philosophy of history. The Christianization of the Empire was not irreversible, and future persecutions, he noted, could never be ruled out.[2] The two cities will be intermingled until the final judgment.[3] This provides an anticipatory antidote for the visions of progress that dominate the modern world.[4] We need tolerance "in unhappiness," Augustine writes, and this unhappiness is not a specific unfortunate situation, but rather a description of the whole of our existence in history. On this side of the *eschaton* there is happiness, but a happiness that even in the case of Christian emperors can only exist "in hope."[5]

A happiness "in hope," however, is not a concession to crass pessimism nor an abandonment to pure otherworldliness. As Michael Lamb has argued at length, for Augustine hope is important not only in the expectation of eternal blessedness but also as a political virtue. As he notes, Augustine distinguishes the two cities by their loves but also by their hopes.[6] As Lamb further highlights, Augustine is aware of the deviations from this virtue that threaten from opposite extremes. "There are two things . . .that kill souls, either despair or perverse

[1] *civ.* XII, 27. Immanuel Kant, "Idea for a Universal History with a Cosmopolitan Purpose," in *Kant: Political Writings*, ed. H.S. Reiss (Cambridge: Cambridge University Press, 1991), 44.

[2] *civ.* XVIII, 52.

[3] *civ.* I, 35.

[4] On the whole one can say that the Middle Ages share with Augustine this view of history. Its consequences for toleration, however, were sometimes relativized by the inclusion of other ingredients. The parable of the wheat and the tares was, for instance, read with the aid of Titus 3:10, which calls for the heretic to be tolerated only up to a third warning (see Aquinas *Super Mt.*, cap. 13 lect. 2).

[5] *civ.* V, 24.

[6] Lamb, *A Commonwealth of Hope. Augustine's Political Thought* (Princeton: Princeton University Press, 2022), 167.

An Augustinian Essay on Toleration. Manfred Svensson, Oxford University Press. © Manfred Svensson 2026.
DOI: 10.1093/9780197912737.003.0009

hope."[7] Like love, hope can be misdirected and stand in need of formation. The cultivation of hope guards against both despair and presumption, which is the vice of excess. Hope thus plays a fundamental role in shaping tolerance. As Lamb concludes, "Without hope, human beings would lack the motivation and resolve to patiently endure the difficulties and delays that accompany the pursuit of difficult future goods here and now."[8]

In the Augustinian tradition, this idea reappears in different ways. The rites of unbelievers, Aquinas wrote in his *Summa*, can be tolerated "either on account of some good that ensues therefrom, or because of some evil avoided."[9] It is not difficult for us to sympathize with the second of these arguments, the one that calls us to avoid greater evil. It is clear that great evils—the curtailing of freedom and the violation of dignity—can be avoided by not interfering. But what does it mean to tolerate because of the good that may come? In Aquinas' example, that good is the conversion of the tolerated unbelievers. Those who are tolerated, he explains, "might gradually be converted to the faith."[10] Many will be tempted to dismiss this hope of conversion as a reasonable ground for toleration in a liberal society. But we can recast Aquinas' words as a statement about the place of hope among the grounds for toleration. As noted in the previous chapter, we tolerate after pondering goods and evils, but not only present ones. Toleration depends on a judgment about the present and some expectation about the future. We tolerate evils not only because of the greater harm that would result from not tolerating them, but also because we cherish hopes regarding the fruits of patience; conversion is just the highest of these hopes, the fullest realization of the fact that God can bring about greater good from the evil he has permitted.

But this is not the only kind of expectation that shapes our thinking about toleration. While conversion was a central object of hope in the world of Aquinas, our contemporary debates are dominated by expectations about the future of humanity and the course of history. Our thinking about toleration has been decisively shaped by the modern belief in progress and its promise of an inner-worldly *eschaton*. What is distinctive about this faith in progress? On closer inspection, it is not its attention to the inner-worldly good. Hope can also be directed toward earthly goods, so the idea of an immanent good is not peculiar to the belief in progress. A belief in the *possibility* of progress toward certain earthly goods is a belief that remains within the realm of hope. Modern

[7] *s.* 87, 8, 10. Lamb's translation. Lamb, 47.
[8] Lamb, 30.
[9] *S. Th.* II-II, q. 10, a. 11.
[10] *S. Th.* II-II, q. 10, a. 11.

philosophies of history, however, tend to suggest a *necessity* rather than belief in a possibility. Not all modern hope for progress assumes such a necessity, but this is the characteristically modern belief.

But how can a belief in necessary progress be sustained? Arguably, it first became thinkable in connection with the understanding of evil we have already explored. There is much evil in the world, but given the way in which our deviation is conceived, improvement seems likely. Instead of finite and fallen, man is seen as ignorant, recalcitrant, or as deeply entangled in the sources of evil. For this sort of evil, one can think of remedies. Since man is not a sinner, improvement can be expected. This improvement can come through the market or the State, through education or revolution, but in any case, it will liberate us from the external sources of evil. In the work of Rousseau, as Ruth W. Grant has noted, this understanding of evil had not yet been united with the tremendous force of the idea of progress.[11] The fusion of these two ideas would prove decisive.

For all their diversity, philosophies of history have shaped the way in which we evaluate all sorts of human phenomena: how we think about the role of technology in our lives, about the legitimacy of nation-states, or about the future of religious belief. This teleological conception of history suggests linear development in all these fields. It also posits that growing tolerance goes hand in hand with these developments. Indeed, one of the more influential by-products of this mentality has been a belief in the combined expansion of secularization and toleration: the more progress, the more secularization; the more secularization, the more toleration. And we should take stock of the effects of such narratives. "Progress" sometimes behaves intolerantly, and this is a form of intolerance to which this lens renders us blind. This view of history must exclude the murders, invasions, exclusions, and other forms of intolerance which have taken place under the expectation of ascending secular tolerance.[12] This is one of the reasons why students of both toleration and secularization have largely abandoned this framework. However, the idea that both are manifestations of progress continues to shape much of our public debate.[13]

But the fact that this belief in progress has survived the horrors of the past century requires further explanation, and here a third reason for its

[11] Grant, "The Rosseauan Revolution and the Problem of Evil," 55.

[12] See Thomas Albert Howard, *Broken Altars. Secularist Violence in Modern History* (New Haven and London: Yale University Press, 2025).

[13] On the many aspects of this debate, see Vyacheslav Karpov and Manfred Svensson, eds., *Secularization, Desecularization, and Toleration. Cross-Disciplinary Challenges to a Modern Myth* (New York: Palgrave MacMillan, 2020).

prevalence—beyond a vision of evil and of history—needs to be noted. The concept of progress, Christopher Lasch has argued, "can be defended against intelligent criticism only by postulating an indefinite expansion of desires, a steady rise in the general standard of comfort, and the incorporation of the masses into the culture of abundance."[14] This, Lasch contended, is not only the reason for the persistence of the idea of progress but also the fundamental impetus for its original emergence: insatiable appetites ceased to be the object of condemnation and began to be seen as the driving force of unending expansion.[15] From this emerges a more flexible version of belief in progress. Perhaps no final point of destination will ever be reached. Perhaps there will be many obstacles and setbacks, and no happy ending. But there will be steady improvement and constant satisfaction of new desires.

Whatever we think of Lasch's genealogy of progress, it is true that the idea has survived the collapse of the more rigid philosophies of history. And progress, conflated with every possible good, is imagined to converge naturally with tolerance. It is this convergence that concerns us here. Tolerance is seen as part of the path to progress, or progress is seen as necessarily including tolerance (for instance, as the non-condemnation of those insatiable desires). They are assumed to go hand in hand in some of these unproblematic ways.[16] But is this belief in a natural harmony between progress and tolerance justified?

From Progress to Liberating Intolerance

The harmony that we have just described would be a reasonable expectation if human affairs behaved like other affairs; if our practical life consisted of a cumulative growth over generations similar to that which we see in scientific progress. But this is not the case. In the words of John Gray, "Science and technology are cumulative, whereas ethics and politics deal with recurring

[14] Christopher Lasch, *The True and Only Heaven. Progress and Its Critics* (New York and London: W. W. Norton, 1991), 78.

[15] For a classical discussion of this transformation, see Albert O. Hirschman, *The Passions and the Interests. Political Arguments for Capitalism before Its Triumph* (Princeton: Princeton University Press, 1997).

[16] Some are prepared to see a slight tension between the two ideals: belief in progress, they recognize, happens to be a part of the dominant Western canon, a belief that invites us to intolerantly judge other cultures as below the standard of civilization. This is the argument developed in Gordon Graham, "Toleration and the Idea of Progress," in *Philosophy, Religion, and the Question of Intolerance*, ed. Mehdi Amin Razavi and David Ambuel (New York: State University of New York Press, 1997), 125–33. Solving this may simply require reminding us of the compatibility between tolerance and judgment (see next chapter).

dilemmas."[17] People respond differently to such recurring dilemmas, and so they often reopen debates that the belief in progress would lead us to imagine as closed. Instead of a harmony between toleration and progress, we should then posit a harmony between tolerance and an awareness of this openness of history. Tolerance requires that we remain aware of the fragility of social life, of the fact that certain goods cannot be taken for granted as already acquired and definitively stored, that old pathologies will reappear under a different guise, and, perhaps, that some things heretofore considered pathological were not.

But the persistence of such recurring dilemmas is hard to understand in a culture deluded by a pervasive illusion of steady progress. For this widespread mentality, being tolerant is a quality of positions or causes that go hand in hand with progress. But this is a misleading place to locate toleration. There are, of course, political arrangements that are more tolerant than others, but it is less obvious that some substantive positions are more tolerant than others. Tolerance is not one of the parties in a given conflict. It is a way in which one party deals with the other in such conflicts. In the seventeenth century, Christians could be divided over questions of free will and predestination; but there is no reason for imagining that toleration was necessarily aligned with only the champions of free will. People are today divided over how equity should guide social policy, over the understanding of marriage that should undergird support for families, over the level of immigration to which a country should be open, but the stand we take in such controversies does not reveal whether we are tolerant or not. When any side in such discussions is seen as an inherent ingredient of progress, a progress that is simultaneously identified with the advance of toleration, this basic insight is undermined. Glen Newey has noted how something analogous happens every time that tolerance is grounded in substantive values like autonomy or mutuality. Theorists of toleration, he writes, then "feel free to advocate their favored solutions to political problems, which now acquire the added allure of being 'tolerant.' "[18]

Like autonomy, the idea of progress shapes our political imagination in decisive ways. It doesn't make anyone necessarily intolerant. It is, of course, possible for a progressive citizen to judge the "backwardness" of his countrymen sharply, to see them as on the "wrong side of history," and still think of this as a tolerable evil. Occasionally, however, this view leads to explicit justifications

[17] John Gray, *The Silence of Animals. Of Progress and Other Modern Myths* (New York: Farrar, Straus, and Giroux, 2013), 75.

[18] Glen Newey, "Toleration, Politics, and the Role of Murality," in *Toleration and Its Limits*, ed. Melissa Williams and Jeremy Waldron, NOMOS, XLVIII (New York and London: New York University Press, 2008), 368.

for liberating intolerance. Evils that otherwise might be tolerated will not be endured if they are separating us from a new heaven and a new earth. The dignity of individuals and the integrity of institutions may have to be transgressed as a means for the improvement of society. This is a reasoning that has been made explicit over generations. In 1947, Maurice Merleau-Ponty stated that "for the moment the question is not to know whether one accepts or rejects violence, but whether the violence with which one is allied is 'progressive' and tends towards its own suspension or toward self-perpetuation."[19] A perhaps more influential version of this position is that of Herbert Marcuse, writing in the next generation. He claimed that one could easily distinguish "between true and false tolerance, between progress and regression."[20] The true tolerance identified with progress is a liberating one, and this liberation can legitimize intolerance against the movements identified as regressive.[21] In a way, Marcuse's argument is a simple and old one: intolerance is bad when our rivals practice it, but it may be necessary when it advances good causes. In this simple form, this vicious argument can be found in almost any political camp. But seasoned with belief in the laws of history, the belief that ours is a violence that "tends towards its own suspension," it can become particularly self-deluding and radical. The intolerance to end all intolerance can be like the war to end all wars.

But can there not be a justified liberating intolerance? Surely racism, for example, would count as a regressive position deserving of just intolerance. Racists should not be called to tolerance, it has been reasonably argued, but to overcoming their racism.[22] But racism, we should also make clear, is perhaps better understood not as *regressive*, but as one of those *recurring* pathologies in ethics and politics mentioned by Gray. If we are aware of its recurrent character, we will be better prepared to face its presence. And being better prepared may well include assigning a merely secondary role to tolerance and intolerance when we address this issue. One may have to temporarily tolerate some manifestations of racism. However, it is decency, respect, and justice that one invokes to correct it, not intolerance. Otherwise, the justifications of liberating intolerance can end up undermining all forms of tolerance. Indeed, while the idea of a liberating intolerance can often justify an intolerance that is rather

[19] Maurice Merleau-Ponty, *Humanism and Terror*, trans. John O'Neill (New York: Routledge, 2023), 3.

[20] Herbert Marcuse, "Repressive Tolerance," in *A Critique of Pure Tolerance*, by Robert Paul Wolff, Barrington Moore, and Herbert Marcuse (Boston: Beacon Press, 1965), 105.

[21] Marcuse, 109.

[22] So, for instance, Jürgen Habermas, "Intolerance and Discrimination," *International Journal of Constitutional Law* 1, no. 1 (2003): 3.

selective, only directed at "regressive" positions, it easily ends in the realization that our whole situation is regressive. Marcuse himself believed that "the conditions under which tolerance can again become a liberating and humanizing force have still to be created."[23] This justifies not only the selective practice of intolerance but its general rationalization as well.[24] But if we do not want to follow this path, what exactly should we reject? Should we rule out all search for perfection from political life? Should we rule out hope, which we previously recognized as a reason for toleration? Let us conclude this chapter by discussing the relation between these questions and the Augustinian idea of the self.

Toleration and the Future Self

Is it morally sound to bear with a person in view of the self she may turn out to become? We can tolerate a person's present condition in the hope of his or her conversion, enlightenment, or some other profound change. But this, some critics suggest, is a weak ground for toleration. The distinction between a present and a future self, it is argued, despises the present existing empirical self. This point is central to the critique of Augustine that Rainer Forst has presented in *Toleration in Conflict*, where Augustine serves to illustrate what Forst calls the "Janus face of Christian toleration."[25] Forst's main contention is that Augustine's reasons for toleration were of such a kind that, under changed conditions, they naturally faded into their opposites: from reasons for tolerance to reasons for intolerance. Augustine's reasons for toleration, as we have seen, derive in part from ancient philosophical teachings about the endurance of the wise, but Forst focuses especially on the reasons drawn from Christian theology: love of neighbor, the distinction between the spiritual and the temporal realm (and the intermingling of the two cities), the preservation of the unity of the Church, the non-coercibility of conscience, and the "involuntary witness" to Christianity offered by the Jews if they were tolerated. Forst is obviously right that these arguments can morph into their opposites: if conscience can be influenced by strong external measures, if the unity of the Church can

[23] Marcuse, "Repressive Tolerance," 111.

[24] According to at least one study, intolerance of racism correlates with intolerance of Muslims and for political communication more in general. April Kelly-Woessner, "The New Left and Political Intolerance," in *The End of the Experiment. The Rise of Cultural Elites and the Decline of America's Civic Culture*, ed. Stanley Rothman (New Brunswick: Transaction Publishers, 2015), 187–200.

[25] Forst, *Toleration in Conflict: Past and Present*, 48.

be enforced, if love can paternalistically guide our neighbor to his highest good, reasons for tolerance can mutate into reasons for intolerance.

But Forst's main point is that this shift happened because of a deficient view of the self. Love of one's neighbor consists in care for his salvation; but this care can sometimes lead us to put up with his sins and sometimes to force him out of darkness even against his will. "Salvation in this sense—Forst writes—is an objectively definable matter and has nothing to do with the individual's 'carnal' preferences and desires or 'false' convictions."[26] Once we know what the salvation of the self means, so the critique goes, we will be tempted to ignore preferences and desires of the actual self and respond, in Augustine's words, with "benign severity."[27] And although this critique is initially directed at the Christian view of salvation, Forst rejects any ethical perfectionism that strives for "independently definable, supreme human goods and ends."[28] Following Isaiah Berlin, he writes that this perfectionism also takes secular forms, for instance in the belief that we must be liberated from our heteronomous selves in order to become truly free.[29] In this case, a secular reason for toleration—autonomy—morphs into an argument for intolerance against the actually existing forms of heteronomy. Any form of perfectionism, so the argument continues, will disregard the will of the empirical selves; it will try to open their eyes to what is really good for them, justifying a coercion subtly conceived as liberation. This all involves, according to Forst, "a structural division of the individual into the existing and the 'true' self and the duty to enable the latter to prevail over the former."[30] The dignity of the actually existing neighbor is denied in the name of some future version of himself. In the words of Camus, "He who loves his friend loves him in the present, and the revolution wants to love only a man who has not yet appeared."[31]

The great question, however, is whether this argument conflates different phenomena. It is true that, under the logic of historical necessity, we can be tempted to sacrifice the concrete human beings with whom we live to the promise of a future humanity. This, as we have seen, is the risk of liberating

[26] Forst, 56.

[27] *ep.* 138, 2, 14.

[28] Forst, *Toleration in Conflict: Past and Present*, 56.

[29] Forst, 57.

[30] Forst, 56. And it is hard to deny that Augustine sometimes writes in terms that lend themselves to this interpretation. In *Contra Faustum*, he writes that it is human nature (rather than the individual or empirical self) that we must love in our enemy, while "the vice which we rightly hate in him is condemned" (*c. Faust.* XIX, 24, a text not considered by Forst). It is also true, however, that the same argument is often made pointing to the "empirical" person. "Love the sinner not as sinner but as a man (*in quantum homo est*)" (*s.* 4, 20), an expression also included before *humana natura* in *c. Faust.*

[31] Albert Camus, *The Rebel*, trans. Anthony Bower (New York: Vintage Books, 1956), 239.

intolerance. But is such disregard for concrete existing persons entailed in every form of perfectionism? Does an Augustinian vision rule out not only historical necessity or progressivism, but all forms of perfectionism? Not without reason, Augustine has been called an "apostle of imperfection."[32] But in these discussions much obviously depends on how terms such as "perfectionism" are understood. If we define realism and perfectionism as mutually exclusive, it is obvious that only one of these can be applied to Augustine (and we already described him as a realist). However, there is little reason for such a disjunction. The classical philosophical tradition, as Gerald Mara has written, saw the "possibilities of conclusive knowledge and perfected practice" as an essential condition for coherent dialogue and practice, not as "rigid standards used to condemn imperfect thoughts and actions."[33] Augustine, furthermore, approached this in terms of his distinctive view of earthly life as pilgrimage. He writes of "seeking that kind of perfection that is appropriate to our condition as pilgrims."[34] He portrays Noah, for instance, as perfect "insofar as one can be perfect in this pilgrimage."[35] Whether we should describe this as perfectionism or not is a secondary matter, but if we do, this is a moderate perfectionism that remains deeply aware of human limits.[36] In any case, it seems hard to describe the search for such a perfection as "an objectively definable matter" that has nothing to do with our carnal "preferences and desires."

But this is not a sufficient answer to Forst's objections. After all, Augustine is not simply concerned with how we seek *our own* perfection in terms that are appropriate to our condition as pilgrims. The question is how we seek the perfection of others. This problem can also be addressed, perhaps more directly, by asking what it means to treat persons as ends. We must treat persons as ends and not as mere means, as Augustine, Aquinas, and Kant agree, and as liberating intolerance forgets. But the crucial question for our enquiry is what it means to treat them as ends, and to what degree treating someone as an end is compatible with a tolerant practice of correction, persuasion, or reorientation. One common approach in the contemporary debate, drawing on Kantian sources, sees human beings as ends in the sense that they can assign themselves ends. To recognize them as ends, in other words, is essentially to respect their autonomy thus understood. Augustine's overarching sense of

[32] Kaufman, *Incorrectly Political*, 98.
[33] Gerald M. Mara, "Socrates and Liberal Toleration," *Political Theory* 16, no. 3 (1988): 489.
[34] *perf. iust.* 8, 18.
[35] *civ.* XV, 26.
[36] On Augustine's "perfectionism," see Gregory, *Politics and the Order of Love. An Augustinian Ethic of Democratic Citizenship*, 73, and Martin Westerholm, "On the Structure and Significance of Augustine's Moral Grammar," *Journal of Religious Ethics* 49, no. 4 (2021): 715–38.

the tension of human life pushes in a different direction. The question (*magna quaestio*) is what kind of love is appropriate in dealing with "the great reality" of persons "made in the image and likeness of God."[37] Should they be enjoyed in themselves, or should they be treated with reference to God as their end? Twentieth-century critics often evaluated Augustine's discussion of "use" (*uti*) and "enjoyment" (*frui*) in the light of Kant's categorical imperative, and they found it wanting. Did it not imply "using" the neighbor as a means? It did not, and such misunderstandings have now been largely corrected.[38] But it is crucial to insist on the point that Augustine was positively making. He rejects the idea of *resting* in our neighbor—being content with the mere empirical self—as an adequate understanding of persons as ends. Such a form of resting in one another without orientation "towards something unchanging" is a "relaxation" that makes us "converted to ourselves" (*cum inde vel ad seipsum relaxatur*).[39] It is a loss of existential tension. It is the path suggested in Rousseau's *Reveries*, in which the soul enjoys nothing external to itself, "nothing if not ourselves and our own existence."[40] Instead of such incurved and defective enjoyment of the self, we are called to refer ourselves and others to God. This is the ultimate meaning of the *Confessions'* well-known lines about the restless hearts that will only find final rest in God.[41] These words are the declaration of a pious heart, but they are also an insight into the tense structure of human life and into the way we should relate to the surrounding reality and to our neighbors. We are called to a type of love that preserves us and others in tension toward our good.

This does not entail loving "only a man who has not yet appeared."[42] Respecting the "empirical self," which is made in the image of God, means keeping this restlessness alive while we reciprocally tolerate our many imperfections. If tolerance, like sacrifice, has tension built into its nature, then it may be particularly compatible with the tension toward God that is central to Augustine's vision of the person. There is no inconsistency in affirming this while at the same time rejecting some of Augustine's conclusions regarding

[37] *doctr. chr.* I, 22, 20.

[38] For nuanced discussions, see Jean-Michel Fontanier, "Sur l'analogie Augustinienne Honestum/Utile//Frui/Uti," *Revue Des Sciences Philosophiques et Théologiques* 84, no. 4 (2000): 635–42; K.-Y. Burchill-Limb, "The Actuality of Augustine's Distinction between Uti and Frui," *Augustiniana*, no. 56 (2006): 183–97; and Michael Lamb, *A Commonwealth of Hope. Augustine's Political Thought* (Princeton and Oxford: Princeton University Press, 2022), 32–46.

[39] *doctr. chr.* I, 22, 2.

[40] Jean-Jacques Rousseau, *The Reveries of the Solitary Walker, Botanical Writings, and Letter to Franquières*, ed. Christopher Kelly, trans. Charles E. Butterworth, Alexandra Cook, and Terence E. Marshall, The Collected Writings of Rousseau 8 (Hanover and London: University Press of New England, 2000), 46.

[41] *conf.* I, 1, 1.

[42] Camus, *The Rebel*, 239.

religious coercion. We reject them because not all means are legitimate for keeping this tension alive, not because "benign severity" as such is always inadequate. As Jacob Levy writes, "We wish—we really wish—to sometimes have our fellows cajole, persuade, preach to, or pressure us, when we are going to fall off the path we have chosen. We sometimes wish for our fellows to tell us what to do; and we trust them to do so."[43] Some forms of social pressure are genuinely rooted in justice and love. Which of these are legitimate—as we will discuss further ahead—will often be settled by the nature of our relationship to one other.

[43] Jacob T. Levy, *Rationalism, Pluralism, and Freedom* (Oxford: Oxford University Press, 2014), 33.

7

Judgment, Limits, and the Intolerable

Judgmental Toleration

In this chapter we will address the problem of limits and the intolerable. First, however, we must return to the non-judgmental pretense of our culture, mentioned in passing when we discussed the problem of evil. How did this non-judgmentalism arise? What are its forms? In our second chapter, we considered the doctrinally minimalistic approaches that developed in the sixteenth century and their place in the way of thinking about toleration that we find in Erasmian liberalism from Castellio to Locke. Let us turn again to this period, but now to the city of Geneva, where, under the leadership of John Calvin, the boundaries of the tolerable are often imagined to have been particularly strict. They were indeed strict, though not paradigmatically so: Geneva's legislation was not very different from that prevailing in the rest of Europe.[1] But if we leave aside the image of Calvin as an arch-authoritarian, his work still illuminates two contrasting ways in which the boundaries of toleration and the legitimacy of judgment were treated in the early modern period.[2] As in the rest of the Augustinian tradition, his exposition of Matthew 13 is a revealing text to consider. Calvin is familiar with Augustine's understanding of the text, and he quite naturally explains the parable in terms that remind us of the mixed condition of the Church: hypocrites and unprincipled people will mingle with true believers, and believers themselves are subject to the many weaknesses of the flesh. As for moral vices, Calvin concludes, we have little more to do than "bear those human faults that cannot be mended."[3] He thus affirmed without question the morally mixed nature of the political and ecclesiastical community. "Absolute purity is nowhere to be found," Calvin states unequivocally.[4] Regarding right worship and doctrine, however, his view is

[1] For this comparison see Coffey, *Persecution and Toleration in Protestant England 1558–1689*, 102.

[2] For a broader discussion of his view of tolerance see Manfred Svensson, "Crucis Tolerantia: John Calvin's Theology and Ethics of Toleration," *Political Theology* 24, no. 2 (2023): 183–99.

[3] Calvin, *Commentarius in harmoniam evangelicam*, CO 45, 368.

[4] CO 45, 368. Comm. Mt. 13:24–43.

An Augustinian Essay on Toleration. Manfred Svensson, Oxford University Press. © Manfred Svensson 2026.
DOI: 10.1093/9780197912737.003.0010

quite different. Here, he writes, he was "not at liberty to extend tolerance."[5] It is not that discipline should be renounced in moral matters, but there Calvin could at least imagine a toleration he found inconceivable when it came to doctrine and worship.

The contrast with his adversaries is instructive. Sebastian Castellio is often portrayed as the tolerant nemesis of the intolerant Calvin. In the midst of the prevailing theology of religious persecution, he seems to be the one man who calls a spade a spade: "To kill a man is not to defend a doctrine, but to kill a man."[6] In this he was right. For our current thinking about toleration, however, it may be fruitful not only to reassert this basic truth, but also to critically look into Castellio's reversal of the domains of life in which Calvin thought that toleration could be granted. This reversal was based on Castellio's disagreement with Calvin about the proper place for judgment. "To make judgments on doctrines is not as easy as making judgments on behavior,"[7] he writes. This would become a standard position among later anti-Augustinians. Since the distinction between virtue and vice is "by all man kinde perfectly & certainly knowne,"[8] Locke wrote, magistrates could leave behind "the imposition of creeds and ceremonies" and instead "severally and impartially set themselves against vice."[9] Calvin's skepticism about the moral reformation of humanity fades, replaced by a greater skepticism about the possibility of agreement on matters of doctrine. This would become commonplace. Another important Genevan, Jean-Jacques Rousseau, would later reproach d'Alambert even for *praising* the Enlightened religious convictions of the city's pastors: such praise rests on judgment, a judgment that is incompatible with respect for "the secrets of consciences."[10] Having thus boasted of his non-judgmentalism (as far as doctrine is concerned), however, Rousseau echoes Castellio's and Locke's writings almost *verbatim*: "let us judge the actions of men and leave it to God to judge of their faith."[11] Rousseau's words are a good indication of where the pretense of non-judgmentalism often ends up: in the uncritical repetition of

[5] CO 45, 368. Comm. Mt. 13:24–43.
[6] Sebastian Castellio, *Concerning Heretics* (New York: Octagon Books, 1965), 271.
[7] Castellio, 131–32.
[8] Locke, *An Essay Concerning Toleration: And Other Writings on Law and Politics, 1667–1683*, 304.
[9] John Locke, "A Second Letter Concerning Toleration," in *Works in Ten Volumes* (London: W. Otridge et al., 1812), 6:65–66.
[10] Jean-Jacques Rousseau, *Politics and the Arts. Letter to d'Alambert on the Theatre*, ed. Allan Bloom (Ithaca, NY: Cornell University Press, 1968), 14. See also the "Seventh Walk" of his *Reveries*, where he describes his own inclinations as innocent and the judgments of men as "null." Rousseau, *The Reveries of the Solitary Walker, Botanical Writings, and Letter to Franquières*, 57.
[11] Rousseau, *Politics and the Arts. Letter to d'Alambert on the Theatre*, 14.

the predominant judgments; in this case, that it is easy to judge about morals, difficult about doctrines.

Lest we delude ourselves with the illusion of non-judgmentalism, it then seems better to recognize judgment as inescapable. Following Charles Taylor, we must think of persons as "strong evaluators."[12] Judgment may often be a delicate matter, but it is inevitable. Judgment is sometimes difficult, but, writes Augustine, "everything that exists is worthy of some evaluation."[13] If we look again at Augustine's work, we will perhaps find some judgments that we would refrain from making. He sometimes writes as if the clear, undisputable identification of an evil were enough to place it beyond the pale of the tolerable. When an evil is evident, "discipline should not delay."[14] Perhaps this depends on what we mean by discipline. In any case, where judgment is due it must be exercised with care. We must recognize our fallibility, the partial nature of our knowledge, the need for some skepticism about the conclusions we find agreeable. Both the Bible and the Stoics combine calls to a life governed by discernment with calls to control our tendency to rush to judgment. Charles Mathewes has hence written about "intelligent judgmentalism" as one of the important things we learn from the various traditions of religious ethics.[15] Our spontaneous judgments must pass through the filter of self-examination, of the search for impartiality, in order to set aside mere prejudices, erroneous and undifferentiated judgments. These cautions, however, all relate to a judgment that is inevitable. For Augustine, this is part of the very description of the good life: "He lives in justice and holiness, who is a sound judge of all things (*integer rerum aestimator*)."[16] Whatever a vulgar conflation of prejudice and judgment may suggest, the exercise of judgment is part and parcel of the good life.

But can judgment be part of a tolerant life? That much should already be clear. As we have seen, and as much of the contemporary literature on toleration affirms, a component of objection is in fact one of the defining elements of toleration.[17] Trivial identifications of tolerance with skepticism, fallibilism, or relativism routinely ignore this fact. Whatever one otherwise thinks of these perspectives, that identification must be resisted. In the words of Geoffrey Harrison, "Advocating tolerance or being tolerant are activities which are internal to particular moral systems. . . . There is nothing that the relativist, qua

[12] Taylor, "What Is Human Agency?," 23.
[13] *ep.* 11, 4.
[14] *c. ep. Parm.* III, 2, 13.
[15] Charles Mathewes, *Understanding Religious Ethics* (Oxford: Wiley-Blackwell, 2010), 7–9.
[16] *doctr. chr.* I, 27, 28
[17] King, *Toleration*, 44–51.

relativist, can say either for or against tolerance from a moral point of view."[18] Fallibilism or skepticism perhaps merit a milder approach. It is often suggested that we must temper the strength of our convictions if we wish to be tolerant. Tolerance must act as a check on moral certitude. If we are "convinced beyond doubt about the correctness of our beliefs or about the immorality of the practices of others," writes Chandran Kukathas, "there is less reason to tolerate those whose beliefs or practices differ from our own."[19] This is very different from presuming a natural affinity between relativism and tolerance, but is it more convincing? As our argument thus far suggests, it is not a less intense judgment that is required for toleration to be possible, but rather the combination of that judgment with other good reasons for toleration (reasons which, presumably, also require some certitude and intensity in order to be efficacious). There may, of course, be other reasons to cultivate some form of fallibilism or skepticism, but not because they are required for toleration. When toleration has been based on skepticism, as Alan Levine points out, it has typically been "limited or supplemented by some other conviction, idea, or aim in order to reach a tolerant conclusion."[20]

So there is nothing paradoxical about Michael Sandel's call for a "judgmental toleration." This is how he characterizes an approach that "assesses the moral worth or permissibility of the practice at issue and permits or restricts it according to the weight of those moral considerations in relation to competing moral and practical considerations."[21] The outcome of such a deliberation is, of course, unpredictable, but it invites finding the grounds for toleration in the substantive moral claims themselves, not in avoiding them. What kind of judging is implied here? What kind of judgment is tolerance based on? Tolerance, we can say, is a suspension not of judgment but of the sentence. If a sentence can be suspended, it is because it is derived from a complex judgment. In this sense, tolerance is the fruit of a web of judgments. Something is judged negatively, but that negativity is not the only thing present in this judgment. Tolerance requires not any kind of moral objectivism or realism, but a significantly differentiated moral judgment. Relativism will not lead to toleration, but neither will any kind of alternative to relativism. What we need is not the mere detection of good and evil. As Rainer Forst has put it, toleration is "*the*

[18] Geoffrey Harrison, "Relativism and Tolerance," *Ethics* 86, no. 2 (1976): 132.

[19] Chandran Kukathas, *The Liberal Archipelago. A Theory of Diversity and Freedom* (Oxford: Oxford University Press, 2003), 126.

[20] Alan Levine, "Introduction: The Prehistory of Toleration and Varieties of Skepticism," in *Early Modern Skepticism and the Origins of Toleration*, ed. Alan Levine (Lanham: Lexington Books, 1999), 6.

[21] Michael J. Sandel, "Judgemental Toleration," in *Natural Law, Liberalism, and Morality. Contemporary Essays*, ed. Robert P. George (Oxford: Clarendon Press, 1996), 107.

ability to say yes and no in a differentiated manner."[22] It is the fruit of a complex judgment in which something is not simply seen as good or evil. It is the fruit of pondering what other evils result from a prohibition, on what goods a given evil depends. Undifferentiated maximalism is not the alternative we need to moral minimalism. Tolerance requires a culture in which the development of a differentiated moral discourse is encouraged, a moral culture in which making distinctions and clarifications is not disqualified as hypocrisy, as concession or accommodation, as lack of commitment or resolve. In the words of Michael Walzer, "in moral discourse, thinness and intensity go together, whereas with thickness comes qualification, compromise, complexity, and disagreement."[23] A culture of toleration is not only a culture of dignity, moderation, or self-control but also a culture shaped by this aspiration to qualified judgment.

Evils We Must Stop: Harm and Intolerance

Qualified judgment, however, is still judgment, and it often leads to limiting toleration. In some circumstances, the enforcement of certain limits can even help us to tolerate. We can tolerate our neighbor's music in part because after a certain hour he must be silent. Some things are tolerable up to a certain point. But there are also things that cannot be deemed acceptable for any length of time. Even the most differentiated judgment will arrive at the conclusion that some things are intolerable. In fact, unlimited toleration is absurd. When we call for toleration, we appeal to reasons, principles, or motives that justify this call.[24] These very same reasons, principles, or motives indicate how far that tolerance will go: the reasons for toleration always reveal reasons for non-toleration. We defend toleration in the name of freedom, privacy, the search for knowledge, or basic sociability, and the protection of such goods immediately suggests that some attacks on them should not be tolerated. How, then, should boundaries be drawn? Usually with prudential considerations aligned with the pursuit of these goods. "Toleration, being a part of moral and political prudence," as Burke writes, "ought to be tender and large."[25] But two further

[22] Forst, *Toleration in Conflict: Past and Present*, 505–06. Italics in the original.

[23] Michael Walzer, *Thick and Thin. Moral Argument at Home and Abroad* (Notre Dame: University of Notre Dame Press, 1994), 6. For an exposition of Augustine's moral thought that represents this kind of "thickness" see Clair, *Discerning the Good in the Letters and Sermons of Augustine.*

[24] Here I draw on Alejandro Vigo's reading of Popper's paradox. Alejandro Vigo, "Liberalismo, tolerancia y bien," *Anuario de Filosofía Jurídica y Social* 17 (1999): 358–59.

[25] Edmund Burke, *A Letter from the Right Hon. Edmund Burke, M.P., to Sir Hercules Langrishe on the Subject of Roman Catholics of Ireland* (London: J. Derrett, 1792), 23.

approaches to this question deserve special attention, since, apart from such prudential considerations, they are frequently invoked to draw limits. It is often held that the limit of toleration can be drawn in terms of harm. It is likewise held that intolerance is the truly intolerable phenomenon. After considering these two common approaches, we must ask whether an appeal to intrinsically evil acts might be an appropriate Augustinian alternative (a question I answer partly in the negative).

Let us first consider the question of harm. Its mention seems to give us access to something universally acknowledged as limit of the tolerable. In the modern world, this question of harm has moreover found a home in the projects of minimal ethics discussed earlier. The dilemma from which such projects arise is easy to understand. On the one hand, there is a desire to avoid imposing moral convictions on others; on the other hand, there is a desire to avoid relativism. What is offered then is a middle way that seeks a clear distinction between autonomy, human rights, tolerance, and other basic principles that should command universal assent and the rest of our thick ethical discourse. Whatever ethical conflicts may exist, there is a core that is safely set apart. In that core, at its very center, we find the prohibition of intentional harm to others. Tolerance should be extended to all practices that do not constitute such harm. This is a widespread view, and one which John Stuart Mill famously defended as a "very simple principle."[26] It has also been argued that this reflects a view of society and liberty not very different from that of Aquinas.[27] For him the human law should prohibit only the more serious vices "that are harmful to others."[28] The agreement between Aquinas and Mill seems to be substantial, suggesting that we have indeed arrived at an uncontroversial minimum.

There is an important sense in which we all hold harm to be intolerable. Murder and theft, to take the more obvious cases, cannot be tolerated. But how significant is this consensus around the intolerable nature of harm? There is a general consensus, but the consequences that people draw from the criterion of harm in fact differ widely. In light of this principle, some consider that our society continues to be unjustifiably restrictive, that we should tolerate much more than we now do. Contemporary discussions ranging from the use of marijuana to euthanasia are approached by Andrew Jason Cohen in these terms, concluding that if "we take the harm principle in its strict form seriously,

[26] John Stuart Mill, "On Liberty," in *Essays on Politics and Society*, The Collected Works of John Stuart Mill (Toronto and Buffalo: University of Toronto Press, 1977), 18:223.

[27] John Finnis, *Aquinas: Moral, Political and Legal Theory* (Oxford: Oxford University Press, 1998), 228.

[28] *S. Th.* I–II, q. 96, a. 2.

there would be a very limited class of things we would not tolerate."[29] Nearly all questions of toleration would, according to this perspective, need to be resolved in the positive. In the ideal society in which toleration reigns, writes Cohen, "drug dealers are simply purveyors of drugs, in the same line of work as any pharmacy today."[30] This understanding of the harm criterion seems to push us in the direction of a more permissive society. But the recent transformation of the public understanding of harm—the expansion in our understanding of abuse, bullying, trauma, and other phenomena[31]—seems to open the way for a development in a very different direction. When "civic harm," "status injury," or "dignitary harm" are added to the more limited forms of harm, it seems inevitable that the limits of tolerance will shrink, and the possibilities of legitimate interference will widen. The harm principle was first presented as a criterion that would serve to expand tolerance; as our conception of harm is expanded, however, it is tolerance that becomes minimal. It is not clear, moreover, that this problem can be solved by a simple return to the original form of the harm principle. Mill is often presented as an antidote to the "new intolerance" of contemporary society, but in his writings this principle was already operating in a more expansive way than the conventional interpretation of his thought supports.[32] Bringing a child into existence without the prospect of providing for its body and its mind was for Mill "a moral crime, both against the unfortunate and against society."[33] Far from being a trivial observation, this was for him a central example of intolerable harm. When the "ordinary chances of a desirable existence" are out of reach, to bestow a life "is a crime against that being."[34] This is just one illustration, but it inevitably raises the question about the extent to which the avoidance of harm is such a clearly identifiable and uncontroversial a criterion for drawing the limits of toleration, a criterion that is uncontested across traditions such as those of Mill and Aquinas.

This question cannot be satisfactorily addressed by simply negotiating between minimal and maximal views of harm. As John Horton has discussed in more detail, it makes no sense to imagine that the content of the concept of harm is independent of the competing visions of what constitutes a good life.[35]

[29] Cohen, *Toleration*, 52.

[30] Cohen, 119.

[31] See Nick Haslam, "Concept Creep. Psychology's Expanding Notions of Harm and Their Moral Basis," in *The Social Psychology of Morality*, ed. Joseph P. Forgas, Lee Jussim, and Paul A.M. Van Lange (New York and London: Routledge, 2016), 293–319.

[32] For one such appeal to Mill against the new intolerance see Furedi, *On Tolerance: A Defence of Moral Independence*, 102.

[33] Mill, "On Liberty," 302.

[34] Mill, 304.

[35] John Horton, "Toleration, Morality, and Harm," in *Aspects of Toleration: Philosophical Studies*, ed. John Horton and Susan Mendus (London: Methuen, 1985), 113–35.

Mill claimed to be offering a "very simple principle," but the notion of harm is as controversial as any other moral concept. Indeed, what people consider harmful depends on what they consider valuable; and since reasonable people disagree about what is most valuable—even concerning such fundamental questions as the value of life itself and their own freedom—it is to be expected that the notion of harm will remain controversial. As Susan Mendus writes, "it is not necessarily the case that we all understand what harms are, but are unsure whether the law should restrict itself to them alone. Rather, we are divided from the outset about what harm essentially is."[36] Moreover, the role of harm as a moral criterion is much more culturally conditioned than is often acknowledged. Harm is also relevant beyond the educated circles of the liberal West, but elsewhere, as Jonathan Haidt has shown, other moral "taste buds" such as sanctity or loyalty can carry more substantial weight.[37] This is not to say that the concept of harm is irrelevant to our reflection about tolerance. But often it is not the only principle to appeal to, and there is not always an uncontroversial way to determine what is harmful.[38] One can appeal to the harm principle, but since this principle is not independent of our broader disputes around the human good, such an appeal lacks the simplicity that much of liberal theory aspires to.

Let us turn to our second question. Ever since Rousseau declared intolerance to be the only "negative dogma" of his civil religion, it has been common to ask whether intolerance should be tolerated.[39] Writing in 1763, just one year after Rousseau published his *Social Contract*, Voltaire stated that "men must avoid fanaticism in order to deserve toleration."[40] Intolerance, it is still often said, is the only intolerable evil, and fanaticism is often included under that label. Alexander Vinet seems to have been alone in his time in counting intolerance as an especially significant object of *tolerance*, since "this virtue is beautiful as the sacrifice is great."[41] But how can we choose between Voltaire and Vinet? There is perhaps a deeper grasp of toleration in Vinet. As his words reveal, he sees its family resemblance to sacrifice. But we can think of many sacrifices that are not beautiful, many forms of intolerance that it would be more beautiful to

[36] Susan Mendus, *Toleration and the Limits of Liberalism* (London: Macmillan, 1989), 124.

[37] Jonathan Haidt, *The Righteous Mind. Why Good People Are Divided by Politics and Religion* (New York: Vintage, 2013), 111–216.

[38] See Horton, "Toleration, Morality, and Harm," 113.

[39] Rousseau, *The Social Contract and Other Late Political Writings*, 151 (IV, 8).

[40] Voltaire, *Toleration and Other Essays*, trans. Joseph McCabe (New York and London: G.P. Putnam's Sons, 1912), 73.

[41] Vinet, *Outlines of Philosophy and Literature*, 275. In the contemporary discussion Glen Newey comes closest to this point. Far from being a paradoxical anomaly, tolerating the intolerant comes closer for him to being the norm in political toleration. Newey, *Toleration in Political Conflict*, 15 and 51.

remove. There is a sense, in other words, in which Rousseau and Voltaire may be right in highlighting intolerance and fanaticism as particularly pernicious. The psychology of fanaticism refuses ambiguity or tension in any form, either in the world or in ourselves. Seen in this light, intolerant fanaticism is not one evil among others but rather an evil that undermines conditions for tolerance across the board. But even if this may be true, it sheds no evident light on how that disposition must be opposed. As harmful as a spirit of intolerance is, it may be an evil we must tolerate. We only know that once we have judged about concrete manifestations of that spirit and the actions to which it leads. The abstract idea of intolerance as our only "negative dogma" is thus rather useless.

This conclusion converges with Karl Popper's famous "paradox of tolerance." According to this paradox, "in order to maintain a tolerant society, the society must be intolerant of intolerance."[42] How should this be interpreted? The key insight in this formulation is that an unlimited tolerance would be self-destructive. This, as we have seen, is certainly true. It is less clear, however, that a banishment of all forms of intolerance—and of intolerance alone—should follow. The absence of justice or mercy, after all, is also destructive to a society, but there is no clear rule about the sense in which injustice or mercilessness should be excluded from society. Some forms of injustice must be excluded, and likely some specific forms of intolerance as well. In their original setting, Popper's words in fact had a precise meaning that they often lack when abusively quoted today. When Popper wrote these pages, in 1945, the "intolerants" were easy to identify. His reflections were written for a post-war context, and in his brief discussion he did not even need to name the totalitarian projects that he labeled as intolerant. The preachers of intolerance and persecution had a concrete face that everyone recognized. When today the same label is crudely applied to any strong conviction, to traditions, cultures, and doctrines that the dominant culture perceives as fanatical, Popper's paradox loses all its intuitive usefulness. The notion of intolerance, like that of harm, does not tell us all we need to know in order to adequately draw the boundaries of what is tolerable. Those who are positively shutting others down must be met at that level, but there is no clear implication for how loosely identified "fanaticism" or "intolerance" must be met.

As our two preceding discussions suggest, the question of limits poses challenges that the conventional appeal to harm and intolerance obscures. Harm is not a "very simple principle," and there are other unbearable evils

[42] Karl Popper, *The Open Society and Its Enemies* (Princeton: Princeton University Press, 2013), 581 n. 4.

besides intolerance. But if we reject such simple solutions, another temptation may arise. We may conclude that the limits of tolerance should be drawn with appeal to natural law or to the notion of intrinsically evil actions. This would seem particularly appropriate within an Augustinian approach. After all, the existence of such intrinsically evil actions, as we have noted in Chapter 4, is an important component of Augustine's own moral thought. There are manifestly evil actions that are completely incompatible with right intention.[43] It is moreover true that actions that are always evil—such as murder, rape, or torture—also tend to be exceedingly evil actions. The "more serious vices" (*mala graviora*) are also, in Aquinas' formulation, "harmful to others" (*in nocumentum aliorum*).[44] Intrinsically evil actions seem to be intolerable actions. Why did I then describe this as a temptation? For the simple reason that not even exceptionless moral rules offer an unproblematic list of intolerable actions. Lying is the evil that prompts Augustine's most detailed discussion of actions that are always evil. But while it is paradigmatically evil, it is only intolerable in a specific sense and in specific contexts.[45] When we say that lying is intolerable, we are expressing how deeply evil it is; we are not affirming that it should be legally prohibited in all its forms. It is a way of saying that whether such actions are permitted or not, lying cannot be condoned.

The idea of intrinsically evil actions, then, plays a role in our thinking about limits, but just as in the discussion of harm and intolerance, we are inevitably thrown back to the need for practical wisdom.[46] While some evils must always be prohibited, the limits of toleration must be approached in essentially prudential terms. Indeed, Popper himself counseled a prudential approach to "the intolerant": if they can be kept in check by argument, he writes, "suppression would certainly be most unwise."[47] Harm is often a good guide, intolerance must often be resisted, and many intrinsically evil acts must always be restrained. But a list of intolerable evils cannot be constructed in the abstract.

[43] Augustine's locus classicus on intrinsically evil actions is *c. mend.* 8, 17. For a further discussion which distinguishes "intermediate" actions from those that are manifestly evil, see *s. dom. m.* II, 18, 59–60.

[44] *S. Th.* I-II, q. 96, a. 2.

[45] For an Augustinian discussion of the morality of lying see Paul J. Griffiths, *Lying. An Augustinian Theology of Duplicity* (Grand Rapids: Brazos Press, 2004).

[46] As Cohen notes, even the strict application of the harm principle tells us only when interference is permissible, not when it is advisable. Cohen, *Toleration*, 63. A similar prudential approach to "unreasonableness" as a criterion can be found in Kerstin Budde, "Unreasonable or Evil?" in *Evil in Contemporary Political Theory*, ed. Bruce Haddock, Peri Roberts, and Peter Sutch (Edinburgh: Edinburgh University Press, 2011), 81–100.

[47] Popper, *The Open Society and Its Enemies*, 581 n. 4. Also Rawls' approach to this issue can be described as fundamentally prudential. John Rawls, *A Theory of Justice. Revised Edition* (Cambridge, Mass: Belknap Press of Harvard University Press, 1999), 192–93.

A tolerant society must exclude some invariably evil actions, but even regarding these, concrete judgment is called for. A variety of circumstances, not just the degree of evil, come into play when we need to establish boundaries. One ponders, for instance, the chances of keeping an evil in check, its capacity for expansion. We must also note that in the classical texts of Aquinas and Mill, the issue is only inclusion and exclusion from the political community. But we can also ask about the limits of toleration in other communities, and other criteria will then come to mind. The specific goods we seek in each community help to define what is tolerable within them, as we will discuss further in Chapter 11. Before turning to such problems, however, we need to complete our discussion of the conditions of tolerance with a dive into the different conceptions of personhood that are present in the debate.

8

Identity and the True Self

The limits of toleration are neither arbitrary nor reducible to a list of intolerable evils. They depend on the goods that we seek in particular associations, on the broader visions of the good that guide our whole lives, and on the concrete judgments that we draw in relevant contexts. These are some of the general conclusions of the previous chapter. But these judgments are directed at what we might call different layers of the self. Implicitly or explicitly, we often distinguish between the present actions and inclinations that we tolerate and the self that the person in question may turn out to become. As discussed in Chapter 6, we often tolerate in the knowledge (or hope) that change will come. We tolerate not only because we respect the person, but also because more than her present state appears on our horizon. We also distinguish between an evil action and the person who commits it. These are very basic distinctions, some of which are essential to tolerance and some of which frequently come with it. But in the contemporary critique of toleration, these layers of human personhood often fade away. A person and his or her inclinations are fused into a single "identity"—cultural, religious, or sexual—and the question then arises as to whether this identity can be the object of toleration or only of recognition. It is to these questions, all broadly concerned with the nature of personhood and with the perspective of the tolerated, that this chapter will turn.[1]

Culture and Recognition

What idea of personhood does toleration require? How does toleration relate to contemporary discussions of identity and cultural recognition? How do these questions, in turn, relate to other dimensions of human life, such as religion? And how does all this relate to the centrality of judgment? Can one judge and tolerate cultures, religions, persons? One possible response to these

[1] For a broader discussion of Augustine's conception of personhood see Peter J. Burnell, *The Augustinian Person* (Washington, DC: Catholic University of America Press, 2005).

An Augustinian Essay on Toleration. Manfred Svensson, Oxford University Press. © Manfred Svensson 2026.
DOI: 10.1093/9780197912737.003.0011

questions is that persons *are* the proper object of toleration, that we are tolerant when we focus our attention on persons *instead of* making judgments about their actions or beliefs.[2] This is the concept of toleration that David Heyd calls "perceptual," because of the perceptual shift that it requires. It shifts from the disapproved action or thought to the subject who freely or authentically chose it. As we will see in a later chapter, this has important consequences for Heyd's approach to education in the virtue of tolerance. But here I follow instead the standard position shared by Augustinians, Kantians, and many others, namely that the object of judgment and of tolerance is a practice or a belief rather than a person. Indeed, this can be seen as a typical assumption of the traditional conception of toleration.[3] We necessarily judge when we tolerate, but the judgment does not fall on the person as such.

Typically, however, we interact not simply with persons and their actions, but with persons who belong to particular cultures. And the relationship between a person and her culture, however we describe it, is different from her relation to her actions. To say that I tolerate your fondness of smoking is very different from saying I tolerate your Southeast Asian culture. The background and the action may be related, but the action seems to be a more reasonable object of toleration than the cultural belonging. Are cultures appropriate objects of toleration? A significant part of the turn to recognition stems from the sensible realization that cultures call for something other than toleration. Recognition, respect, and other affirmative dispositions are not only pertinent as responses to persons but also as response to cultures. Cultures can of course be shaped by perverse ideas and patterns of behavior, and disentangling a culture from the tolerable and intolerable traditions that shape it is sometimes a difficult task. But it is not always difficult, and it is for the most part possible. In the words of Oliver O'Donovan, making such distinctions is "the first requirement of moral consciousness, a requirement as old as civilization itself."[4] We can respect or value a culture—our own majority culture, a foreign culture, a domestic minority culture—and barely tolerate some of the forces that shape it.[5] With a slightly different terminology, this distinction between cultures and ethico-religious orientation is explicitly present in Augustine: "Though there are many and great peoples on earth, living with diverse rites and customs,

[2] For a defense of this view see Heyd, "Introduction," 10–17.

[3] On this see, among others, Churchill, "On the Difference between Non-Moral and Moral Concepts of Tolerance: The Case for Toleration as an Individual Virtue," 200–01.

[4] Oliver O'Donovan, "Reflections on Pluralism," *The Princeton Seminary Bulletin* 29 (2008): 59.

[5] In what follows I integrate Augustine with the distinctions discussed in Jonathan Chaplin, "Rejecting Neutrality, Respecting Diversity. From 'Liberal Pluralism' to Christian Pluralism," *Christian Scholar's Review* 35 (2006): 143–76.

distinguished by their different languages, weapons, and dress, yet there are no more than two types of society, which we may rightly call two cities according to our Scriptures."[6] There are many cultures, "many and great peoples on earth," but only two loves or basic orientations. These basic orientations cannot, therefore, be identified with any culture. This is no disparagement of cultural difference. In making this distinction, the Augustinian conception of the goodness of the created order makes a respectful engagement with the cultural dimension of human life a natural conclusion. Augustine does not "celebrate" cultural difference, because another dimension of human life—our ultimate love—is much more central to his understanding of persons. But he takes cultures into account. As it journeys through this earth, the city of God "gathers a pilgrim society with citizens from all the peoples and all the languages, regardless of the different customs, laws, and institutions by which they conquer and preserve earthly peace."[7] This can be described as an attitude of integration into the single city of God, with relative indifference to culture. But not total indifference. The right attitude toward those customs, laws, and institutions, Augustine goes on to write, "is not to cut them off or destroy them, but even to preserve and follow them."[8] At least mild forms of cultural recognition can be interpreted as compatible with this view. Such mild forms will not demand approval, but they rest on due acknowledgment that our different languages, customs, institutions, and historical traditions are a relevant dimension of human life.

As we have already seen, however, not all calls for recognition are equally mild. One of the problems in the contemporary discourse is the reduction of human reality to its cultural dimension: we treat our differences as cultural differences, drawing the conclusion that all differences demand recognition. The UNESCO Declaration on Tolerance, a symptomatic text that we have already considered, invites us to "respect, acceptance and appreciation of the rich diversity of our world's cultures, our forms of expression and ways of being human."[9] This inevitably makes judgment and toleration superfluous. If cultural difference becomes the paradigm through which we understand all difference—our "ways of being human," our rival political, moral, religious, or philosophical visions—any kind of judgment will be a form of misrecognition. And this is an important aspect of the contemporary discussion of toleration,

[6] *civ.* XIV, 1.
[7] *civ.* XIX, 17.
[8] *civ.* XIX, 17.
[9] UNESCO, *Declaration of Principles on Tolerance*, November 16, 1995, arts 1.1 and 1.2, available at: https://unesdoc.unesco.org/ark:/48223/pf0000151830 [accessed 2 January 2023].

one which affects both our understanding of its judgment- and of its power-component. Consider, for example, the way in which our understanding of political tolerance is distorted under this view. In political life we need toleration because politics revolves quite centrally around contested visions. This is neither a passing feature nor a remnant of older political configurations. Rival political projects—often inspired by rival moral visions—are essential to democratic politics, with its fluctuating majorities and minorities. If this is essential to political life, then it is clear why tolerance is fundamental to its health. But if our political life is observed through the lens of cultural rather than political difference, things change substantively. Political life is then understood in terms that consider the very existence of power and majorities an affront. Legitimate political majorities or legitimate rival parties hardly have a place in this picture. Instead of being fundamental to the health of political life, tolerance here is necessarily suspect.

Against the prevailing hyperculturalism, we need to restrict the field to which recognition can reasonably be applied. There is no need to ignore the role of cultural majorities and minorities, but political toleration requires that we refocus the discussion on political visions—not cultures—and their capacity for mutual toleration. The fact that policies and practices of recognition extend to cultures or collective cultural practices, moreover, does not mean that they can always be extended to collective identities or identity-claims as well.[10] Insofar as such identity-claims seek to guide human lives, to give direction, to influence policies and offer ultimate meaning, they are closer to worldviews or philosophies than to cultures. And there are crucial reasons why we do not offer recognition to such visions or philosophies. Appreciating one's own culture entails no necessary judgment, positive or negative, about other's cultures. But a conception of the good, as Glen Newey writes, "is also a conception of the badness of others' conceptions of the good."[11] Visions can logically exclude each other in ways that cultures do not; we can convert from one vision to another in ways in which we cannot change between cultures. Visions are universalistic where cultures are particular; for many such reasons, we reasonably judge about visions in a way that makes less sense about cultures.

None of this makes cultural difference irrelevant. Cultures, like visions, are encompassing. Cultures can and do collide in the same ways that visions do. The point of distinguishing them is not to blind us to the depth of possible

[10] Here I follow Bader, "Moral Minimalism and More Demanding Moralities: Some Reflections on 'Tolerance/Toleration,'" 38.

[11] Newey, *Toleration in Political Conflict*, 60.

cultural misunderstandings or to ignore the ways in which toleration may be necessary in cultural conflict. But recognition *can* be the appropriate response to cultural difference. We *can* look at different cultures as something that a single vision—such as that of the city of God—can hope to "preserve and follow."[12] This is the Augustinian view. It implies, quite obviously, the primacy of religion over culture. But it also requires first that we distinguish between the two dimensions and thus avoid reducing the former to the latter. As we shall see next, this distinction, while in some ways "as old as civilization," is also the result of a specific revolution.

Religion as Culture?

In previous chapters we have touched on other aspects of the debate over religion, such as the myth of a necessarily tolerant secularization or the way in which a "theology of conflict avoidance" underlies Locke's understanding of toleration. But here we need to ask how religion relates to the cultural dimension of personhood. In its general outline the dilemma is simple: if we treat religion as nearly indistinguishable from a culture, it cannot be the object of either judgment or toleration. Is it thus indistinguishable? Religion seems to be intertwined with culture, but it also calls for acknowledgment of its distinctive nature. Here Jan Assmann's distinction between primary and secondary religions may be helpful. He calls primary religions those that evolved in forms that are inextricably intertwined with a specific culture, language, and society. Secondary religions, in contrast, is his title for monotheistic religions, which are also religions of the book and world religions. These are colossal differences. For Assmann, however, the key aspect of the revolution that separates primary and secondary religions is the "Mosaic distinction." With this formula he refers not to "the distinction between One God and many gods but the distinction between truth and falsehood in religion, between the true and false gods, true doctrine and false doctrine, knowledge and ignorance, belief and unbelief."[13] There is, of course, much room for discussion about the uniqueness of the Mosaic moment, and the question of truth in religion, as Joseph Ratzinger has objected, may be more universal than Assmann claims.[14] But Assmann

[12] *civ.* XIX, 17.

[13] Jan Assmann, *The Price of Monotheism*, trans. Robert Savage (Stanford, CA: Stanford University Press, 2010), 2.

[14] See Ratzinger's discussion of Assmann in Ratzinger, *Truth and Tolerance. Christian Belief and World Religions*, 140–53.

captures a fundamental insight that places religion on the side of visions instead of cultures. This was also, quite obviously, the view of Augustine. It is a "chief head of man's salvation that philosophy, which is search for wisdom, is not different from religion," he writes in *On True Religion*.[15] And if they stand or fall by their truth claims, secondary religions are a type of "counterreligion." They arose in acts of revolution against the primary religions, which they would therefore necessarily denounce as pagan, idolatrous, and superstitious. This is why Assmann writes of the "price" of monotheism: the Mosaic distinction seems to demand the exclusion of all that is incompatible with the truths it proclaims. This was also Augustine's point after affirming the identity between philosophy and religion: "Those whose doctrine we do not approve, do not partake in our sacraments."[16]

What happens with tolerance in this account? Though he has often been read along those lines, Assmann was not interested in the thesis that "monotheism is intrinsically and necessarily intolerant," which he admits is rather cheap and crude.[17] What he sought to demonstrate was not the intolerance of world religions but their "power of negation," the "antagonistic energy" that comes from the distinction between true and false religion.[18] He sometimes described this "antagonistic energy" as "intolerance," but he acknowledged that this "power of negation" can be channeled in both tolerant and intolerant ways.[19] In fact, it would be meaningless to describe them as intolerant in contrast to the tolerance of ancient paganism. For however much we may want to quantify and compare the violence of primary or secondary religions, in the primary ones "the criterion of incompatibility is missing."[20] Without the distinction between false and true religion, if religion is simply a dimension of culture, the relationship to other religions cannot be meaningfully described in terms of either religious tolerance or intolerance. So it is with monotheism, or, rather, with the "Mosaic distinction," that the question of religious tolerance arises. The question of tolerance is known to humanity aside from the "Mosaic distinction," precisely because moral and political judgment is such an essential element of human history. For this question to arise as one of *religious* tolerance, religious judgment must exist, the question of religious truth

15 *vera rel.* 5, 8.
16 *vera rel.* 5, 8.
17 Assmann, *The Price of Monotheism*, 22. There are, one must concede, passages in which he seems to uphold that crude thesis. "Secondary religions must be intolerant," he writes (p. 14). But such expressions only reflect a momentarily vague language.
18 Assmann, 22.
19 "How they deal with their structural intolerance is another matter," he admits. Assmann, 14.
20 Assmann, 18.

and falsehood must become central, religion must be more than an element of culture.

What this teaches us is obviously not that religions should be primarily characterized by their "power of negation." The "antagonistic energy" is rather a consequence—one that can be rightly or wrongly channeled—of the "directional" nature of religion.[21] Like philosophy, religions address questions of meaning and orientation, not just of belonging. This is, in fact, a new way of being comprehensive. The unity of culture and religion (which we can call the original comprehensiveness) was broken by secondary religions, and a new comprehensiveness emerged in its place, one that brought together religion and the concern for ethics. In the words of Assmann, with the Mosaic distinction "justice, law, and freedom are declared to be central themes of religion and the sole prerogative of god"[22] for the first time in religious history. And Augustine was still a witness to this revolution. "What kind of gods are these?" he asked with surprise about the Roman gods, noting that they "did not teach a good living" to the people that adored them.[23] The question was not obvious to the Romans, but it comes naturally to the bishop who has been taught by the Jewish prophets about the vanity of a worship devoid of justice and mercy. This unity of religion and moral formation has multiple manifestations in Augustine's work.[24] To preach Christ, he writes, one must "not only say what things are to be believed about Christ, but also what things are to be observed by him who enters the structure of the body of Christ."[25] Some ethical positions are quite unequivocally bound up with orthodoxy. Religion may also be an element of culture, but not in the terms that prevailed in primary religions. Questions of truth and orientation, explicitly or under the surface, are central wherever secondary religions have left their trace (including in indigenous cultures). This is not a development that we can reasonably try to overcome, and it is crucial for an appropriate treatment of tolerance. Distinguishing culture and religion—distinguishing them as fundamental but different dimensions of the human self—is in fact crucial for the preservation of both the toleration of religions and the recognition of cultures.

[21] For the meaning of "directional" I here follow Chaplin, "Rejecting Neutrality, Respecting Diversity. From 'Liberal Pluralism' to Christian Pluralism," 147–48.
[22] Assmann, *The Price of Monotheism*, 44–5.
[23] *civ.* II, 22.
[24] For this question in the *City of God*, see Oliver O'Donovan, "Book 2. Augustine on Religion without Morality," in *The Cambridge Companion to Augustine's City of God*, ed. David Vincent Meconi (Cambridge: Cambridge University Press, 2021), 39–52.
[25] *f. et op.* 9, 14.

Love the Person

It is the multidimensional nature of the human person that allows us to make the distinctions that have guided us so far. Religion and culture may be entangled, but different aspects of the human condition are at play in each case, and this makes room for the different responses of recognition and toleration. We can respect and preserve the customs and traditions of a people while we oppose and tolerate its religion. This is no impossible acrobatics, but it requires that these dimensions of the self be treated each in their own terms. But to a significant extent, identity politics is the abolition of this multidimensional nature of persons. This is so not only in questions about cultural and religious identity. It is a broader trend in much of our thinking about identity. Hence the questions raised at the beginning of this chapter—questions about the distinction between a person and her actions. A typical formula for expressing the link between these questions and toleration is the idea that we should "love the sinner and hate the sin." The formula certainly represents ancient wisdom, but Augustine played a key role in giving it its definitive form.[26] This should come as no surprise, given the coherence between such a distinction and an anti-Manichaean view of persons: it is precisely because "no one is evil by nature," Augustine writes, that we must train our loves and hates. The purpose of such training is that neither our hatred for vice should lead us to hate persons, nor our love of persons lead us to love vices.[27] In terms of toleration, this means to "bear with the sinner not so that you love the sin in him."[28]

Like the rest of the constitutive elements of toleration, this component has been subjected to severe criticism. For its critics, it is precisely the link to toleration that damns the act/person distinction. In *Love the Sin*, Janet Jakobsen and Ann Pellegrini write that "the distinction between sin and sinner, act and person, seems to offer a middle ground, a compromise in which all are welcomed to the table."[29] The distinction between act and person is thus rejected because it allows harsh moral judgments to remain in place, while those who formulate them can experience themselves as tolerant. This, Jakobsen and Pellegrini continue, "sets up an us-them relation in which 'we'

[26] Its origin is often (sometimes even disparagingly) attributed to Gandhi. For its early development see William Mattison, "Jesus' Prohibition of Anger (Mt 5:22): The Person/Sin Distinction from Augustine to Aquinas," *Theological Studies* 68, no. 4 (2007): 839–64.

[27] *civ.* XIV, 6. The result may be described as a perfect love, but Augustine actually describes it as "perfect hate" (*perfectum odium*).

[28] *s.* 4, 20.

[29] Janet R. Jakobsen and Ann Pellegrini, *Love the Sin: Sexual Regulation and the Limits of Religious Tolerance* (New York and London: NYU Press, 2003), 1.

tolerate 'them.' "[30] Since an "us–them relation" is characteristic of both hate and love, they see tolerance as fatally tainted. Has something new been added in this critique of toleration? In a sense, this is only the echo of the by now familiar indictment of tolerance's arrogance and condescension. And to this, as we have already seen, one can reply that tolerance is indeed occasionally arrogant, but that no necessary connections can be established here. Power ("us–them relations") and judgment are ingredients of both tolerance and intolerance, but this highlights their ambivalence rather than a fatal flaw. So one might respond to these recurrent arguments. But however recurring they may be, in the present phase a new ingredient has been added to the Enlightenment critique of toleration: the rejection of the very possibility of meaningfully distinguishing between a person and his actions. In the inaugural version of this argument, Nietzsche wrote that the agent "is a mere accessory to the action." "There is no 'being' behind doing, acting, becoming," he tells us in *On the Genealogy of Morals*. Liberated from the idea of a subject, of an agent that is distinguishable from his action, "the doing itself is everything."[31] This reversal of the classical "action follows being" (*operari sequitur esse*) underlies much of the contemporary thinking about identity, and it is difficult to reconcile with toleration.

And there are further problems with the language of identity. As Peter Jones has written, "the language of identity sinks people's particularities into their very being." Under such circumstances, "tolerating someone's identity becomes tantamount to tolerating their very existence."[32] But the good of existence cannot be the object of toleration. Indeed, this is a fact acknowledged by all parties to the discussion. But while Augustine believes that our loves must be trained to see this good of existence in the midst of our sinful lives, Jakobsen and Pellegrini write off toleration as the result of a confused "love-hate relation."[33] Is there a way out of this impasse? The way out likely lies not in overcoming the act/person distinction, but in remembering that beyond persons and their actions we often deal with a more deep-seated reality, something that seems to be the source of our acts and beliefs and that relates to the self in an obviously more intimate way. There is more than persons and actions, namely inclinations or orientations; it is about these that we must think carefully. Since we are bundles of loves, since we are driven by those

[30] Jakobsen and Pellegrini, 50. The formula is targeted for similar reasons in Maykel Verkuyten, Kumar Yogeeswaran, and Levi Adelman, "The Negative Implications of Being Tolerated: Tolerance from the Target's Perspective," *Perspectives on Psychological Science* 15, no. 3 (2020): 545.

[31] Friedrich Nietzsche, *On the Genealogy of Morals* (Oxford: Oxford University Press, 1996), 29 (I, 13).

[32] Jones, "Toleration, Recognition and Identity," 140.

[33] Jakobsen and Pellegrini, *Love the Sin*, 45.

loves (*amor meus, pondus meum*[34]), we often experience the orientations that underlie our actions as our very self, as something that cannot easily be detached from our person.[35] But not everything that emerges from the depths of personal life is our very self, an identity to be affirmed. Even though our loves and inclinations may be something more basic than our actions, they can obviously be disordered and subject to correction. And there is, furthermore, the way in which we consciously relate to our self and its basic orientations. As we suggested in Chapter 5, "self-understanding" may in fact be a more fruitful category than "identity" for at least some of these discussions. Judging about self-understandings, while different from judging a person, is a more delicate matter than judging about specific actions or beliefs. But self-understandings are obviously among the realities that can be judged to be wrong and thus appropriate objects of toleration.

All of this is also relevant to the discussion about the "perspective of the tolerated." It is a recurring theme in the critique of toleration that tolerance sounds friendlier from the perspective of the tolerator than from the perspective of the tolerated. Tolerance is less than equality, and this fact is obviously more palpable to the tolerated party. This criticism seems to gain strength in the context of the identity-saturated thinking we just described. Given the psychological harm of being tolerated, the situation is described in terms of the "identity threats posed by tolerance."[36] The taxing effects of being tolerated are treated as equivalent to those of being discriminated against, and this psychological impact is assumed to be greater the more central the defining aspect of the identity tolerated.[37] Culture, religion, and gender would be inappropriate objects of toleration precisely because they are central to the self. Is this true? We must first point out the fundamental sense in which it must necessarily be true. For it is in the nature of tolerance that it will be experienced and described differently by the tolerators and the tolerated. This disparity may take acceptable and unacceptable forms, but the disparity itself is something with which we must reconcile ourselves if we regard tolerance as a necessary element of our social life. It is also true that some dimensions of the self are more central than others, and it will naturally be more painful to experience toleration for the things that matter most. It is not surprising, then, that efforts are made to

[34] *conf.* XIII, 9, 10.

[35] I take "bundles of loves" from Gregory, *Politics and the Order of Love. An Augustinian Ethic of Democratic Citizenship*, 21.

[36] Maykel Verkuyten et al., "Coping with Being Tolerated: Trans Experiences," *Psychology of Sexual Orientation and Gender Diversity* 11, no. 1 (2024): 31–41.

[37] Verkuyten, Yogeeswaran, and Adelman, "The Negative Implications of Being Tolerated: Tolerance from the Target's Perspective," 553.

take some of the sting out of toleration. But if, in the process, every remnant of negative judgment is dissolved, one will have eliminated tolerance altogether.[38]

If we do not want to eliminate toleration, we must remember that it is rarely "mere" toleration. Sometimes it is. Toleration can take forms that not only have the painful "sting" of its objection-component, but which constitute a literal exclusion from citizenship, or from the relevant moral community (such as a family), and which are in this substantial sense disrespectful. But the wrong committed in such cases is that of exclusion, not the infliction of pain by toleration. By contrast, we must note that there is no "erasure" of the self when toleration goes hand in hand with other dispositions such as hospitality or respect for persons. Under such circumstances, toleration may still be painful, but that is not the level at which the appropriateness of toleration should be decided. Indeed, the preservation of a humane society requires that we maintain this combination, and with it the possibility of our self-understandings being challenged in non-devastating ways. This requires an approach to human persons that integrates tolerance with affirming dispositions, as well as a fundamental recognition of the multidimensional life of persons. Once we see it in this context, many of the objections raised against it fall away.

[38] For an attempt at this balancing see Leslie Green, "On Being Tolerated," in *The Legacy of H.L.A. Hart. Legal, Political, and Moral Philosophy*, ed. Matthew H. Kramer et al. (Oxford: Oxford University Press, 2008), 225–38.

III

THE SUBJECTS AND SPACES OF TOLERATION

9
Patience or Tolerance as a Personal Virtue

A Common Virtue

The first chapters of this book fleshed out different conceptions of toleration. Over against toleration as indifference and toleration as recognition, a "traditional" understanding of toleration as restraint in the face of objectionable actions or ideas was defended. But rather than leave this "traditional" understanding underspecified, I have argued for a more specifically Augustinian version of toleration of evil. Its specificity is found above all in its vision of evil itself, and from there we moved to an Augustinian understanding of history and of judgment, of limits and of the self. Although it is about character, actions, and beliefs—not persons—that we judge, our understanding of persons is central to toleration. As it turns out, this view makes room for objecting to (and tolerating) a person's self-understanding, as well as for admonishing, moving, and persuading one another. These are aspects of existence in tension. Thus we have considered the nature, object, and conditions of toleration. In the final three chapters, I will extend this approach to what we can call the subjects and spaces of toleration. We often say that we want a tolerant society. But where is tolerance located in such a society? Can only individuals be tolerant? Can a State tolerate? What is the place of tolerance within and between intermediate associations? These questions, in turn, will help us to further unpack the need to keep alive distinctions like the one between intolerance, manipulation, and persuasion.

I will begin with a discussion of tolerance as a moral disposition of persons. If we are incapable of coping with the tensions involved in tolerance, we may of course still be capable of specific tolerant acts. But it is the possession of the virtue—tolerance as a constant disposition—that we are primarily concerned with here. Treating it as a virtue, however, is not the most common way of dealing with tolerance. The modern prominence of toleration is not the prominence of a virtue. Locke begins his *Letter* by speaking of virtues, of kindness and gentleness, but after this initial appeal he sets out almost exclusively to defend policies of toleration. To take a more recent example, Michael Walzer

An Augustinian Essay on Toleration. Manfred Svensson, Oxford University Press. © Manfred Svensson 2026.
DOI: 10.1093/9780197912737.003.0013

has dealt with varieties of tolerance under the label of different "regimes of toleration."[1] There are also, of course, attempts in contemporary literature to treat tolerance as a moral disposition. But treating it as a moral disposition or asking about its moral justification is not the same as treating it as a virtue. Brian Leiter, for example, addresses the question of the moral justification of tolerance, the possibility of a "principled toleration," but in doing so he explicitly tells us that for him "moral arguments divide, predictably enough, into Kantian and utilitarian forms."[2] Not a mention of virtue ethics. An abundant literature likewise presents respect for autonomy as the adequate moral basis for toleration.[3] Even more striking than this is the fact that contemporary philosophers and theologians who cultivate a moral philosophy centered on the virtues have not had much to say about tolerance. In recent decades, we have witnessed the production of a vast literature on the virtues and a rich discussion of tolerance; but with notable exceptions such as John Bowlin, these two tendencies have barely crossed paths.[4]

Some have even considered tolerance to be impossible to conceive of as a virtue. It is hard to see, writes David Heyd, how it perfects us; moreover, it is not clear that it is acquired by habituation. He denies, then, that it is a virtue.[5] Bernard Williams has likewise written that of all virtues, tolerance is the closest to a "conceptual impossibility."[6] Tolerance requires that we suppress our desire (or the actions that would follow from such a desire) that an objected practice or idea disappear, but at the same time it requires that we retain those convictions that make us judge about rival conceptions. If these convictions were suppressed or suspended, the result would not be tolerance, but once again only indifference or affirmation. George Fletcher has made a similar analysis by describing tolerance as an unstable virtue that would always quickly shift toward intolerance or toward affirmation, to the extent that we incline more to the component of rejection or to that of acceptance, both of which are present in tolerance.[7] It is difficult to have objections against something and put up with it at the same time. It is not surprising that when we try

[1] Michael Walzer, *On Toleration* (New York and London: Yale University Press, 1999).

[2] Brian Leiter, *Why Tolerate Religion?* (Princeton and Oxford: Princeton University Press, 2013), 15.

[3] For the more unusual explicitly utilitarian approach, see Jonathan Harrison, "Utilitarianism and Toleration," *Philosophy* 62, no. 242 (1987): 421–34.

[4] Bowlin, *Tolerance Among the Virtues.*

[5] David Heyd, "Is Toleration a Political Virtue?" in *Toleration and Its Limits*, ed. Jeremy Waldron and Melissa Williams, NOMOS, XLVIII (New York and London: New York University Press, 2008), 183–86.

[6] Bernard Williams, "Tolerating the Intolerable," in *The Politics of Toleration in Modern Life*, ed. Susan Mendus (Edinburgh: Edinburgh University Press, 1999), 66.

[7] George P. Fletcher, "The Instability of Tolerance," in *Toleration: An Elusive Virtue*, ed. David Heyd (Princeton: Princeton University Press, 1998), 158–72.

to resolve this tension, we tend toward either pure rejection, pure acceptance, or indifference. The tension of tolerance, thus, seems to make it "unstable" or an "impossibility." But is this such an unusual situation? Are these difficulties exclusive to tolerance? Or is this tension a rather common feature of many of the more important moral dispositions? "If we assume that tolerance is an ordinary human excellence, and if we place it among the other moral virtues," Bowlin writes, "we soon discover that this psychological dynamic distinguishes virtue in general, not tolerance in particular."[8] Tolerance is difficult. That much is true. But the nature of the difficulty is not intellectual, making it a "conceptual impossibility." It is the hard but ordinary process of acquisition that makes it difficult. So tolerance is not only a virtue; to the extent that virtues can be called common, it is also a common virtue.

We can further note that in the ancient tradition of virtue ethics no one questioned the status of tolerance as a virtue. The link with patience, a link that is still present in our ordinary language, confirms this fact. As Fletcher has noted, in several languages there is an evident connection between the roots of both terms: "the same root generates both tolerance and patience in German (*Geduldsamkeit* and *Geduld*), Hebrew (*sovlanut* and *savlanut*), and Russian (*terpimost'* and *terpenie*)."[9] In late antiquity, this view was as common among the Stoics as among the Church fathers: tranquility, simplicity, liberality, perseverance, equanimity, and tolerance are dimensions of a single virtue of the wise. Encyclopedic works are also instructive. A sixteenth-century theological dictionary sums up the tradition by affirming that "tolerance is the same as patience; it comes from 'I tolerate', which means 'I bear patiently.'"[10] A century ago, this was still a standard equivalence.[11] And as long as tolerance was identified with patience, there was no question that tolerance was a virtue. Both are dispositions of calm endurance of adversities while striving for certain goods; they control our distraction, frustration, and anger; they make us capable not only of waiting but also of active perseverance.[12]

But what do we gain by looking at tolerance in this way? Thinking about tolerance as patience, and of patience as a virtue, may first help us rethink what

[8] Bowlin, *Tolerance Among the Virtues*, 34.

[9] Fletcher, "The Case for Tolerance," 237. Pianalto similarly notes that "In Tibetan Buddhist thought, patience and tolerance are coextensive and are captured in a single term, *soe-pa*." Matthew Pianalto, *On Patience. Reclaiming a Foundational Virtue* (Lanham, MD: Lexington Books, 2016), 25.

[10] Johannes Altensteig, "Tolerantia," in *Lexicon Theologicum* (Antwerp: Peter Beller, 1576), 328.

[11] The more recent versions of the *Lexikon für Theologie und Kirche*, for instance, include detailed articles on tolerance, as one would expect them to do. The entry on tolerance of its first edition (1930–38), however, simply remits to the entry on patience.

[12] For an illuminating contemporary discussion of patience, see Pianalto, *On Patience. Reclaiming a Foundational Virtue.*

an education for toleration means. In the significant field of "tolerance education," one can ask both how tolerance is being understood and also which understanding of education prevails. The answer is one with a strong focus on theoretical education. The path to toleration runs through the removal of prejudices. Toleration educators work to dismantle our wrong preconceptions and perhaps put something else in their place. In the more complex approach of David Heyd, such education must involve a "complete abandonment of the judgmental perspective," combined with an "assessment of the individual who happens sincerely to believe otherwise."[13] This "radical separation" is a sophisticated intellectual feat, involving, in Heyd's own words, "a schizophrenic, two-level view of the nature of moral judgement."[14] One can wonder about both the feasibility and the desirability of such an exercise. But a very different approach follows when we understand tolerance as a virtue. "Arguments and teaching surely do not prevail on everyone," Aristotle warned, explaining why virtue must be acquired through early habituation.[15] If tolerance is a virtue, then we acquire it in the usual ways of character formation. This will often come to involve theoretical reflection, since mature judgment goes hand in hand with good character; but it requires a substantial process of habituation into basic decency. This process is difficult, but not "schizophrenic." Understanding this is perhaps the first thing we gain from seeing tolerance as a virtue.

Second, as in all reflection on the virtues, this invites us to consider our understanding of happiness. The problem we face here was well identified by John Calvin: many understand patience to be at odds with the happy life (*adversam esse beatae vitae patientiam*).[16] If happiness is the end of life, then our tolerance will depend on the place for suffering included in our image of that happiness. An understanding of happiness that can accommodate strong obstacles, dissension, and loss will plausibly prepare us to endure many different evils. The absence of such a conception of happiness may be more central to the contemporary crisis of tolerance than we think.

We can approach this question more directly by asking to what extent a hedonistic culture is a fertile ground for toleration. This culture often sees itself as particularly tolerant: to live and let live is a formula that can express both its hedonism and its tolerance. Indeed, the modern assumption has often been

[13] David Heyd, "Education to Toleration: Some Philosophical Obstacles and Their Resolution," in *The Culture of Toleration in Diverse Societies. Reasonable Tolerance*, ed. Catriona McKinnon and Dario Castiglione (Manchester and New York: Manchester University Press, 2003), 201.

[14] Heyd, 205.

[15] Aristotle, *Nicomachean Ethics*, 2nd ed., trans. Terence Irwin (Indianapolis: Hackett Publishing, 1999), X 9, 1979b 24.

[16] CO 45, 162. Comm. Mt. 5:2.

that people fight over their ideas of the good in a way that makes them prone to intolerance. This civil war over the good had, therefore, to be replaced by peaceful mechanisms for the attainment of each's individual pleasure. A philosophy that in the ancient world was rather oriented to private life thus became a political project.[17] As a means to attain peace, however, this project can hardly claim success. As Jean-Claude Michéa has written, once these pleasures are understood as rights, we have already reached the conditions for a new civil war.[18] Augustine himself saw the earthly city as involved in such a civil war precisely because everyone is "seeking his own interests (*utilitates*) and pleasures."[19] There is, in other words, more tension between hedonism and tolerance than modern political hedonism suggests. As Augusto del Noce has noted, the coincidence between full satisfaction of the passions and the disappearance of aggressiveness may in fact belong to the realm of utopia.[20] Resisting instant gratification is, after all, a fundamental aspect of self-control. The cultivation of tolerance thus requires that we rehabilitate the view of happiness with substantive place for suffering and adversity.

Augustine, as we have seen, affirms this in rather counter-conventional terms when he states that "patience is needed not in happiness, but in unhappiness."[21] Here he seems to be saving patience rather than happiness: if one of these must be sacrificed, it is to patience that we must cling, admitting that we are in a valley of tears. Some have even interpreted his work as a departure from classical eudaimonism. But there is no reason to endorse that interpretation.[22] He certainly considered the idea of purely temporal happiness to be impossible, as the prospect of losing happiness in the future would make us miserable in the present. "For how can a life be blessed if the blessed one does not love it? And how can we love it if we are indifferent to its permanence or undoing?"[23] But

[17] Two very different but illuminating studies are Frederick Vaughan, *The Tradition of Political Hedonism. From Hobbes to J.S. Mill* (New York: Fordham University Press, 1982), and Robert J. Roecklein, *Machiavelli and Epicureanism: An Investigation into the Origins of Early Modern Political Thought* (Lanham: Lexington Books, 2012).

[18] Jean-Claude Michéa, *The Realm of Lesser Evil* (Cambridge: Polity, 2009), 23.

[19] *civ.* XVIII, 2.

[20] Augusto del Noce, *The Crisis of Modernity*, trans. Carlo Lancellotti (Montreal & Kingston: McGill-Queen's University Press, 2014), 139. With these pleasures understood as rights, Michéa argues, we have already reached the conditions for such a new civil war. Michéa, *The Realm of Lesser Evil*, 23.

[21] *s.* 359a, 2.

[22] Nicholas Wolterstorff finds such a break, but this is only because he cannot see how other-regarding actions are compatible with eudaimonism (p. 194). For all his emphasis on this break, tranquility as condition for happiness and a universal search for happiness reemerge in the later part of his exposition of Augustine (p. 200). Nicholas Wolterstorff, *Justice. Rights and Wrongs* (Princeton and Oxford: Princeton University Press, 2008), 180–206. Anti-eudaimonism is central to Brian Harding's interpretation of Augustine as well, but he paints in broad strokes that do not come close to his own fine discussion of the Augustinian critique of Roman virtue. Brian Harding, *Augustine and Roman Virtue* (London: Bloomsbury, 2008).

[23] *trin.* XIII, 8, 1.

though he severely critiques overenthusiastic expectations of temporal happiness, he writes of a "happiness in hope" that is adequate to temporal life.[24] Sorrow is thus integrated into a long-term expectation of happiness, and in the context of that quest patience is fundamental. This happiness does not consist, then, in simple prosperity, but in clinging to God.[25] And if happiness exists "in hope," virtue exists in combat. In contrast to Aristotle's view of virtuous action as naturally flowing from those who have acquired virtue, Augustine writes of the virtues in our earthly lives as in perpetual conflict. Virtues are in "perpetual war against the vices."[26] In consequence, it is only a partial tranquility that we attain in this life.[27] We reach a justice "consisting more in the remission of sins than in the perfection of virtue."[28] This is an understanding of virtue in conflict whose traces can still be found in Kant. Given the radical evil in human nature, virtue for him is a "moral disposition in conflict."[29] Tolerance can well be said to be particularly at home in this conception of life as a struggle.

But we should be careful with how we understand this idea of struggle. As some scholars have noted, this conception of struggle is different from a heroic ethic. Contrasting Augustine with the Pelagians, Peter Iver Kaufman has written that "they looked to achieve; he hoped to endure."[30] If virtue was formerly described in terms of achievement, Augustine's theology of grace acknowledges the importance of a certain passivity.[31] Apart from this, however, Augustine's approach is naturally linked to that of his predecessors. Like other virtues, tolerance is a mean between vicious extremes; like other virtues, it is part of a web of dispositions and goes hand in hand with practical knowledge; like other virtues, it is not only the source of specific actions but of a specific way of performing them. What matters, Augustine writes, is not the kind of evils that we suffer, but how we suffer them (*non qualia, sed qualis quisque patiatur*).[32] Tolerance is not only something we owe to others. Like other virtues, contra Heyd, it perfects those who possess it. No wonder that,

[24] See *civ.* V, 24, XVIII, 49, and XIX, 4.
[25] For some versions of this statement, see *conf.* VII, 11, 17 and *civ.* X, 18 and 25.
[26] *civ.* XIX, 4.
[27] *civ.* XV, 6.
[28] *civ.* XIX, 27. For a discussion of inner conflict "under grace" see *s.* 154.
[29] Immanuel Kant, *Critique of Practical Reason*, trans. Mary Gregor, Cambridge Texts in the History of Philosophy (Cambridge: Cambridge University Press, 2015), 5:84.
[30] Kaufman, *Incorrectly Political*, 65.
[31] See Mathewes, *The Republic of Grace: Augustinian Thoughts for Dark Times*, 33; and Pieter Vos, *Longing for the Good Life: Virtue Ethics After Protestantism* (London: T&T Clark, 2020), 61. For patience in particular see 178–79. Jean Bethke Elshtain has also described this as "a profound and radical shift away from the dominant heroic ethic of the antique world." Elshtain, *Augustine and the Limits of Politics*, 15.
[32] *civ.* I, 8.

in the words of Augustine, though "no one loves what he tolerates, he loves tolerating it."[33]

Power and the Golden Mean

But patience and tolerance are not strict synonyms. Tertullian wrote of the "virtue of tolerance" as something by means of which martyrs are "perfected in weakness."[34] These words adequately convey the perfecting nature of virtue, but they only describe acquiescence, patience—the virtues of martyrs—not tolerance. Patience is rather a virtue of the weak, or of the one who is in a situation or moment of weakness. It would be absurd for the martyr to say that he is giving permission to the one who persecutes him. That would be making virtue out of necessity. The weak, the powerless, simply bear; they don't permit.[35] They may bear evils virtuously, and then we call them patient; but it is not permitting that they do. Patience is a right relation to evils that we cannot avoid; tolerance, on the contrary, is a disposition regarding avoidable evils.[36] Evils we can remove, evils with which we can interfere. Ricoeur has thus described tolerance as an "asceticism in the exercise of power."[37] The tolerant person permits something that he has the power not to permit. Calls for tolerance are addressed to people for whom it would be quite possible not to tolerate.

The call for tolerance is made primarily to the person who might interfere, who has the ability or strength to impose his will on what he perceives as evil. It is a call made to the powerful, or to any of us in even a temporary situation of power. For "powerful" can mean different things. Indeed, the lack of a differentiated discourse on power is a stumbling block for our reflection on tolerance. Consider Stanley Hauerwas, who has written that "humility, not tolerance, is a Christian virtue." The reason for his disjunction between humility and tolerance is precisely the connection between tolerance and power. "I would find it surprising for Christians to have positions of power that would

[33] *conf.* X, 28, 39.
[34] Tertullian, *De fuga in persecutione* 2, 8.
[35] Preston King has suggested "acquisence" for the bearing by the weak and "tolerance" for that of the strong. King, *Toleration*, 21.
[36] But we should not overstress this contrast. See Pianalto's definition of patience as "a disposition to accept unavoidable burdens as well as those avoidable burdens that one can reasonably judge it to be wise to accept." Pianalto, *On Patience. Reclaiming a Foundational Virtue*, 54.
[37] Paul Ricoeur, "The Erosion of Tolerance and the Resistance of the Intolerable," *Diogenes* 44, no. 176 (1996): 189.

make it necessary for them to be tolerant," he writes.[38] Augustine would not have found this fact surprising, and he was actively engaged in counseling Christians who had assumed the responsibilities of power.[39] Nothing is more fruitful for human affairs, he writes, than to have in power those who are pious and lead a good life "if they have the science of government."[40] Having that science of government is not a secondary condition, but those called to such duties will also need virtues that are specific to the situation, among them not merely patience, but also tolerance. We should stress, moreover, that this does not apply only to those in highest political office. Emphasizing political and economic power as the only instances of real power arguably makes us blind to the share of power we all have and to the extended need for this virtue.

This difference between patience and tolerance is worth pondering when we see tolerance criticized for its harshness or for its weakness. In this book, I have mostly highlighted critics who follow the first of these lines of criticism, rejecting toleration as arrogant and judgmental. But the other line is also worthy of attention. For Nietzsche tolerance is "the fear to judge,"[41] "mistrust of one's own ideals,"[42] "a lazy peace, a cowardly compromise" which "*forgives* everything because it is *understanding* of everything."[43] It is possible to interpret this as a critique of tolerance as indifference, leaving room for a deeper kind of tolerance in Nietzsche.[44] But it is also possible to make a more straightforward reading of his statements. Nietzsche sees morality itself as brought to life by the weakness he denounces.[45] If, according to his genealogy of our moral concepts, weakness has transformed its "I can't" into an "I shouldn't," it is rather surprising that Nietzsche did not make the rejection of tolerance even more central to his work. For him tolerance is indeed a virtue, but that is precisely what makes it suspect. Tolerance is as vicious as any virtue. In the argument we are advancing here, in contrast, tolerance is a sign of a strong character, not to be confused with mere passivity, indifference, or an undifferentiated

[38] Stanley Hauerwas, "Hauerwas on 'Hauerwas and the Law': Trying to Have Something to Say," *Law and Contemporary Problems* 75, no. 4 (2012): 249.

[39] See, for example, *ep.* 189 and 220 (to Boniface), and 153 and 155 (to Macedonius).

[40] *civ.* V, 19. See also *civ.* IV, 2.

[41] Friedrich Nietzsche, *Nachgelassene Fragmente 1885–1887* (Munich: DTV, 1988), 275.

[42] Friedrich Nietzsche, *Nachgelassene Fragmente 1880–1882* (Munich: DTV, 1988), 477.

[43] Friedrich Nietzsche, *Antichrist* (Munich: DTV, 1888), 169.

[44] To my knowledge, the best attempt is Werner Stegmaier, "Nietzsches Kritik der Toleranz," in *Toleranz als Ordnungsprinzip? Die moderne Bürgergesellschaft zwischen Offenheit und Selbstaufgabe*, ed. Christoph Enders and Michael Kahlo (Paderborn: Mentis, 2007), 195–206. Since this leads Stegmaier to arrive at several "paradoxes of toleration" that I do not recognize as such, I remain unconvinced. However, see Nietzsche's profound observations on patience discussed in Pianalto, *On Patience. Reclaiming a Foundational Virtue*, 6–10.

[45] Nietzsche, *On the Genealogy of Morals*, 17-25 (I, 6-10).

acceptance of ambiguity. It is a virtue in the responsible exercise of power, any kind of power.

Responsible exercise of power, however, does not consist in merely tolerating. It is often wrong to tolerate. What does this entail for the way we speak about the virtue of tolerance? How should we speak of those instances in which the tolerant do not and should not tolerate? Do they display a "virtuous intolerance"?[46] Is it a "just" intolerance? Should the limits of tolerance be defended by arguing that "intolerance is also an exercise in virtue"?[47] In discussing the idea of liberating intolerance, we have already seen why this approach is not advisable. It reveals an inability to frame our problems in terms of justice, and the selective intolerance it justifies may turn out to become a general one. Our ordinary language, and the specific language of virtue, suggests a different approach. Virtues, as Augustine remarks, are the kind of goods that cannot be used badly.[48] One can have too much money or too many books, but one cannot be too just or too tolerant.[49] This does not mean that toleration is always the virtue to be exercised; a virtuous person will know *when* to exercise that particular virtue. But if it is a virtue, then of course it is always a virtue. Likewise, we never speak of intolerance as a virtue. We never praise someone by saying that he is an example of intolerance, or that intolerance was one of his most laudable character traits. There is no reason to distance ourselves from this ordinary way of speaking.

This may seem to be a mere question of words, but it is not without importance. Speaking of a "virtue of intolerance" may seem to reinforce the idea of limits, it may convey an appropriate message: that it is often wrong to tolerate. But it can also reinforce an impoverished moral vocabulary that knows of nothing beyond tolerance and intolerance. To speak of the virtue of intolerance is to fall prey to a monolithic standard of moral evaluation. And this problem is present not only in the praise of intolerance, but also at the other vicious extreme. We lament excessive tolerance, and there are plenty of fields where that lament is pertinent. We can deplore that governments allow part of their territory to escape the rule of law, we can lament lax parenting, we can deplore a permissive approach to technology, gambling, or the use of opioids.

[46] For an older version of that position, see Sir Mortimer Wheeler, *The Virtue of Intolerance* (Lincoln and London: Printed for Birckbeck College by J.W. Ruddock and Sons Ltd, 1957), 5. For a more recent version, Henryk M. Broder, *Kritik der reinen Toleranz* (Berlin: Pantheon, 2008), 24.

[47] See Alasdair MacIntyre, "Toleration and the Goods of Conflict," in *Ethics and Politics. Selected Essays, Volume 2* (Cambridge: Cambridge University Press, 2006), 223.

[48] *lib. arb.* II, 18, 50.

[49] For the same observation regarding patience, see Pianalto, *On Patience. Reclaiming a Foundational Virtue*, xii.

But the question is whether such things are adequately described in terms of an "excess of tolerance." Instead of bemoaning an excess of tolerance, we might want to recover an older way of describing it: permissivism. Like the other virtues, tolerance is a golden mean between two vicious extremes, those of intolerance and permissivism. Because we are more attuned to the dangers of the first extreme than of the second, we often lack the word to describe it. We know very well that intolerance can cause immediate and tangible harm, but we ignore that permissiveness is a damaging vice—that it makes education, for example, impossible, or that it is negligent in the face of the multiple self-destructive tendencies of human beings—and so we have even forgotten how to name it.[50]

The awareness that tolerance is a virtue, and that it is rooted in a set of virtues, helps us to describe both excess and lack of toleration in more helpful ways. Intolerance always refers to a vice, not because there are no limits to tolerance, but because we defend those limits through the exercise of other virtues. When someone correctly prevents an evil, we do not praise him for being intolerant. Rather, we mention the other virtues that might have motivated his action, such as justice or responsibility, courage, or loyalty. Augustine says as much when he comments on Jesus' interrogation by the high priest. While Jesus endures the interrogation patiently and in this sense is tolerant, he questions the justice of the proceeding. "If what I said is wrong, bear witness about the wrong; but if what I said is right, why do you strike me?" (Jn 18:23, ESV). In Augustine's interpretation, this is an example of cherishing "patience together with benevolence" in the inward heart, while in outward action (*in manifesto*) doing that which seems "most likely to benefit those whose good we must seek."[51] The beneficial outward action, in this case, is to make manifest an injustice at the same time that it is patiently borne. We have touched on the compatibility between such actions at various points, but now we need to address it more directly.

Resisting and Correcting

It is perfectly tolerant to strive to banish certain actions while patiently enduring them as long as they persist. In the words of Leslie Green, toleration "is not a principle of *complete* restraint."[52] Calling surrogacy or euthanasia

[50] Discussions of permissivism were still common in the mid-1970s. See, for instance, Christopher Lasch, *Haven in a Heartless World. The Family Besieged* (New York: Basic Books, 1979), 167–90; and del Noce, *The Crisis of Modernity*, 137–86.

[51] *ep.* 138, 2, 13.

[52] Green, "On Being Tolerated," 278. Italics in the original.

intolerable does not obligate us to take justice into our own hands, but neither does tolerating them temporarily require resignation. We can tolerate while at the same time trying to resist or change the facts that led to the toleration of certain evils in the first place. As this suggests, there is no necessary line from patience to passivity. Indeed, we might well describe contemporary culture as one in which a passive impatience sometimes prevails, one to which patient action might be the right response. Our whole idea of the tolerant society may need to be reconsidered in light of this point. As we noted in discussing hedonism, the tolerant society is typically thought of as the society of a simple "live and let live." But if we think of it as a society that avoids the twin problems of permissiveness and intolerance, *laissez-faire* will only partially characterize it. It is true that avoiding the *hybris* of intolerance will often lead to a generous practice of permission. But this permission can go hand in hand with a wide variety of attitudes and practices. One can tolerate and simultaneously challenge current conditions. One can allow something and still call others to reconsider or abandon an objected practice. One can refrain from interfering, while simultaneously praying for God's intervention. As Peter Königs has written, the "acceptance component" of toleration only rules out certain uncivil forms of "interference." This is why there is nothing paradoxical about toleration as a moral ideal. As he writes, "in view of exactly what kind of acceptance toleration involves, the moral value of tolerance is readily intelligible."[53]

Augustine himself was well aware of the different ways of accepting present conditions, and he knew that some forms of acceptance are vicious. There are those who believe they are enduring the sins of others because they pass over such sins in silence. "This feigning (*simulatio*) should be abhorred," he comments.[54] In the opening chapters of the *City of God* he goes into such reasons for non-interference in detail. There can be good reasons for avoiding interference, but often we refrain from correction "not because of the duty of love, but out of self-serving lust."[55] We fear damage to our reputation or safety. We love the flattery and fear the judgment of others. But integrity requires that we do more than refrain from agreeing with those doing wrong. It also requires that we sometimes rebuke them.[56] He is writing about the Church here, about rebuking the faithful rather than passing over their faults in silence. But, though in a different manner, he extends this to the discussion of the political community as well. If the good and the evil suffer from the same external evils,

[53] Königs, "The Simplicity of Toleration," 9.
[54] *s.* 4, 20.
[55] *civ.* I, 9.
[56] *c. ep. Parm.* II, 21, 40.

he writes, it may be that this is in part a deserved punishment of the former for their failure to correct the latter.[57]

Some, he writes, believe that leaving vices unpunished is the way to secure the stability of the republic, a view that he attributes to the later Romans in contrast to the early ones. "If we cannot correct" those who hold these views, he comments, "we may patiently tolerate them."[58] But though he tolerates these later Romans, he sides with earlier ones who believed in the necessity of correction. Augustine's famous eulogy of Christian emperors also dwells on this theme. We consider such emperors happy when they grant pardons "not that iniquity may go unpunished, but in the hope of correction."[59] Correction is indeed a recurring theme in Augustine's dealings with both friends and authorities.[60] In these exchanges it is not only evildoers who are corrected. Augustine's exchange with the imperial vicar Macedonius is a particularly important example of a corrective interaction with a political leader who seeks cover in a lazy form of realism. Although Augustine praises his character, he rejects the goal he attributes to Macedonius, "that men may suffer no inconvenience according to the flesh."[61] Satisfied with the peace achieved through the political virtues, Macedonius lacks ethico-religious ambition. Augustine's approach, in contrast, takes the present conditions as something to be accepted in frank terms, but not as definitive. His own political activity has been described by Robart Dodaro as "respectful, but not complacent or passive, toward the existing political order."[62] Concern for justice will unravel any seemingly definitive consensus, and justice is an "inseparable companion" of tolerance.

This relationship with justice prevents tolerance from becoming complacent. It also indicates the scope of toleration. "Reflect on the principle that all rational animals are born for each other's sake, that tolerance is a part of justice," writes Marcus Aurelius.[63] If we are bound to each other in relations

[57] *civ.* I, 9.
[58] *ep.* 138, 4, 17.
[59] *civ.* V, 24.
[60] Among other examples, it has been suggested that he revolutionized ancient letter writing by introducing an element of correction in the genre of friendship letters. His expectation was that adressees would write back and engage in a mutually corrective correspondence. Jennifer V. Ebbeler, *Disciplining Christians. Correction and Community in Augustine's Letters* (Oxford: Oxford University Press, 2012). See also her application of this reading to the Donatist controversy. Jennifer V. Ebbeler, "Charitable Correction and Ecclesiastical Unity in Augustine's Contra Epistulam Parmeniani," in *The Donatist Schism. Controversy and Contexts*, ed. Richard Miles (Liverpool: Liverpool University Press, 2016), 284–96.
[61] *ep.* 155, 3, 10.
[62] Robert Dodaro, "Between the Two Cities: Political Action in Augustine of Hippo," in *Augustine and Politics*, ed. John Doody, Kevin L. Hughes, and Kim Paffenroth (Lanham, MD: Lexington Books, 2005), 110.
[63] Marcus Aurelius, *Meditations, Books 1–6*, trans. Christopher Gill, Clarendon Later Ancient Philosophers (Oxford: Oxford University Press, 2013), 4.3.

of justice, he continues, "we must do good to them and put up with them."[64] A "just and pious man," adds Augustine, must strive to patiently endure the evils of those he wishes to make good.[65] Pagan and Christian voices thus describe tolerance as part of justice. It is true that Augustine has both theological and philosophical reasons for denying that political justice can be had without the *vera iustitia* of regeneration. On such matters, however, his approach is often more gradual than his rhetoric at first suggests. The fact that we cannot govern ourselves *rightly* does not imply a denial of all self-government. Nor does the fact that Pagans do not give God his due suggest that they are always incapable of giving others their due.[66] If we have described toleration as something as old as humanity, the same is true about justice. There are no societies in which all justice is absent, and it is within the relationships shaped by that justice that tolerance finds its place. This is one of the important conclusions drawn out by Bowlin: tolerance is not a virtue principally aimed at strangers held at a distance, as is often assumed in the various contemporary approaches to toleration. It is, like justice itself, "a creature of social relationships."[67] If tolerance is a part of justice, it is always a part of our social relationships. It is a personal virtue necessary for the maintenance of that social life. But it is also a practice that can become established as a stable policy of a just order, and hence its place in the politico-philosophical discussions to which we now turn.

[64] Marcus Aurelius, 5.20.
[65] *ep.* 138, 2, 12.
[66] For this reading (and a discussion of rival interpretations) see Katherin Chambers, "Augustine on Justice: A Reconsideration of City of God, Book 19," *Political Theology* 19, no. 5 (2018): 382–96.
[67] Bowlin, *Tolerance Among the Virtues*, 159.

10

Permission and Toleration in Political Life

A Form of Relationship

"Man is in some way moved by the laws of his nature, to have fellowship and peace with other men," writes Augustine.[1] We closed the previous chapter noting that toleration serves precisely this purpose. It maintains peace with others who are already part of our social life. In the face of human disagreement and conflict, that peace does not emerge spontaneously. It requires that reasons for permission prevail over our objections, so that we remain in relationship with those with whom we are in conflict. Ingrid Crepell even counts this as an additional component next to the traditional ingredients of tolerance. Tolerant persons, she writes, restrain themselves "not strictly because of an abstract belief in everyone's rights to freedom but also because one wants to continue to live together with a specific set of persons who hold beliefs or ways of life that one cannot or does not accept as being one's own."[2] Aside from the specifics of Creppell's position—which go beyond this initial "will to relationship" to a more demanding "mutuality"[3]—this relation between toleration and the commitment to a life in common deserves our attention. It is within a political community that questions of toleration arise. The very language of toleration is one to which we turn less often when it comes to the relationship between different political communities. In the relationship between different nations we find evil, judgment, tension, restraint, and yet we do not typically characterize these relationships as tolerant or intolerant.[4] As this suggests, tolerance is indeed an element of life *within* a community. Even strangers, as Bowlin notes, "become objects of tolerance only as they are included in this matter and connected to us in some way as participants in some kind of social

[1] *civ.* XIX, 12.

[2] Creppell, *Toleration and Identity. Foundations in Early Modern Thought*, 24. Further developed in Ingrid Creppell, "Toleration, Politics, and the Role of Mutuality," in *Toleration and Its Limits*, ed. Melissa Williams and Jeremy Waldron, NOMOS, XLVIII (New York and London: New York University Press, 2008), 315–59.

[3] For a sharp critique of her proposal, see Newey, "Toleration, Politics, and the Role of Murality."

[4] For one exception in which international relations are discussed within the framework of toleration see Cohen, *Toleration*, 112–15.

An Augustinian Essay on Toleration. Manfred Svensson, Oxford University Press. © Manfred Svensson 2026.
DOI: 10.1093/9780197912737.003.0014

order."[5] Within such a shared order, toleration obviously allows for many different degrees of communion, and for forms of separation too. There is, as Paul Griffiths has written, a "letting be by removal."[6] But even the most radical versions of such "separatist" toleration imply the preservation of some kind of relationship. That relationship must not even be willed; it may be that we only accept coexistence as an inevitable fact. But if this fact were not present, we would be talking about something other than toleration.

This raises several questions. What community do we have in mind when we speak of preserving our social life? What sort of cohesion or shared vision of the good must characterize such communities? And in what sense is it acceptable to give in or yield for the sake of peace or social life? Let us begin by identifying the relevant community. In our next chapter we will consider the questions of tolerance that arise for local or intermediate communities. But here we ask about the encompassing political community. How broad is it? Can we speak of a fellowship of all humanity? There is a sense in which Augustine writes with that unlimited community in mind. "With 'neighbor' we refer not to proximity of blood, but to the community of reason by which all human beings are associated," he writes in his Letter 155.[7] But our political community is not the planet. Human life is organized in concrete communities, and the structure of our responsibilities derives from this organization. It is within a political life with boundaries and specific responsibilities that questions of toleration emerge. Augustine famously addresses this problem in terms of an "order of love." We must love all equally, but we have "a greater duty of care for those who by a sort of lot are tied to us by accident of time, place, or some other circumstance," he writes in *On Christian Doctrine*.[8] Passages like this include both a universalist orientation and a recognition of particular commitments. It is important to lay out both these dimensions of the *ordo amoris*. We belong to concrete communities in which hierarchical ordering and prudential preference will determine some of our positive duties. But Augustine does not forget the "perspective of humanity." His universalism is present not only in the duty to love all, but also in the universal prohibition of harm that is part and parcel of his discussion of ordered love. Ordered concord requires "first that we harm no one and next that we do good to whomever we can."[9]

[5] Bowlin, *Tolerance Among the Virtues*, 159 (see 106–59 for tolerance as a part of justice).
[6] Paul J. Griffiths, *Problems of Religious Diversity* (Oxford: Blackwell, 2001), 112.
[7] *ep.* 155, 4, 14.
[8] *doctr. chr.* I, 28, 29.
[9] *civ.* XIX, 14.

To whom can we do good in the first place? In *On Christian Doctrine*, Augustine responds in quite general terms, mentioning ties that arise from "accident of time, place, or some other circumstance." In the *City of God*, in contrast, he emphatically focuses on the household as the first locus of our duties, only then moving outwards. The home should be "the beginning or particle of the city."[10] But the outward movement apparently stops here. Augustine was a citizen of an Empire, but he rejected its claims to being an ideal polity. His critique, as is well known, partly draws from the Roman historians themselves, and partly on the parallels between soul and city that he inherits from the Platonic tradition.[11] If expanding our domains is a bad recipe for individual happiness, the same rule applies to the political community as a whole.[12] Augustine could also write with his sight set beyond the city, but then his hopes were placed on "small kingdoms enjoying neighborly concord."[13] But what about modern nations, which are somewhat bigger than the kingdoms Augustine had in mind? How should we think about their relation to toleration? When toleration is conflated with cosmopolitan or universalist perspectives, nations are inevitably seen as exclusionary and thus intolerant. Toleration, according to such perspectives, is a virtue of societies that are open, not only in the sense of having a regime of toleration, but in the sense of being literally open to the movement of people across boundaries or without boundaries.[14] Augustine's "neighborly concord" suggests something different: one can defend degrees of openness that are compatible with boundaries, by analogy with the many "houses of citizens in a city."[15] As we have seen, however, questions of tolerance and intolerance only properly emerge within the political community, and the concept of toleration is not the adequate tool for addressing how porous its borders should be. Once this point is clarified, there is place for a range of judgments about modern nations and their treatment of those within their community. Much can be said about the consequences of their enormous centralizing power, and about their aggressive dealing with their own minorities. But nation-states have also allowed for massive experiences of coexistence that cannot be portrayed in terms of homogenizing intolerance. Throughout their history very different cultural and religious groups have

[10] *civ.* XIX, 14–16.

[11] For the debt to Roman historians and intellectuals see Harding, *Augustine and Roman Virtue*; for Plato see Rowan Williams, "Politics and the Soul: A Reading of the City of God," *Milltown Studies* 19/20 (1987): 55–72.

[12] *civ.* IV, 3.

[13] *civ.* IV, 15.

[14] For one version of this anti-nationalist argument see Chandran Kukathas, *Tolerating the Intolerable*, no. 33, Papers on Parliament (Parliament of Australia, 1999).

[15] *civ.* IV, 15.

been articulated at a large scale. What kind of loyalty does such a community command? Augustinians will naturally be critical of any understanding of nationhood that portrays it as the *primary* form of personal belonging. But such a critique is compatible with seeing national belonging as often the primary *shared* allegiance in a territory. As such, it can soften the divisions that arise from our other commitments and thus foster civic peace.

With this in mind, we can turn to our second question. What type of concord should be expected from this type of political community? To what extent does the capacity of nations for tolerance depend on a shared vision of the good? Modern nations arose as communities of conviction, but they developed as communities of language and memory, of shared tradition and law. One can identify difficulties for tolerance in both these stages of development. In cohesive communities of conviction toleration does not seem to be needed; in thin communities of shared law there is less of a common good in virtue of which to tolerate. But this radical contrast actually suggests that there is a large middle ground in which toleration is both necessary and possible. Communities of conviction are seldom lacking in conflict, and thin modern communities are not held together by pure contract. Augustine's whole vision of two cities passing intertwined throughout human history, present in every political community, also aligns with a gradual approach to this question of social concord. The city of God can come to prevail in a political community, making it more substantially cohesive. There is nothing anti-Augustinian in the historical existence of Christendom or in a present hope for something like it. But such dreams will at best be realized incompletely, never making toleration redundant. And it is equally Augustinian to accept that for long stretches of history no fundamental orientation will prevail decisively over the other, that bodies of citizens with opposed visions will have to share a political community. In that case, each city will perhaps realize its goals less perfectly, but they will still be able to find the resources that are necessary for a shared life. There is a concord "in things pertaining to this life" that does not depend on a fully shared vision of human and divine things. The existence of a common history and law can often continue to provide members of a political community with reasons for toleration. However, the well of resources for sustaining social life is not bottomless. The city of man, as understood by Augustine, is defined by its antisocial dynamic.[16] The bonds of a society can disintegrate to a point where calls for tolerance become empty, where nobody has eyes for a shared good in virtue of which to tolerate.

[16] See Roberts Ogle, *Politics and the Earthly City in Augustine's City of God*, 19–25.

But is the value of social life and civic peace such that one must always yield? This was our third question. Is giving in for the sake of peace a form of morally justified toleration or a capitulation of moral reason to social acceptability? Augustine was aware that there are situations in which the city of God cannot "share the laws of religion with the earthly city."[17] There are things that cannot be done for the sake of civic peace. But these lines deserve further attention, because Augustine acknowledges that burdens can arise for both sides. If the city of God remains faithful in such a clash, it "becomes a burden to those who think differently, and it must endure the onset of their anger, hatred, and persecutions."[18] The city of God becomes a burden to others, and it must endure their reaction. This may be lamentable, but it is sometimes necessary. Augustine is obviously not pleading for submission to an unjust peace. Social life is a good to be maintained, but sometimes we must put some strain on our life together. However, the resulting conflicts will sometimes end in loss, and accepting this passive loss is obviously different from actively violating one's conscience. This is not an argument for capitulation or submission, but rather a recognition of the element of tragedy that is often part of social life.

But if acceptance of loss is one of the things needed for a culture of toleration, we need to be very specific about what we mean by that acceptance, and what we mean by remaining in community or having the will to relate. Consider, for example, Jeremy Webber, who writes that toleration "is willing to subordinate, at least to some extent, an insistence upon substantive values to the preservation of community."[19] While this seems to converge with what we have said so far, a simple call to subordinate "substantive values" to the preservation of community may in fact lead us back to the problems diagnosed in our earlier chapters: toleration can become too costly. It may be more helpful to think of the preservation of community itself as one of these substantive values. To put it in other words, in every particular controversy we are deciding not only the specific issue at stake—the nature of sexual difference, the right interpretation of the past, the future of educational policy, and so on—but also in what terms we continue to live together. Caring for that life together is not a "pragmatic" toleration that one should contrast to a "principled" approach to its limits. The will to relate transcends this divide between pragmatic and principled considerations. The common good may be conceived in rather thin or more robust terms, but living together is itself one of the goods it encompasses.

[17] *civ.* XIX, 17.
[18] *civ.* XIX, 17.
[19] Webber, "The Generosity of Toleration," 283.

When conceived in this way, neither common life nor any other good is reduced to something instrumentally negotiable.

Pride and Prejudice?

Toleration requires that we see a good in human fellowship, that we are ready to accept losses within our shared life. But these are requirements for all the members of a political community, not just for those in authority. Our focus in the previous section in fact falls wholly on the requirements of social rather than political tolerance. Beyond the toleration thus exercised by all citizens in their different capacities, however, political toleration has the State and its branches as main agents. And the general objections to the concept that we have discussed in previous chapters naturally take a more specific and more intense form when we deal with toleration as a regular feature of political power. If judging is seen as arrogant, combined with the idea of State neutrality it will even look impossible: incapable of objections, the State cannot tolerate. If it judges, it is because it has not yet purged itself of all prejudices. If tolerance's relationship to power generally makes it suspect, if it makes even the *virtue* suspect, then toleration as a governmental policy will be even more contested. Finally, the passivity that is often described as typical of toleration seems to be an undesirable characteristic for our common institutions: we want them to be limited, but active. We have already considered the critique of power, judgment, and passivity that lurks behind many rejections of toleration, but in the discussion of political toleration, these arguments often take a more specific form.

Let us begin with the question of neutrality. State toleration is often rejected in the belief that States do not judge in the ways that make toleration necessary. If tolerance presupposes judgments, and if these presuppose a vision of reality, a vision that guides judgment, then modern States do not qualify as potential tolerators. Individuals may be "judgmental," and so we expect them to be tolerant; but a modern State hardly judges, and thus would not need to be tolerant. The State has not only ceased to be confessional, it has also ceased to be personal, and this seems to make neutrality even more inevitable. It is not only that the monarch upholds no confession that needs to tolerate others, but in the monarch's place we have impersonal institutions that are incapable of personal attitudes toward specific citizens.[20] So we can summarize the main

[20] In a slightly different version, this argument was already developed in the early nineteenth century. According to Vinet, States cannot be tolerant since they lack virtues. Vinet, *Outlines of Philosophy and Literature*, 276.

arguments for seeing States as neutral (and hence as not fulfilling a basic condition for being counted as tolerant).

It is not clear, however, that contemporary politics is as impersonal or as neutral as this portrayal suggests. As Sune Laegaard has noted, institutions "can be disposed to act in certain ways whether or not we think of them as subjects of attitudes."[21] The impersonal nature of the State does not render it neutral. Moreover, in all branches of the State's activity, actual governmental agents operate with personal discretion. As Jeremy Webber notes, there is also more continuity between the levels of State and society than we like to imagine.[22] The case for neutrality, even in sober or limited forms, is thus less than obvious. These and other arguments against it notwithstanding, one can perhaps see reasons to affirm neutrality as "never real," but as "an important fiction."[23] This fiction, so the argument of Alasdair MacIntyre goes, not only protects those citizens who dissent from the views promoted by the State; it also protects such views from the distorting effects of the endorsement by that modern State. Up to a certain point this seems to be a sound approach. But if it leads us to ignore the fact that at least implicit endorsements exist, the fiction notwithstanding, it will make us blind to the uneven way in which burdens are distributed.

What would an Augustinian approach to this question then look like? We might start with the obvious fact that Augustine sees individuals and communities as inevitably shaped by one of two loves. There is no third, neutral way, only a choice between a life oriented primarily toward love of God or a life oriented primarily toward a love of self. No neutrality, and certainly not secularity as neutrality. Our life in the *saeculum* should not be understood in terms of the modern "secular." Augustine's *saeculum* refers not to the earthly city, but to this age in which both cities intersect.[24] But for all the critique of State neutrality one might derive from here, Augustine also believed that different individuals and communities could have a common life in this *saeculum*, a common peace under common laws.[25] At least "in things pertaining to

[21] Laegaard, "State Toleration, Religious Recognition and Equality," 60.

[22] Rightly noted by Webber, "The Generosity of Toleration," 271.

[23] MacIntyre, "Toleration and the Goods of Conflict," 214. For MacIntyre's view of tolerance as integral to practical rationality see Nathan Pinkoski, "Why Alasdair MacIntyre Is Not a Conservative Post-Liberal," *The Political Science Reviewer* 43, no. 2 (2019): 531–63.

[24] For the understanding of the *saeculum* and its consequences see Griffiths, "Secularity and the *Saeculum*."

[25] Augustinians do not frame this in terms of neutrality, but a shared concern can exist with some who frame it in that way. Cécile Laborde understands her version of public reason as a search for "reasons that actual (not idealizaed) publics find accessible," and in this non-idealized approach there may be a good point of encounter with the Augustinian tradition. Cécile Laborde, *Liberalism's Religion* (Cambridge, Mass: Harvard University Press, 2017), 121. For a broadly Augustinian approach that takes this empirically realist road see Jonathan Chaplin, "An Institutionalist Reframing of the Religion and Public Reason Debate," *Social Theory and Practice* 47, no. 3 (2021): 589–602.

this life," as we have seen, our shared norms can be grounded in appeals to goods shared by different ways of life present in a society, although members of both cities will often think differently about the nature, origin, and end of such norms. In any case, the rejection of neutrality is not affirmed here to support an agonistic program, as is often done, nor to underscore the legitimacy of promoting a conception of the good politically. It is the reverse side that interests us: a government that exercises judgment satisfies not only the condition for promoting the good, but also that for determining which evils ought to be tolerated.

The denunciation of toleration's power-component follows a slightly different path. While some doubt that its objection-component can be fulfilled in modern political life, no one raises that doubt about the power-component. It is precisely the reality of power that makes us face toleration with distrust. The natural and healthy suspicion vis-à-vis power often turns into cynicism, and our cynicism regarding power can easily become cynicism regarding tolerance: it is nothing more than pride and prejudice. Across the political spectrum we now find a denunciation of tolerance for creating a climate conducive to commercial progress, for making the world a safe place for political and economic conquest.[26] This presumably arrogant nature of tolerance, which grants permission instead of recognizing rights, is one of the major sources of the current discrediting of tolerance. In multiple variations, as we have seen in previous chapters, it is described as arrogant or insulting. Those who raise this criticism have obviously gotten something right: they point to the potential and often real arbitrariness of arrangements in which the sovereign grants a tolerance that he may well rescind once certain circumstances change. If an edict of toleration is granted with a view to the attainment of peace, it may also be revoked when peace is perceived to have been attained. The revocation of the Edict of Nantes did not contradict the stated purpose of the original Edict: it proclaimed that "our endeavors have attained their proposed end," and that peace could henceforth be maintained without the granting of toleration.[27] The question is whether pointing this out strikes at the heart of political toleration.

Let us consider that heart more closely. It is possible for each of us to engage in tolerant acts without being tolerant, but this toleration becomes more stable with the presence of the virtue. But rules and institutions that secure toleration add another kind of stability: we can expect certain policies and laws to

[26] For different variations see A. J. Conyers, *The Long Truce: How Toleration Made the World Safe for Power and Profit* (Waco: Baylor University Press, 2009); and Brown, *Regulating Aversion*.

[27] J.H. Robinson, *Readings in European History. Vol. 2* (Boston: Ginn, 1906), 288.

guarantee tolerance also among those who lack the virtue. Stability is achieved not by ignoring the link between toleration and power, but by controlling arbitrary power. The integration of toleration into the system of constitutional democracy, as Habermas has argued, corrects the one-sidedness at which the critique of tolerance as concession or indulgence has typically aimed.[28] Today, as Gadamer once wrote, "it cannot be proclaimed in an edict."[29] The very idea of tolerant policies or laws implies some distinction between politics and morality, an advisable call to secure a tolerance that will not depend on the limited virtue of those in power. We hope that certain minimal practices of toleration will prevail among all citizens, whatever their virtues, and we expect that a politics of toleration will restrain vicious rulers. This is not to deny that the virtue is fundamental, that we cannot trust a purely procedural approach. But there is no need to see moral and political constraints on power as competing alternatives. They are complementary, and both start from the reasonable premise that power will continue to exist among us.

Acknowledging this fact is obviously compatible with a critical approach to the human *libido dominandi* and its occasional link to toleration.[30] Augustine himself connects this lust for domination with a vicious form of tolerance in the justification of Roman expansion. In the prologue to the *City of God* he cited the Roman motto, to "spare the vanquished and to crush the proud," as evidence of that *libido dominandi*.[31] These lines by Virgil may in fact be the best expression of a tolerance that is also a strategy of domination.[32] And Augustine denounced it not only as *libido dominandi*, but as a usurpation of divine prerogative. It is God who legitimately "resists the proud but gives grace to the humble" (Prov. 3:34; Jas. 4:6, 1 Pet. 5:5), he reminds his readers.[33] It is worth noting, moreover, how Augustine's position is lost in some later moments of Christian thought. Ptolemy of Lucca, who completes Aquinas' *On Kingship*, quotes the same passage from Virgil as a proof of the benevolence by virtue of which the Romans deserved to rule the world.[34] There is a

[28] Borradori, *Philosophy in a Time of Terror: Dialogues with Jürgen Habermas and Jacques Derrida*, 40–41. Further developed in Habermas, "Intolerance and Discrimination."

[29] Hans-Georg Gadamer, "The Idea of Tolerance 1782–1982," in *Praise of Theory. Speeches and Essays*, trans. Chris Dawson (New Haven and London: Yale University Press, 1998), 100.

[30] As Harding notes, this is often seen as a characteristically Augustinan theme, but the formula is borrowed from Sallust. Harding, *Augustine and Roman Virtue*, 47–66.

[31] Virgil, *Aeneid*, Revised edition, trans. H. R- Fairclough, Loeb Classical Library (Cambridge, Mass: Harvard University Press, 1999), VI, 853.

[32] These lines are discussed again in *civ*. I, 6 and V, 12.

[33] *civ*. prol.

[34] Ptolemy of Lucca (with portions attributed to Thomas Aquinas), *On the Government of Rulers/De Regimine Principum*, trans. James M. Blythe (Philadelphia: University of Pennsylvania Press, 1997), 160–62 (III, 6).

legitimate suspicion of power in Augustine that not all Augustinians retain. But Augustine's insight can be taken seriously without demanding the conclusion that we can dispense with power and tolerance. Augustine did not denounce power itself as diabolical.[35] The inherent goodness of created beings quite explicitly includes the goodness of power. "Pride is not a vice in the one who gives power, nor in the power itself, but in the soul that perversely loves its own power and despises that of the just and omnipotent."[36] As Joyce Schuld writes commenting on this passage, Augustine conceives of power as "coterminous with relationality."[37]

If power is coterminous with relationality, we all have power in some form or other. This confirms that we all need to practice toleration, whether we be "rich or poor, free or slave, of either sex."[38] We have already quoted these words about the universal need for toleration. But in this passage Augustine actually stresses vocations in which power is particularly central. Toleration is needed by "kings, princes, judges, soldiers, or provincial magistrates."[39] In political life power appears in concentrated forms. When Aquinas writes that "those who are in authority rightly tolerate certain evils," he explicitly frames this by analogy to the permission of evil granted by an all-powerful God.[40] Political authority—on another dimension than God—is the great tolerator of our shared life. Given its considerable concentration of power, as Preston King has concluded, "the state may generally be regarded as the most important tolerating agent in a society."[41] Unless we see all power as in itself fatally tainted, this should be taken as a simple assessment of the nature of toleration. There is nothing inherently problematic about recognizing the most powerful agents as the main tolerators.

But some imbalances of power can, of course, corrupt a relationship, and in light of that we can stress the benefits of political arrangements that keep that imbalance in check. It is crucial, however, that we do not mistake such arrangements for a politics in which the regular ingredients of toleration disappear. Given the tendency to imagine imbalances of power as out of place in democratic politics, this is worth keeping in mind. There is a tendency to believe that democracy cannot include power relationships, and the defense

[35] There are, moreover, many other *libidines* aside from the *libido dominandi*. See *civ.* XIV, 15.

[36] *civ.* XII, 8.

[37] J. Joyce Schuld, *Foucault and Augustine. Reconsidering Power and Love* (Notre Dame: University of Notre Dame Press, 2003), 11.

[38] *civ.* II, 19.

[39] *civ.* II, 19.

[40] *S. Th.* II–II, q. 10, a. 11.

[41] King, *Toleration*, 62.

of toleration then tends to explain away its power-component.[42] Against that illusion, we must remember that some imbalances of power are a legitimate part of democratic politics, and that these imbalances do not taint the tolerant practices that power enacts. We must ask which asymmetries of power are illegitimate, improperly paternalistic, or incompatible with basic principles of reciprocity. But democratic politics and democratic tolerance suppose the reality of power. And acting tolerantly, as we will now further consider, is not limited to abstention in the use of this power.

Beyond Simple Permission

That the State fulfills the power-component of toleration has never been doubted. It is superlatively fulfilled, and we have seen that there is no reason for this to taint the very practice of toleration. The judgment component of toleration is also fulfilled by the State. It may fulfill it in a form that differs from the one taken under personal rule, but our laws and institutions burden some citizens more than others. Sometimes toleration is the mechanism required to soften this imbalance. But at the beginning of this chapter, we also mentioned a third objection that might be raised against the tolerant State, that of its passivity. No one doubts that this passivity, the "hands-off" model of toleration, is possible. But there is an important question about its desirability.

In order to address this question, we should first note that the conceptions of toleration described in the initial chapters of this book each can lead to different views of the ideal scope of the State. A weakened objection-component fits well with a minimal State, while the turn from tolerance to recognition naturally implies more positive action by the State. This does not necessarily translate into corresponding responses at the level of social tolerance. A liberal society may combine a weakened objection ingredient at the level of State toleration with a more traditional conception of tolerance operating at other levels of social interaction; its social tolerance may sometimes be traditional and can sometimes go beyond toleration. The ways in which the turn to recognition alters the social landscape is also open to multiple routes. A State can engage in benign or moderate forms of symbolic recognition that support the agency of neglected groups of civil society, but it can also take a more interventionist turn that, in its quest for inclusion and abolition of prejudice, uproots that civil society. I will consider this scenario in the next chapter, but at present

42 On this see Eduardo Fuentes, "The Power to Tolerate," *Trans/Form/Ação* 45, no. 3 (2022): 65–84.

it is worth noting how flexible the traditional conception of toleration is with respect to the State.

The traditional conception of toleration can accommodate both very limited and more expansive conceptions of legitimate State action. This discussion is typically muddled, however, by the tendency of advocates of recognition and related dispositions to conflate the liberal and the traditional conceptions of toleration. The move beyond toleration towards recognition, hospitality, and agonistic respect, as we saw in Chapter 3, is marked by a relentless critique of the shortcomings of liberal political theory, rashly treating its views of toleration as the standard by which to measure the whole practice. The idea of toleration is then seen as tied not only to a minimal State but also to a negative conception of citizenship for which non-interference is the primary social virtue. Whether justice is done to the liberal tradition in such portrayals is a legitimate question. But however one may answer that question, none of this follows once we have disentangled the history of toleration from an exclusive link to liberalism. The traditional conception of toleration is not tied to any particular conception of the State, nor of citizenship. It is tied neither to a pronounced form of negative citizenship nor to a necessarily minimal State.[43] However, non-interference is part of the nature of toleration, and such a form of "asceticism" will come harder to forms of political power to which limits in general are alien.

Within the State's limited duties not all, obviously, relate to toleration. But what is the nature of the duties it does have in this field? As many today agree, the State tends to act primarily as an arbiter between other parties. The State's chief aim with regard to toleration is to guarantee that the different groups within a society tolerate each other. In the words of Peter Jones, "its commitment to toleration is manifest not in its refraining from acting on its own disapproval, but in its establishing arrangements that prevent others from acting on theirs."[44] Hence also the tendency to imagine it as neutral: if the State is primarily an arbiter, it is natural to emphasize its impartiality.[45] There is an instructive medieval precedent for this combination of non-interference and impartial judging between conflicting groups. In addition to simple permission (*permissio simplex*), medieval legal literature recognized a permission that actively removes obstacles (*permissio tollens impedimentum*). A permission

[43] For discussion of citizenship, see Gregory, *Politics and the Order of Love. An Augustinian Ethic of Democratic Citizenship*.

[44] Peter Jones, "Toleration, Recognition and Accommodation," *European Journal of Philosophy* 23, no. 3 (2012): 130.

[45] See Newey, *Toleration in Political Conflict*, 42–43.

may not only passively grant the right to do something, but may actively involve the removal of obstacles placed by third parties on the practices that the authorities permit.[46] The typical case that led to positing this distinction was the permission for Jewish worship: not only was it to be allowed, but it also fell to the authorities to prevent others from obstructing it. It is not difficult to see how such questions arise in our context as well. The State often has to adjudicate between the demands of different groups, demands that cannot always be met in terms of mere equality under the law.

Sheldon Leader has provided a useful characterization of the different "faces of toleration" in a contemporary democracy, in terms of basic, equal, and special rights.[47] In the next section I will return to the question of special rights, albeit rather obliquely. But the other two categories fit with the medieval terminology well. When we ask for a basic right, we are asking for non-interference, or the medieval *permissio simplex*; when we ask for an equal right, we ask for access to a common space, where we will actually interfere with others who also claim that space for their activities. This use of a common space, though it involves no special accommodation or special rights, already raises questions that cannot be resolved with a simple "live and let live" approach. As Jeremy Waldron has written, "people pursue not only different aims, but aims with different and disparate shapes."[48] A shared park cannot be used for worship, for playing soccer, and for enjoying a peaceful afternoon at the same time.[49] The tensions that emerge here are frequently solved by the citizens themselves, who in diverse ways negotiate the extent to which they will accept interference from each other. But there are also situations where the use of public space can only be regulated by a common law that goes beyond passive non-interference.

The limited nature of tolerance does not mean that those in power are limited to tolerating/permitting or ceasing to do so. It does not mean that the establishment of a regime of tolerance implies pure passivity on the part of the State. A just regime of tolerance, it seems, will require an active State, one that not only grants tolerance but is also capable of securing it. A limited but solid State. But how much can such a State interfere in the life of its civil society? Since its duties in this regard involve some kind of pacification of society, the

[46] On this see István Bejczy, "Tolerantia: A Medieval Concept," *Journal of the History of Ideas* 58, no. 3 (1997): 365–84.

[47] Sheldon Leader, "Three Faces of Toleration in a Democracy," *The Journal of Political Philosophy* 4, no. 1 (1996): 45–67.

[48] Jeremy Waldron, "Toleration and Reasonableness," in *The Culture of Toleration in Diverse Societies. Reasonable Tolerance*, ed. Catriona McKinnon and Dario Castiglione (Manchester and New York: Manchester University Press, 2003), 18.

[49] Leader, "Three Faces of Toleration in a Democracy," 46.

problems that we have discussed throughout this book arise again. The State may be tempted to see its task as that of filing off the offensive edges of different groups or forcing them to reciprocal recognition. It is with this problem that we will conclude this book. Before addressing it, however, we must first turn to the more general question of how our thinking about toleration has shaped our views of human groups and associations.

11
Communities of Conviction and Tolerance as a Local Practice

Communities, Roots, and Flexibility

In the two previous chapters we have considered tolerance as a personal virtue and as a political practice. Disputes about tolerance, its necessity, and its limits, often revolve around these two poles: toleration granted by States and toleration between individuals. But this dual focus is to some extent an accident of our history. It depends, as Benjamin Kaplan notes, on the radical individualism of contemporary society. It is this feature, the centrality of voluntary individual choice in our way of life, that reduces questions of tolerance to these two subjects. A State and a society are tolerant, we assume, if they make room for the changing practices and beliefs that result from such individual choices. And it is true that this is a significant realization of the idea of tolerance. But as Kaplan further notes, there is another historical model that has stressed not the autonomy of individuals but the autonomy of communities (especially, but not only, religious ones).[1] The Ottoman Empire is a well-known example of such a system, where the Jewish and Christian communities could organize their social life with great independence from the officially Muslim Empire. But the independence of these communities did not mean that their individual members would be seen as fundamentally autonomous. Will Kymlicka therefore described this model as a sort of hypercommunitarianism.[2] From the perspective of an individualistic culture, such models are easily dismissed as simply intolerant. But, as Kaplan, again, notes, "what the second model really offers is a different kind of toleration from the first, with advantages as well as

[1] For a brief comparison between a toleration structured around individuals and one structured around communities, see Kaplan, *Divided by Faith. Religious Conflict and the Practice of Toleration in Early Modern Europe*, 239–41.

[2] Kaplan refers to Kymlicka's seminal contribution, which helped turn the Ottoman Empire such a frequent point of reference in this discussion. Will Kymlicka, "Two Models of Pluralism and Tolerance," *Analyse & Kritik* 14, no. 1 (1992): 33–56. For a historically more balanced discussion see Philip Jenkins, *The Lost History of Christianity: The Thousand-Year Golden Age of the Church—and How It Died* (New York: HarperOne, 2008), 148–64.

An Augustinian Essay on Toleration. Manfred Svensson, Oxford University Press. © Manfred Svensson 2026.
DOI: 10.1093/9780197912737.003.0015

disadvantages."[3] This alternative model offers less in terms of individual autonomy, less mobility between groups, and more segregation; but it also offers more space for each tradition and community to order its existence as it sees fit. We should add, moreover, that this model is not absent from the contemporary world. Some deeply divided modern societies (also in nineteenth- and twentieth-century Europe) have arranged their existence in analogous terms. We often think of this "segmented pluralism" as an exception to modern developments, but as Staf Hellemans has written, perhaps we should recognize it as one of the manifestations of modernity.[4]

But this model also exists in less drastic forms. An analogous form of smaller communities norming substantial parts of their lives within a larger political community can be found wherever nation-states include a vibrant civil society. Since the nineteenth century, the call for the revitalization of this sphere has come from a variety of quarters: it has been rooted in secular and Christian traditions, and it has channeled socialist, conservative, and liberal concerns.[5] This modern discourse on subsidiarity, civil society, little platoons, or intermediate societies does not suggest any necessarily segmented society. The communities and organizations designated with these terms have developed in cultures of strong individual rights. They admit individual choice, mobility between groups, and conversion, and they are thus different from the "hypercommunitarian" or "segmented" model. But they remain at odds with contemporary individualism, and this is often reason enough for certain currents of thought to subject them to the critique of intolerance. Although such communities or traditions may be merely "communitarian," they are seen as "hypercommunitarian." As this suggests, it is not only that groups receive less attention than they deserve in the toleration debate but also that our lens seems to be designed to see them as intolerant.

Why? Behind this inclination, as Maurizio Passerin d'Entrèves has noted, stands a mentality in which "community" is associated with "strong identities, fixed by custom and tradition," while tolerance "suggests more flexible identities, less rooted in history and collective memory and more open to the acceptance of difference, of plurality and of alternative life-styles."[6] If tolerance

[3] Kaplan, *Divided by Faith. Religious Conflict and the Practice of Toleration in Early Modern Europe*, 241.

[4] Staf Hellemans, "Pillarization ('Verzuiling'). On Organized 'Self-Contained Worlds' in the Modern World," *The American Sociologist* 51 (2020): 124–47.

[5] For a brief but instructive survey see Jonathan Chaplin, *Herman Dooyeweerd: Christian Philosopher of State and Civil Society* (Notre Dame: University of Notre Dame Pess, 2011), 14–16. For a long-term view of intermediacy in the liberal tradition see Levy, *Rationalism, Pluralism, and Freedom*.

[6] Maurizio Passerin d'Entrèves, "Communitarianism and the Question of Tolerance," *Journal of Social Philosophy* 21, no. 1 (1990): 77; see also Roger Crisp, "Communitarianism and Toleration," in *Toleration: Philosophy and Practice*, ed. Peter Nicholson and John Horton (Aldershot: Averbury, 1992), 108–25.

suggests "flexible identities" rather than the capacity to endure what we object to, then groups with strong commitments and fixed roots, be they "communitarian" or "hyper-communitarian," will by definition count as intolerant. And this mentality has deeper roots in the history of philosophy than we might think. One classical philosophical expression of this perspective can be found in the work of John Stuart Mill, and especially in the cultural politics contained in chapter three of *On Liberty*. While the conventional reading of his work stresses Mill's defense of freedom of thought and discussion, in this chapter readers will find a sustained critique of "received opinion," "hereditary creed," and "despotism of custom."[7] This "despotism" must give way to individuality and genius, to spontaneity and "experiments of living."[8] Those who have been raised in this Millian critique of custom naturally tend to identify rootedness with intolerance.[9]

But this is also a deep-seated view in our culture beyond any explicitly stated philosophies. "Travel is fatal to prejudice," Mark Twain once observed. An expanded version is often (though falsely) attributed to Miguel de Unamuno: "Fascism is cured by reading, and racism is cured by traveling." Such statements reveal where we imagine the source of intolerance lies. Breaking with our immediate circle, whether through actual mobility or through the practice of reading, prepares us for tolerance. Or so these oft-quoted phrases suggest. This one-sided critique of custom and belonging is obviously in need of revision. Reading and travel may make us more tolerant; but so may the ability to remain in the same neighborhood, in the same marriage, in the same conversations. It is patience that to some extent sustains marriages, communities, and polities, but it is also the case that these structures and forms of living together teach patience.[10] Tolerant societies are sustained not only by their curiosity, flexibility, and openness but also through custom, belonging, and other features of "fixed" communities. Curiosity and flexibility may teach a community how to tolerate alien or new groups or ideas, but its customs and sense of belonging can teach it why to endure failures and deviations that emerge in its own bosom.

Why have we lost touch with this last insight? How did the prevailing view become dominant? Why is it so central to our thinking about toleration?

[7] Mill, "On Liberty," 247, 248, and 272.

[8] Mill, 261.

[9] For a general interpretation of his thought with close attention to this problem see Joseph Hamburger, *John Stuart Mill on Liberty and Control* (Princeton and Oxford: Princeton University Press, 1999).

[10] On this see Jean Bethke Elshtain, "The Life and Work of Christopher Lasch: An American Story," *Salmagundi* 106/7 (1995): 152.

One thing to note is that the prevalent mentality is particularly suspicious of institutions that are not purely voluntary. For not all intermediate groups are voluntary, or at least not all of them are voluntary in the same sense. But it is precisely a tradition of writings on toleration that has led us to think of institutions in terms of their voluntary dimension, perhaps blinding us to their non-voluntary dimensions and to the ways in which these are compatible with toleration. To a significant degree, we have inherited this approach from Locke's *Letter*. The description of the Church as a voluntary society (*societas libera et voluntaria*) is as central to the *Letter* as the separation of Church and State.[11] The task of churches is worshipping God in a way that is conducive to the salvation of the soul, while their nature is that of a voluntary society. This description of the Church, as if it were constituted by enlightened adult believers who have finally settled for the Church of their choice, excludes any sense of inheritance, belonging, of being formed by a group instead of constituting it through our will. As Sander Griffioen has written, this substitution of membership for contract implies a denaturation of institutions to which we belong on more than a voluntary basis.[12]

But there is a weighty moral reason behind this development. Locke's aim in describing churches as voluntary societies was to ensure tolerance in the form of freedom of exit. This is a desirable goal, an indispensable ingredient of a plural society. The question is whether we need the description of the Church Locke provides in order to ensure this freedom. We can defend freedom of exit without first reimagining all institutions as purely voluntary. Consider the contrast with Paul Griffiths' Augustinian definition of religion. He describes a religion as a "form of life that seems to those who inhabit it to be comprehensive, incapable of abandonment, and of central importance."[13] Is this inherently intolerant? The question is worth asking in all seriousness, since religion as "incapable of abandonment" seems to frontally collide with the right of exit that we recognize as a basic condition of a liberal society. But this collision is not really necessary. Griffith's words rather suggests that we should be careful not to identify the external and internal descriptions of religion or of the Church. One element of a tolerant society is the possibility of abandonment, conversion, or exit; it is essential for political society to make this possible and thus to see religious communities as groups that can be abandoned. But there is no reason why this should be taken as an adequate internal perspective. An

[11] Locke, *Epistola de Tolerantia/A Letter on Toleration*, 71.
[12] Sander Griffioen, "Is a Pluralist Ethos Possible?" *Philosophia Reformata* 59, no. 1 (1994): 11–25.
[13] Griffiths, *Problems of Religious Diversity*, 7.

internal description must acknowledge that abandoning our religion would in some sense be like abandoning ourselves.[14] If religion is to be taken seriously, we cannot expect the external description to be internalized, and its internalization should not be seen as a condition for counting as tolerant. This does not mean that churches should be blind to their status as voluntary institutions within free societies that include a right of exit. Some institutions may need to see themselves in this double light, attentive to their voluntary and non-voluntary dimensions. A radical internalization of voluntariness, in contrast, is not only unnecessary, but also damaging. Once the logical link between voluntariness and toleration is established, we have a hard time considering how long-term bonds, communities into which we have been born, identities we have not chosen, relate to toleration. This alters the understanding of toleration that is cultivated within the intermediate institutions themselves, restricting them to a "take it or leave it" logic.[15] But it is precisely because some institutions are not governed by this logic that they must resolve their conflicts by means other than pointing to the door that we can voluntarily pass through. Institutions that have a natural, permanent, or inherited character can be prepared to bear particularly heavy burdens, but this capacity depends on not seeing themselves as purely voluntary institutions.

This question also determines the way in which associations are viewed from the outside, by the surrounding society and by the State. If all human associations are conceived of as having grown out of deliberate human decision, we begin to think of communities as tolerant only insofar as they fit into this mold. When they do not fit, they are viewed in terms of their potential for oppression. We then come to see toleration as a goal to be achieved once people have been liberated from these communities. The liberal tradition itself has a mixed trajectory in this regard. Some of its strands aim at defending the freedoms of citizens and their associations, while other strands aim at liberating citizens from contexts they find oppressive.[16] For Stephen Macedo, for example, only "religious communities *of the right sort*" should be treated as an important part of liberal culture.[17] Deborah Fitzmaurice likewise has argued that the liberal State is bound to be inhospitable to traditional ways of life.[18]

[14] Griffiths, 10.

[15] An important point in Griffioen, "Is a Pluralist Ethos Possible?"

[16] For a comprehensive discussion of the liberal tradition in light of this theme see Levy, *Rationalism, Pluralism, and Freedom*.

[17] Stephen Macedo, "Transformative Constitutionalism and the Case of Religion: Defending the Moderate Hegemony of Liberalism," *Political Theory* 26, no. 1 (1998): 65.

[18] Deborah Fitzmaurice, "Autonomy as a Good: Liberalism, Autonomy and Toleration," *The Journal of Political Philosophy* 1, no. 1 (1993): 14.

Since they wrote in these terms, three decades ago, this conviction has become more widespread, with the result that freedom of expression and association are often suspended in the name of liberal values. If liberalism has a liberalizing mission, it will clash with other missions; the more consistently it adheres to this liberalizing mission, the less tolerant it may prove to be.[19] In the words of Susan Mendus, "The pluralism and tolerance which this account of liberalism affords is only between and within life styles which place a high value on autonomy."[20] But if the liberal order rests not on a liberalizing mission, if its core lies instead in the existence of a regime of toleration, very different conclusions follow. This only makes the question raised at the end of the previous chapter all the more important: how must the State understand its duty to enforce toleration? How will this duty be understood when it is nourished by this "inhospitable" perspective? And what does all this mean for the internal diversity of associations and for the conditions under which they will be expected to cooperate with the State?

Mission, Transmission, and the Neutralization of Civil Society

How should we understand the governmental duty to secure toleration? Besides tolerating, we have noted, authorities must safeguard conditions of tolerance between different groups. But how we understand this duty will depend on how we understand tolerance and how we look at groups. Because our thinking about toleration has been developed especially in relation to the State, there is a strong tendency to simply transfer what we think about State toleration to the quite different dilemmas faced by intermediate bodies. Not only do we believe that the State's toleration will depend on its neutrality, but we transfer this belief to our view of groups: as long as their criteria of belonging are minimal, we see them as relatively neutral and tolerant institutions; but when they are structured around strong commitments, when they see their membership as binding, when they hold beliefs *qua* groups, they are regularly suspected of intolerance. Schools and churches, families, hospitals, and businesses can be subject to this implicit or explicit critique. This understanding of groups then intersects with the State's role in calling or compelling groups to reciprocal tolerance.

[19] For a discussion of Nozick, Kymlicka, and Raz with such questions in mind see Jonathan Chaplin, "How Much Cultural and Religious Pluralism Can Liberalism Tolerate?" in *Liberalism, Multiculturalism and Toleration*, ed. John Horton (New York: Palgrave, 1993), 32–49.

[20] Mendus, *Toleration and the Limits of Liberalism*, 107.

The risks that emerge at this intersection can be illustrated by looking at Montesquieu. In *The Spirit of the Laws*, he explicitly states the position that we find in part of the contemporary discussion. A legislator who has decided to tolerate different religions, he writes, must "also oblige them to tolerate each other."[21] The State must not only prevent followers of one religion from using violence against the State or against individuals, but also against other groups. But if groups are thought of in the light of the model of the supposedly neutral State, the State's task will easily be understood as that of curtailing any substantial commitments that might put pressure on the group's individual members or put different association at odds with each other. Toleration will then consist in neutralizing civil society. Montesquieu did already reach this conclusion, which many in today's debates hold up as an ideal. He would only grant religions the title of tolerant to the extent that they renounced missionary activity: "a religion that can tolerate others scarcely thinks of its propagation," he writes.[22] A church or a religion can only be tolerant if it keeps its faith to itself. This is very different from telling churches that they must abstain from coercion, a more normal criterion for evaluating their toleration.

This has important consequences for our understanding of toleration. Montesquieu condemns "agitating" and "disturbing"[23] in a way that easily ends up blurring the distinction between coercion, manipulation, and persuasion. Commenting on the blurring of this distinction, Jean Bethke Elshtain has stressed the way it depends on the privatization of belief. Under these conditions, "proselytizing comes to seem a violation of toleration," as if toleration meant that no one could challenge our faith or spirituality.[24] Persuasion, like manipulation and coercion, becomes a form of imposition. Her critique of this confusion is clearly pertinent. But this tendency is not as recent a development as her discussion suggests. The blurring of these distinctions extends to more foundational moments in modern political thought, and in those foundational moments it is by no means unique to Montesquieu.[25] Hobbes, too, described attempts at religious persuasion not only as crimes, but as violations of our duties of reciprocity. The preacher of a new religion, in his view, "does that which he would not approve in another."[26]

[21] Charles de Secondat Montesquieu, *The Spirit of the Laws* (Cambridge: Cambridge University Press, 1989), 487 (XXV, 9).
[22] Montesquieu, 488 (XXV, 10).
[23] Montesquieu, 487 (XXV, 9).
[24] Elshtain, "Toleration, Proselytizing, and the Politics of Recognition," 90.
[25] For a further example see Kries, "Rousseau and the Problem of Religious Toleration," 275–76.
[26] Hobbes, *Leviathan*, II, 27/456.

This is obviously not the whole of the Enlightenment legacy with regard to toleration, but it is part of that legacy. Its consequences, moreover, are not limited to the way in which we think about religion. Just as the idea of the Church as voluntary association has shaped the way we think about all human communities, so too the rejection of missionary activity as a form of intolerance inaugurates a broader pattern of thought. Education conceived as transmission is often seen in terms that scarcely differ from the Hobbesian critique of missions. In the words of Alain Finkielkraut, after Auschwitz teaching "is permitting, not transmitting."[27] According to this mentality, human dignity can only be respected if every trace of paternalism is eliminated. Education itself thus runs the risk of being seen as intolerant. We have already seen that for David Heyd transmitting the virtue of tolerance is close to an impossibility. But it is not only his understanding of tolerance that underlies this conclusion. It is the fact that for him "the educational relationship itself is often intolerant in its very nature."[28] Teaching is transmitting, and it is thus as intolerant as missions.

A curious circle is thus completed. In a bold and slightly intolerant move, Locke had suggested that a law might be passed "so that all churches were obliged to teach, and to lay down as the foundation of their own liberty, the principle of toleration for others."[29] It was not the simple practice of reciprocal toleration that in this proposal counted as guarantee of civility, but the teaching and owning of toleration. In the name of toleration, however, we have ended up challenging missionary activity and education as transmission, only to find out that the very idea of educating for toleration then becomes impossible or intolerant.

But if this understanding of toleration affects the way the outward action of groups is evaluated—casting doubt on mission and transmission—contemporary thinking about inclusion tends to neutralize their internal composition. Habermas has written that "before we call for tolerance, the norm of full inclusion of all citizens should be accepted."[30] This is an apt way of describing the place of toleration in political society. Criteria such as equal freedom and full inclusion, however, regulate our relations as citizens, not as members of other associations. It is often meaningful to speak of inclusion

[27] Alain Finkielkraut, *Une voix vient de l'autre rive* (Paris: Gallimard, 2000), 109.

[28] Heyd, "Education to Toleration: Some Philosophical Obstacles and Their Resolution," 202.

[29] Locke, *Epistola de Tolerantia/A Letter on Toleration*, 135.

[30] Jürgen Habermas, *Wann müssen wir tolerant sein? Über die Konkurrenz von Weltbildern, Werten und Theorien. Festvortrag zum Leibniztag der Berlin-Brandenburgischen Akademie der Wissenschaften am 29. Juni 2002* (Veröff. v. der Berlin-Brandenburgischen Akademie der Wissenschaften, 2002), 173.

as a general goal for society at large. But it makes less sense to imagine inclusion as the central goal of all intermediate institutions. There is no universal "norm of full inclusion" in them. If anything, this "acceptance without exception" will diminish the actual pluralism of civil society. William Galston has described this in terms of a "paradox of diversity": if each group is expected to reflect the same standard of internal diversity as the overarching political community, "meaningful differences between associations all but disappear."[31] This is, of course, especially obvious for the groups we can call "communities of conviction." Few nations can today be considered as such, but many of their intermediate groups can. And if it is illusory to ground the State's toleration on its neutrality, it is even more distorting to apply that expectation to such communities. There are degrees and types of internal diversity from which all human associations can benefit. But if we recognize a problem in the neutralization of civil society, inclusion must often be subordinated to the purposes for which associations exist.[32] The goals of marriage, schools, churches, and other associations substantially determine the kind of inclusion that is appropriate in each case. As Leo Strauss argued in a very different context, "The prohibition against every 'discrimination' would mean the abolition of the private sphere, the denial of the difference between state and society, in a word, the destruction of liberal society."[33] A tolerant State should leave ample freedom to such communities in matters pertaining of their internal composition.

A somewhat different dilemma arises when the State expects some associations, in virtue of their social role, to participate in practices to which they object. The most prominent example may be that of hospitals that, because of their Christian affiliation, refuse to offer gender affirmative treatments, perform abortions, or offer physician-assisted suicide. This is the focus of particular controversy when such institutions are part of a public network (for example, with some public funding). The issue here is not respect for the inner composition of an association, but one about its role in public life. And in complex societies this public space is indeed one of frequent collaboration between the State and institutions that may oppose some goals of that same State. Significant dilemmas arise in this context. When it comes to individuals, conscientious objection seems to offer a well-established approach. But can

[31] Galston, *Liberal Pluralism*, 20.

[32] So also T.M. Scanlon, "The Difficulty of Tolerance," in *The Difficulty of Tolerance. Essays in Political Philosophy* (Cambridge: Cambridge University Press, 2003), 194.

[33] Leo Strauss, "Why We Remain Jews," in *Jewish Philosophy and the Crisis of Modernity* (Albany, NY: State University of New York Press, 1997), 315.

we imagine something analogous on the part of institutions? There is, in fact, a good argument for sometimes treating groups as agents, with something analogous to moral conscience and the responsibilities that go with it.[34] Just as a government remains in place as an authority if it tolerates the refusals and opposition of some citizens, so it can interact with associations in ways that allow for simultaneous cooperation and opposition. But this, again, supposes a specific way of seeing such associations. If one sees intermediate associations as acting on behalf of the State, with delegated authority (as a long tradition following Jean Bodin has conceived them), then the State will seem to act in a self-contradictory way if it tolerates such deviations from its goals. If, on the contrary, we see the public realm as a domain constituted by the action of the State and of various institutions possessing original authority—institutions that cooperate with the State in many complex ways—this contradiction dissolves. This does not mean that the State abdicates its governing function when it comes to groups. But it does suggest that if groups are to be "controlled and directed," in the words of John Neville Figgis, they must be governed "like persons."[35]

As we have noted, there are different strands within the liberal tradition, and some will be more open to this form of pluralism than others. In any case, the view of toleration that we have developed in this book definitely allows for simultaneous collaboration between the State and such objecting institutions in matters where it is possible. This is in fact another instance in which *just* toleration can differ from *mere* toleration. If the State merely tolerated these institutions, it could not possibly cooperate with them. But if a disposition of tolerance can go hand in hand with other dispositions, the State's toleration of the specific positions of some institutions need not reduce the whole relationship to one of mere toleration, thus allowing for collaboration. Of course, this does not imply that everything that takes place within organized groups gets *carte blanche*. Certain groups can, furthermore, be deemed unworthy of any respect. But once the State and the surrounding society see value in a certain way of life, they may discover that in that value lies a reason for bearing what otherwise are matters of contestation.[36] It is not only the multidimensional

[34] Christopher Tollefsen, "Institutional Conscience, Corporate Persons, and Hobby Lobby," in *Christianity and the Laws of Conscience. An Introduction*, ed. Helen M. Alvaré and Jeffrey B. Hammond (Cambridge: Cambridge University Press, 2021), 395–413.

[35] John Neville Figgis, *Churches in the Modern State* (London: Longmans, Green and Co, 1913), 47.

[36] See, for instance, the argument of Alon Harel, who (with other debates in mind) considers that we may have good reasons for tolerating otherwise intolerable practices if they take place within a respectable way of life. Alon Harel, "The Boundaries of Justifiable Tolerance: A Liberal Perspective," in *Toleration. An Elusive Virtue*, ed. David Heyd (Princeton: Princeton University Press, 1996), 114–26.

nature of individual persons we must take into account when thinking about toleration, but also that of groups.

Limits and Tolerance within Groups

With the foregoing considerations in mind one can more profitably return to the question of limits, the question of legitimate exclusion. In Chapter 7 I have already pointed to the role of prudence when determining the limits of the tolerable. But prudence works in different ways depending on who the tolerating subject is. In thinking about these limits, we must allow for significant differences between the evils that an individual person can endure, the evils that the political community can tolerate, and the evils that a particular group should bear. While practical wisdom can never be replaced, some general criteria can sometimes be given to delineate the areas in which it operates. An individual person may have to endure all kinds of evils in her various activities, but our significant relationships and responsibilities provide a guide for what to tolerate. There are, for instance, things that one tolerates less in one's own children than in the children of others, and vice versa. What about the State? In both Aquinas and Mill we have found what looks like a minimalistic approach: the State cannot tolerate actions that endanger the subsistence of the political community. But can we also think about harms to the community beyond the question of its subsistence? For Marcus Aurelius, only that which is harmful to the city should be considered harmful to ourselves.[37] But what is harmful to the city? How do we appeal to the idea of harm when we think of the political community as a whole? Some question the very notion of a harm to society. If "there simply is no such thing that can be harmed," then the fabric of society cannot be harmed by things like pornography, writes Andrew Jason Cohen.[38] To the extent that one finds the idea of such a fabric defensible, one will make a less minimalistic reading of Aquinas' words. Or perhaps one will think that society must defend itself from such harms, but not always through the means that are distinctive of the State. In any case, the minimalistic answer that partially applies to the State cannot simply be transferred to our question about communities of conviction or other communities with specific substantive goals. If we inquire about the limits of toleration in particular human

[37] Marcus Aurelius, *Meditations, Books 1-6*, 5.22.

[38] Thus, for instance, in Cohen, *Toleration*, 94, who rashly takes for granted that no evidence for such harms exist.

associations, we will have to ask what evils would make the attainment of the goods of each community impossible. It is within this horizon that prudence will operate in these cases.

This is not an abstract criterion. On the contrary, it is one that can be illuminating in many crucial controversies. Different institutions require different drawing of boundaries. A tolerant society has strong policies in defense of freedom of thought and speech, for example, but these are especially central to the university. There we can ask whether humanity is worth preserving, whether tolerance is really a good, whether human dignity extends to all members of the species. Such conversations can be burdensome, but truth-seeking is bound up with this freedom. This does not mean, however, that we should wish for the whole of society to engage in the same radical questioning as the university. Universities are obviously not the only place where fundamental matters are raised, but not every time and place is appropriate for the same range of questioning. On the other hand, to make such discussions possible, the university itself will have to draw boundaries that are not drawn elsewhere. For these issues can only be meaningfully discussed if universities are less permissive towards everything that makes productive discussion and teaching impossible. All of these steps—the ones that expand toleration and the ones that restrict it—require prudential deliberation. However, this deliberation can only take place if we understand the nature and purpose of each institution.

But though communities can be very different in how they draw their boundaries, none of them can achieve their ends without tolerance. To consider why, we must again think about the nature of groups. As Jacob Levy puts it, we tend to look at groups "as big individuals or small states."[39] The problems that we have discussed in this chapter stem from the second of these tendencies, from understanding groups as small states. If we imagine them in these terms, demands for universal inclusiveness will potentially fall on all kinds of groups, with the consequences that we have pointed out. But it is no less a problem to ignore that groups are something different than big individuals. Human associations are not only intermediate in terms of their size. They not only represent a middle magnitude between the State and individuals. They are intermediate in that multiple human wills are united in them. Groups have a unifying principle, but the wills of their members remain distinct from each other. Like an individual agent, a group may have a conviction and pursue a

[39] Levy, *Rationalism, Pluralism, and Freedom*, 57.

goal with determination. But however much they may resemble individuals in this way, in associations we always have a plurality of wills that cannot be reduced to complete unity. This has typically been recognized as the reason why all human communities need authority. It is also the reason why they all need forms and degrees of toleration.

Conclusion

"Remove prostitutes from human affairs, and you will disrupt everything with lust."[1] This was Augustine's approach to the toleration of prostitution in the third of his published works, *De ordine*. Writing in 386, in this work he was concerned with the way in which specific evils are part of the general harmony of the cosmos. Prostitution, like the presence of the hangman, was one of the necessary evils of an ordered world. Not to tolerate such evils would bring greater evils in their place. But these lines would take on a life of their own in the Middle Ages. Sometimes they would appear as part of broader arguments for toleration.[2] But often they would be cited precisely as an argument for tolerating prostitution. Men cannot control themselves, the common interpretation of these lines goes, so tolerating prostitution helps to protect respectable women and to preserve the social order. It is not the best piece of Augustinian philosophy, and one could raise objections to many of its ingredients. But although this passage from *De ordine* is universally cited as Augustine's settled opinion, he had more to say about the toleration of prostitution in his later work. He did not turn decisively to its prohibition, but the tone changes noticeably in the *City of God*.[3] There prostitution is described as a "disgrace made lawful by the earthly city."[4] What members of the city of God should do about it in the realm of secular affairs is thus left as more open a question than he had suggested thirty years earlier. Perhaps this is a disgrace that should continue to be lawful, perhaps not.

How are we to understand this change of mind? It is not that Augustine had become less concerned about the unintended consequences of restraining evil. And it is definitely not the case that he had become more optimistic about our ability to overcome lust. If anything, in his mature work he had become

[1] *ord.* II, 4, 12.

[2] See, for example, *S.Th.* II-II, q. 10, a.11.

[3] The fact that modern scholarship stresses the early text from *De Ordine* is partially understandable in light of its medieval influence. The lack of any mention of the later texts is, however, noteworthy. For an illustrative example of this imbalance, see James A. Brundage, "Prostitution in Medieval Canon Law," *Signs* 1, no. 4 (1976): 830.

[4] *civ.* XIV, 18.

An Augustinian Essay on Toleration. Manfred Svensson, Oxford University Press. © Manfred Svensson 2026.
DOI: 10.1093/9780197912737.003.0016

more aware of the inner conflict in every human life. But perhaps he became more confident that self-control or moderation could be expected from the many converted, not just from the few wise men he had in mind in *De ordine*. This change of mind is instructive about the implications that different anthropologies can have for the discussion of toleration. Augustine's mature view, as can be seen in passages like this, holds on to both the profound fallenness of human beings and their capacity for partial self-governance; and it is this combination, not a simple "realism" or the selective optimism (for the few wise) of *De ordine*, that leaves open the question of whether this particular evil of prostitution should be tolerated or not. Whether it should be banished in fact continues to be debated not only between the two cities but also within each of them. Perhaps that is what we should expect. As our discussion throughout this book has suggested, prudential reasoning can never be avoided when we ask about the limits of the tolerable. So even on matters where we might be more comfortable with Augustine's judgment, what we have sought to learn from him in this book is not about the limits of toleration. Instead, I have emphasized his unique understanding of the nature of this virtue.

The reason for going back to Augustine lies in the impasse that so many in the contemporary discussion acknowledge we have reached. It is not just that we have theoretical doubts about the philosophical justification of toleration and confusion about its implications. There are significant questions to be raised about its compatibility with other ideals we have come to embrace. "The cultural values that dominate our lives," as Frank Furedi writes, "find it difficult to sustain and uphold true tolerance."[5] Writing as a historian of toleration, Benjamin Kaplan comes to a similar conclusion. "If toleration depends on the adoption of certain contemporary Western values, its fate in the rest of the world, and perhaps in our own future, is uncertain."[6] The modern world can count among its achievements some important extensions of toleration, but these have developed in parallel with a culture that in many ways moves and pushes in the opposite direction. We have considered how hedonism, belief in progress, and critique of custom, among other things, can undermine tolerance. Its theoretical negation, in the many critiques of toleration discussed in this book, perhaps reflects a reality that is more central to modern life than we would like to imagine. In any case, this circumstance suggests that looking to the past for wisdom is not an extravagant diversion. The understanding of

[5] Furedi, *On Tolerance: A Defence of Moral Independence*, vii.

[6] Benjamin Kaplan, *Divided by Faith. Religious Conflict and the Practice of Toleration in Early Modern Europe* (Cambridge, MA: The Belknap Press of Harvard University Press, 2007), 357.

toleration advocated in this book is, of course, not exclusively Augustinian. It is a version of the "traditional conception" of toleration, elements of which are present in many different traditions and writers, including much contemporary scholarship on toleration. But the Augustinian views of evil, history, hope, and personhood are directly relevant to the way we see toleration in a context shaped by Manichean, progressive, and identitarian tendencies. Sometimes these ingredients of his thought are explicitly linked to toleration by Augustine himself; at other times we have drawn on connections made in the later Augustinian tradition. To make such insights fruitful for contemporary discussion, I have also drawn on things that Augustine tentatively suggested—such as the distinction between cultures and ultimate orientations—which, once made explicit, help us see why toleration is the appropriate response to some forms of difference but not to all.

Throughout this work, I have tried to recognize where a broadly shared understanding of toleration is possible, but also where clarity can only be achieved by contrasting rival approaches to its nature and purpose. How can this contrast between rival views of toleration be summarized? In the first chapters I drew a contrast between approaches to toleration that, by weakening its objection-component, invite to less than actual tolerance, and those that go beyond it toward a higher affirmative disposition. In opposition to these two approaches, I have defended the traditional conception of tolerance as just enduring. But one can also shed some final light on our subject through another contrast. Wolfhart Pannenberg once wrote that in the contemporary context tolerance is typically rooted in the values of self-expression and self-determination, while in the classical and Christian traditions it is rooted in self-control.[7] This is not a simple clash between more tolerant and less tolerant traditions. Each of these has its darker and brighter moments, but it is at this deeper level that these visions of tolerance are worth contrasting. And it is not only in the place given to self-control and virtue that Stoicism and Christianity differ from the self-expressive approach to toleration. The position described by Pannenberg can be characterized by its attention to tolerance as part of the quest for the good life.

Tolerance is part of that quest, not a renunciation of it. Once we see it in such terms, it is natural that we should understand it as part of a broader web of interrelated habits. Moreover, when we ask about the good life, we are asking not only about self-control and virtue but also about wisdom regarding our

[7] Wolfhart Pannenberg, *Grundlagen der Ethik. Philosophisch-theologische Perspektiven* (Göttingen: Vandenhoeck & Ruprecht, 1996), 119.

place in nature and history, and about the communities in which such wisdom can take shape and be transmitted. And we are also asking about happiness as the goal of this quest. It is precisely because happiness is so imperfectly attainable in this life that tolerance is required here. But only here. In this sense—quite different from Goethe's sense—tolerance is indeed a "passing disposition." It will not pass away because progress brings us to a stage where it is not needed, but it will pass away when eternal happiness is attained. In the "supreme and divine city," writes Augustine, "there will be no need to endure troublesome calamities."[8] "There we shall not have to discern prudently between good and evils, for the latter will not exist; nor valiantly tolerate adversity, for the objects of love will replace the objects of toleration."[9] Tolerance will cease to exist when, like the other virtues, it is transformed into love alone. But until that moment is reached, attempts to overcome toleration belong to the realm of utopian thinking.

[8] *ep.* 137, 5, 20.
[9] *ep.* 155, 3, 12.

Bibliography/Sources other than Augustine

Altensteig, Johannes. "Tolerantia." In *Lexicon Theologicum*, 328. Antwerp: Peter Beller, 1576.

Apel, Karl-Otto. "Plurality of the Good? The Problem of Affirmative Tolerance in a Multicultural Society from an Ethical Point of View." *Ratio Juris* 10, no. 2 (2008): 199–212.

Aquinas, Thomas. *Summa Theologiae*, Leonine edition, vols 4–12. Vatican City: Vatican Polyglot Press, 1888–1906.

Aristotle. *Nicomachean Ethics*. 2nd edn. Translated by Terence Irwin. Indianapolis: Hackett Publishing, 1999.

Assmann, Jan. *The Price of Monotheism*. Translated by Robert Savage. Stanford, CA: Stanford University Press, 2010.

Atkins, Jed W. *The Christian Origins of Tolerance*. Oxford: Oxford University Press, 2024.

Avramenko, Richard, and Michael Promisel. "When Toleration Becomes a Vice: Naming Aristotle's Third Unnamed Virtue." *American Journal of Political Science* 62, no. 4 (2018): 849–60.

Bader, Veit. "Moral Minimalism and More Demanding Moralities: Some Reflections on 'Tolerance/Toleration." In *Tolerance, Intolerance and Respect. Hard to Accept?* edited by Jan Dobbernack and Tariq Modood, 23–51. Basingstoke: Palgrave Macmillan, 2013.

Bainton, Roland. "The Parable of the Tares as the Proof Text for Religious Liberty to the End of the Sixteenth Century." *Church History* 1, no. 2 (1932): 67–89.

Balint, Peter. *Respecting Toleration: Traditional Liberalism and Contemporary Diversity*. Oxford: Oxford University Press, 2017.

Barton, Stephen C. "Paul and the Limits of Tolerance." In *Tolerance and Intolerance in Early Judaism and Christianity*, edited by Guy G. Stroumsa and Graham N. Stanton, 121–34. Cambridge: Cambridge University Press, 1998.

Bauman, Zygmunt. *Modernity and Ambivalence*. Cambridge: Polity Press, 1991.

Bayle, Pierre. *A Philosophical Commentary on These Words of the Gospel, Luke 14:23, "Compel Them to Come In, That My House May Be Full."* Indianapolis: Liberty Fund, 2000.

Beddoe, Paul. "Contagio in the Donatists and St. Augustine." *Studia Patristica* 27 (1993): 231–36.

Bejan, Teresa. "Evangelical Toleration." *The Journal of Politics* 77, no. 4 (2015): 1103–14.

Bejan, Teresa. *Mere Civility. Disagreement and the Limits of Toleration*. Cambridge, MA: The Belknap Press of Harvard University Press, 2017.

Bejczy, István. "Tolerantia: A Medieval Concept." *Journal of the History of Ideas* 58, no. 3 (1997): 365–84.

Bejczy, István, ed. *Virtue Ethics in the Middle Ages. Commentaries on Aristotle's Nicomachean Ethics, 1200–1500*. Leiden and Boston: Brill, 2008.

Bloom, Allan. *The Closing of the American Mind*. New York: Simon & Schuster, 1987.

Bonhoeffer, Dietrich. "Essay about Protestantism in the United States of America, August 1939." In *Theological Education Underground, 1937–1940*, 15: 438–62. Dietrich Bonhoeffer Works. Minneapolis: Fortress Press, 2012.

Borradori, Giovanna. *Philosophy in a Time of Terror: Dialogues with Jürgen Habermas and Jacques Derrida*. Chicago: University of Chicago Press, 2003.

Bowlin, John. "Augustine on Justifying Coercion." *The Annual of the Society of Christian Ethics* 17 (1997): 49–70.

Bowlin, John. "Tolerance Among the Fathers." *Journal of the Society of Christian Ethics* 26, no. 1 (2006): 3–36.

Bowlin, John. "Augustine Counting Virtues." *Augustinian Studies* 41, no. 1 (2010): 277–300.

Bowlin, John. *Tolerance Among the Virtues*. Princeton and Oxford: Princeton University Press, 2016.

Bretherton, Luke. *Hospitality as Holiness: Christian Witness Amid Moral Diversity*. Farnham: Ashgate, 2006.

Bretherton, Luke. *Christ and the Common Life. Political Theology and the Case for Democracy*. Grand Rapids: Eerdmans, 2019.

Broder, Henryk M. *Kritik der reinen Toleranz*. Berlin: Pantheon, 2008.

Brown, Wendy. *Regulating Aversion: Tolerance in the Age of Identity and Empire*. Princeton: Princeton University Press, 2009.

Brundage, James A. "Prostitution in Medieval Canon Law." *Signs* 1, no. 4 (1976): 825–45.

Budde, Kerstin. "Unreasonable or Evil?" In *Evil in Contemporary Political Theory*, edited by Bruce Haddock, Peri Roberts, and Peter Sutch, 81–100. Edinburgh: Edinburgh University Press, 2011.

Burchill-Limb, K.-Y. "The Actuality of Augustine's Distinction between Uti and Frui." *Augustiniana* 56, no. 1–2 (2006): 183–97.

Burke, Edmund. *A Letter from the Right Hon. Edmund Burke, M.P., to Sir Hercules Langrishe on the Subject of Roman Catholics of Ireland*. London: J. Derrett, 1792.

Burke, Edmund. *Reflections on the French Revolution*. London: J.M. Dent & Sons, 1955.

Burnell, Peter J. *The Augustinian Person*. Washington, DC: Catholic University of America Press, 2005.

Burt, Daniel X. "Friendly Persuasion: Augustine on Religious Toleration." *American Catholic Philosophical Quarterly* 74, no. 1 (1990): 63–76.

Calvin, John. *Calvini opera quae supersunt omnia* [abbreviated CO, volume and page]. Edited by Wilhelm Baum, Eduard Cunitz, and Eduard Reuss. 59 vols. Corpus Reformatorum, vols 29–87.

Camus, Albert. *The Rebel*. Translated by Anthony Bower. New York: Vintage Books, 1956.

Carson, D.A., *The Intolerance of Tolerance*. Grand Rapids: Eerdmans, 2012.

Castellio, Sebastian. *Concerning Heretics*. New York: Octagon Books, 1965.

Cavanaugh, William T. *The Myth of Religious Violence: Secular Ideology and the Roots of Modern Conflict*. Oxford: Oxford University Press, 2009.

Chambers, Katherin. "Augustine on Justice: A Reconsideration of City of God, Book 19." *Political Theology* 19, no. 5 (2018): 382–96.

Chaplin, Jonathan. "How Much Cultural and Religious Pluralism Can Liberalism Tolerate?" In *Liberalism, Multiculturalism and Toleration*, edited by John Horton, 32–49. New York: Palgrave, 1993.

Chaplin, Jonathan. "Rejecting Neutrality, Respecting Diversity. From 'Liberal Pluralism' to Christian Pluralism." *Christian Scholar's Review* 35 (2006): 143–76.

Chaplin, Jonathan. *Herman Dooyeweerd: Christian Philosopher of State and Civil Society*. Notre Dame: University of Notre Dame Press, 2011.

Chaplin, Jonathan. "An Institutionalist Reframing of the Religion and Public Reason Debate." *Social Theory and Practice* 47, no. 3 (2021): 589–602.

Chaput, Charles J. "Religious Tolerance and the Common Good." *First Things*, May 23, 2007. https://www.firstthings.com/web-exclusives/2007/05/religious-tolerance-and-the-common-good.

Churchill, Paul Robert. "On the Difference between Non-Moral and Moral Concepts of Tolerance: The Case for Toleration as an Individual Virtue." In *Philosophy, Religion, and the Question of Intolerance*, edited by Mehdi Amin Razavi and David Ambuel, 189–211. Albany, NY: State University of New York Press, 1997.

Clair, Joseph. *Discerning the Good in the Letters and Sermons of Augustine*. Oxford: Oxford University Press, 2016.

Coffey, John. *Persecution and Toleration in Protestant England 1558–1689*. Harlow: Pearson Education, 2000.

Cohen, Andrew Jason. *Toleration*. Cambridge: Polity Press, 2014.

Condorcet, Marquis de. *Outlines of an Historical View of the Progress of the Human Mind*. London: J. Johnson, 1795.

Connolly, William E. *The Ethos of Pluralization*. Minneapolis: University of Minnesota Press, 1995.

Connolly, William E. *The Augustinian Imperative: A Reflection on the Politics of Morality*. Lanham, MD: Rowman & Littlefield Publishers, 2002.

Connolly, William E. *Pluralism*. Durham and London: Duke University Press, 2005.

Conway, Trudy D. *Cross-Cultural Dialogue on the Virtues: The Contribution of Fethullah Gülen*. Dordrecht: Springer, 2014.

Conyers, A.J. *The Long Truce: How Toleration Made the World Safe for Power and Profit*. Waco: Baylor University Press, 2009.

Creppell, Ingrid. *Toleration and Identity. Foundations in Early Modern Thought*. New York and London: Routledge, 2003.

Creppell, Ingrid. "Toleration, Politics, and the Role of Mutuality." In *Toleration and Its Limits*, edited by Melissa Williams and Jeremy Waldron, 315–59. NOMOS, XLVIII. New York and London: New York University Press, 2008.

Crisp, Roger. "Communitarianism and Toleration." In *Toleration: Philosophy and Practice*, edited by Peter Nicholson and John Horton, 108–25. Aldershot: Averbury, 1992.

Curley, Edwin. "Sebastian Castellio's Erasmian Liberalism." *Philosophical Topics* 31, nos 1–2 (2003): 47–73.

Digeser, Elizabeth D. *The Making of a Christian Empire. Lactancius and Rome*. Ithaca, NY: Cornell University Press, 2000.

Dixon, C. Scott. *Contesting the Reformation*. Oxford: Wiley-Blackwell, 2012.

Dobbernack, Jan, and Tariq Modood. "The Acceptance of Cultural Diversity in Europe: Theoretical Perspectives and Contemporary Developments." In *Tolerance, Intolerance and Respect*, edited by Jan Dobbernack and Tariq Modood, 1–20. Basingstoke: Palgrave Macmillan, 2013.

Dodaro, Robert. "Note sulla presenza della questione pelagiana nel De civitate Dei." In *Il De civitate Dei. L'opera, le interpretazioni, l'influsso*, edited by Elena Cavalcanti, 245–70. Rome: Herder, 1996.

Dodaro, Robert. "Political and Theological Virtues in Augustine, Letter 155 to Macedonius." *Augustiniana* 54, no. 1 (2004): 431–74.

Dodaro, Robert. "Between the Two Cities: Political Action in Augustine of Hippo." In *Augustine and Politics*, edited by John Doody, Kevin L. Hughes, and Kim Paffenroth, 99–116. Lanham, MD: Lexington Books, 2005.

Domínguez, Juan Pablo. "Introduction: Religious Toleration in the Age of Enlightenment." *History of European Ideas* 43, no. 4 (2017): 273–87.

Dougherty, Richard J. "St. Augustine and the Problem of Political Ethics in The City of God." In *Augustine's Political Thought*, edited by Richard J. Dougherty, 13–35. Rochester, NY: University of Rochester Press, 2019.

Drew, William. D.W. *Griffith's Intolerance: Its Genesis and Its Vision*. Jefferson, NC: McFarland, 1986.

Dunn, Geoffrey D. "Discipline, Coercion, and Correction. Augustine against the Violence of the Donatists in Epistula 185." *Scrinium* 13 (2017): 114–30.

Dunn, John. *The Political Thought of John Locke: An Historical Account of the Argument of the "Two Treatises of Government."* Cambridge: Cambridge University Press, 1969.

Ebbeler, Jennifer V. *Disciplining Christians. Correction and Community in Augustine's Letters*. Oxford: Oxford University Press, 2012.

Ebbeler, Jennifer V. "Charitable Correction and Ecclesiastical Unity in Augustine's Contra Epistulam Parmeniani." In *The Donatist Schism. Controversy and Contexts*, edited by Richard Miles, 284–96. Liverpool: Liverpool University Press, 2016.

Elshtain, Jean Bethke. "The Life and Work of Christopher Lasch: An American Story." *Salmagundi* 106/7 (1995): 146–61.

Elshtain, Jean Bethke. *Augustine and the Limits of Politics*. Notre Dame: University of Notre Dame Press, 1997.

Elshtain, Jean Bethke. "Toleration, Proselytizing, and the Politics of Recognition." In *Religious Pluralism, Globalization, and World Politics*, edited by Thomas Banchoff, 89–104. Oxford: Oxford University Press, 2008.

Erasmus von Rotterdam. "Epistola Ad Paulum Volzium." In *Ausgewählte Schriften*, vol. 1, edited by Werner Welzig, 1–53. Darmstadt: Wissenschaftliche Buchgesellschaft, 1968.

Evans, Gillian R. *Augustine on Evil*. Cambridge: Cambridge University Press, 1990.

Fiala, Andrew. *Tolerance and the Ethical Life*. London and New York: Continuum, 2005.

Figgis, John Neville. *Churches in the Modern State*. London: Longmans, Green and Co., 1913.

Finkielkraut, Alain. *Une voix vient de l'autre rive*. Paris: Gallimard, 2000.

Finnis, John. *Moral Absolutes. Tradition, Revision, and Truth*. Washington, DC: The Catholic University of America Press, 1991.

Finnis, John. *Aquinas: Moral, Political and Legal Theory*. Oxford: Oxford University Press, 1998.

Fitzmaurice, Deborah. "Autonomy as a Good: Liberalism, Autonomy and Toleration." *The Journal of Political Philosophy* 1, no. 1 (1993): 1–16.

Fletcher, George P. "The Case for Tolerance." *Social Philosophy and Policy* 13, no. 1 (1996): 229–39.

Fletcher, George P. "The Instability of Tolerance." In *Toleration: An Elusive Virtue*, edited by David Heyd, 158–72. Princeton: Princeton University Press, 1998.

Fontanier, Jean-Michel. "Sur l'analogie Augustinienne Honestum/Utile//Frui/Uti." *Revue Des Sciences Philosophiques et Théologiques* 84, no. 4 (2000): 635–42.

Forst, Rainer. *Toleration in Conflict: Past and Present*. Cambridge: Cambridge University Press, 2013.

Forster, Greg. *John Locke's Politics of Moral Consensus*. Cambridge: Cambridge University Press, 2005.

Foucault, Michel. "The Gray Mornings of Tolerance." In *Aesthetics, Method, and Epistemology*, edited by James D. Faubion, 229–31. New York: New Press, 1998.

Frankel, Steven, and Martin D. Yaffe, eds. *Civil Religion in Modern Political Philosophy. Machiavelli to Tocqueville*. University Park, PA: The Pennsylvania State University Press, 2020.

Fredriksen, Paula. *Augustine and the Jews. A Christian Defense of Jews and Judaism*. New York: Doubleday, 2008.

Fuentes, Eduardo. "The Power to Tolerate." *Trans/Form/Ação* 45, no. 3 (2022): 65–84.

Furedi, Frank. *On Tolerance: A Defence of Moral Independence.* London: Bloomsbury, 2011.

Gadamer, Hans-Georg. "The Idea of Tolerance 1782–1982." In *Praise of Theory. Speeches and Essays*, translated by Chris Dawson, 84–100. New Haven and London: Yale University Press, 1998.

Galeotti, Anna Elisabetta. *Toleration as Recognition.* Cambridge: Cambridge University Press, 2002.

Galston, William. *Liberal Pluralism: The Implications of Value Pluralism for Political Theory and Practice.* Cambridge: Cambridge University Press, 2002.

Galston, William. "Moral Pluralism and Liberal Democracy: Isaiah Berlin's Heterodox Liberalism." In *Political Philosophy in the Twentieth Century. Authors and Arguments*, edited by Catherine H. Zuckert, 154–69. Cambridge: Cambridge University Press, 2011.

G.I.G. "Tolerance." *Herald of Truth* (Geneva, NY), August 30, 1834.

Goethe, Wolfgang. *Maximen und Reflexionen.* VI. Werke. Frankfurt: Insel, 1981.

Goldie, Mark. "The Theory of Religious Intolerance in Restoration England." In *From Persecution to Toleration. The Glorious Revolution and Religion in England*, edited by Ole Peter Grell, Jonathan Israel, and Nicholas Tyacke, 331–68. Oxford: Clarendon Press, 1991.

Graham, Gordon. "Toleration and the Idea of Progress." In *Philosophy, Religion, and the Question of Intolerance*, edited by Mehdi Amin Razavi and David Ambuel, 125–33. New York: State University of New York Press, 1997.

Grant, Ruth W. "The Rosseauan Revolution and the Problem of Evil." In *Naming Evil, Judging Evil*, edited by Ruth W. Grant, 53–74. Chicago and London: The University of Chicago Press, 2006.

Gray, John. *Enlightenment's Wake: Politics and Culture at the Close of the Modern Age.* New York and London: Routledge, 2007.

Gray, John. *The Silence of Animals. Of Progress and Other Modern Myths.* New York: Farrar, Straus, and Giroux, 2013.

Green, Leslie. "On Being Tolerated." In *The Legacy of H.L.A. Hart. Legal, Political, and Moral Philosophy*, edited by Matthew H. Kramer, Claire Grant, Ben Colburn, and Antony Hatzistavrou, 225–38. Oxford: Oxford University Press, 2008.

Gregory, Eric. *Politics and the Order of Love. An Augustinian Ethic of Democratic Citizenship.* Chicago: The University of Chicago Press, 2008.

Griffioen, Sander. "Is a Pluralist Ethos Possible?" *Philosophia Reformata* 59, no. 1 (1994): 11–25.

Griffiths, Paul J. *Problems of Religious Diversity.* Oxford: Blackwell, 2001.

Griffiths, Paul J. *Lying. An Augustinian Theology of Duplicity.* Grand Rapids: Brazos Press, 2004.

Habermas, Jürgen. *Wann müssen wir tolerant sein? Über die Konkurrenz von Weltbildern, Werten und Theorien. Festvortrag zum Leibniztag der Berlin-Brandenburgischen Akademie der Wissenschaften am 29. Juni 2002.* Veröff. v. der Berlin-Brandenburgischen Akademie der Wissenschaften, 2002.

Habermas, Jürgen. "Intolerance and Discrimination." *International Journal of Constitutional Law* 1, no. 1 (2003): 2–12.

Habermas, Jürgen. *Between Naturalism and Religion. Philosophical Essays.* Cambridge: Polity, 2008.

Haefeli, Evan. "The Problem with the History of Toleration." In *Politics of Religious Freedom*, edited by Winnifried Fallers Sullivan, Elizabeth Shakman Hurd, Saba Mahmood, and Peter G. Danchin, 105–44. Chicago and London: The University of Chicago Press, 2015.

Haidt, Jonathan. *The Righteous Mind. Why Good People Are Divided by Politics and Religion.* New York: Vintage, 2013.

Hamburger, Joseph. *John Stuart Mill on Liberty and Control.* Princeton and Oxford: Princeton University Press, 1999.

Harding, Brian. *Augustine and Roman Virtue.* London: Bloomsbury, 2008.

Harel, Alon. "The Boundaries of Justifiable Tolerance: A Liberal Perspective." In *Toleration. An Elusive Virtue,* edited by David Heyd, 114–26. Princeton: Princeton University Press, 1996.

Harrison, Geoffrey. "Relativism and Tolerance." *Ethics* 86, no. 2 (1976): 122–35.

Harrison, Jonathan. "Utilitarianism and Toleration." *Philosophy* 62, no. 242 (1987): 421–34.

Haslam, Nick. "Concept Creep. Psychology's Expanding Notions of Harm and Their Moral Basis." In *The Social Psychology of Morality,* edited by Joseph P. Forgas, Lee Jussim, and Paul A.M. Van Lange, 293–319. New York and London: Routledge, 2016.

Hauerwas, Stanley. "Seeing Darkness, Hearing Silence. Augustine's Account of Evil." In *Naming Evil, Judging Evil,* edited by Ruth W. Grant, 35–52. Chicago and London: The University of Chicago Press, 2006.

Hauerwas, Stanley. "Hauerwas on 'Hauerwas and the Law': Trying to Have Something to Say." *Law and Contemporary Problems* 75, no. 4 (2012): 233–51.

Hayek, Friedrich. "Individual and Collective Aims." In *On Toleration,* edited by Susan Mendus and David Edwards, 35–47. Oxford: Oxford University Press, 1987.

Hazard, Paul. *The Crisis of the European Mind 1680–1715.* New York: New York Review Books, 2013.

Hellemans, Staf. "Pillarization ('Verzuiling'). On Organized 'Self-Contained Worlds' in the Modern World." *The American Sociologist* 51 (2020): 124–47.

Herdt, Jennifer A. "Locke, Martyrdom, and the Disciplinary Power of the Church." *Journal of the Society of Christian Ethics* 23, no. 2 (2003): 19–35.

Heyd, David. "Introduction." In *Toleration. An Elusive Virtue,* edited by David Heyd, 3–18. Princeton: Princeton University Press, 1996.

Heyd, David. "Education to Toleration: Some Philosophical Obstacles and Their Resolution." In *The Culture of Toleration in Diverse Societies. Reasonable Tolerance,* edited by Catriona McKinnon and Dario Castiglione, 196–208. Manchester and New York: Manchester University Press, 2003.

Heyd, David. "Is Toleration a Political Virtue?" In *Toleration and Its Limits,* edited by Jeremy Waldron and Melissa Williams, 171–94. NOMOS, XLVIII. New York and London: New York University Press, 2008.

Heyking, John von. *Augustine and Politics as Longing in the World.* Columbia: University of Missouri Press, 2001.

Hirschman, Albert O. *The Passions and the Interests. Political Arguments for Capitalism before Its Triumph.* Princeton: Princeton University Press, 1997.

Hobbes, Thomas. *Leviathan.* Edited by Noel Malcolm. Oxford: Clarendon Press, 2014.

Horkheimer, Max. *Eclipse of Reason.* New York and London: Continuum, 2004.

Horton, John. "Toleration, Morality, and Harm." In *Aspects of Toleration: Philosophical Studies,* edited by John Horton and Susan Mendus, 113–35. London: Methuen, 1985.

Horton, John. "Why the Traditional Conception of Toleration Still Matters." *Critical Review of International Social and Political Philosophy* 14, no. 3 (2011): 289–305.

Howard, Thomas Albert. *Broken Altars. Secularist Violence in Modern History.* New Haven and London: Yale University Press, 2025.

Hunter, James Davison. *Culture Wars. The Struggle to Define America.* New York: Basic Books, 1991.

Israel, Jonathan. *Radical Enlightenment. Philosophy and the Making of Modernity 1650–1750.* Oxford: Oxford University Press, 2001.

Ivanhoe, Philip J. “Pluralism, Toleration, and Ethical Promiscuity.” *Journal of Religious Ethics* 37, no. 2 (2009): 311–29.

Jakobsen, Janet R., and Ann Pellegrini. *Love the Sin: Sexual Regulation and the Limits of Religious Tolerance.* New York and London: NYU Press, 2003.

Jefferson, Thomas. “Notes on Locke and Shaftesbury.” In *The Papers of Thomas Jefferson. Volume 1, 1760–1776*, edited by Julian P. Boyd, 544–50. Princeton: Princeton University Press, 1950.

Jenkins, Philip. *The Lost History of Christianity: The Thousand-Year Golden Age of the Church—and How It Died.* New York: HarperOne, 2008.

Johnson, Kristen Deede. *Theology, Political Theory, and Pluralism: Beyond Tolerance and Difference.* Cambridge: Cambridge University Press, 2007.

Joly, Robert. “L’intolérance de saint Augustin, doctrine ou attitude?” In *Hommage à Marcel Renard, I* 101: 493–500. Collection Latomus. Brussels: Latomus, 1969.

Jones, Peter. “Toleration, Recognition and Identity.” *The Journal of Political Philosophy* 14, no. 2 (2006): 123–43.

Jones, Peter. “Toleration, Recognition and Accommodation.” *European Journal of Philosophy* 23, no. 3 (2012): 542–63.

Kant, Immanuel. “Idea for a Universal History with a Cosmopolitan Purpose.” In *Kant: Political Writings*, edited by H.S. Reiss, 41–53. Cambridge: Cambridge University Press, 1991.

Kant, Immanuel. *Practical Philosophy.* Cambridge: Cambridge University Press, 1999.

Kant, Immanuel. *Critique of Practical Reason.* Translated by Mary Gregor. Cambridge Texts in the History of Philosophy. Cambridge: Cambridge University Press, 2015.

Kaplan, Benjamin. *Divided by Faith. Religious Conflict and the Practice of Toleration in Early Modern Europe.* Cambridge, MA: The Belknap Press of Harvard University Press, 2007.

Karpov, Vyacheslav, and Manfred Svensson, eds. *Secularization, Desecularization, and Toleration. Cross-Disciplinary Challenges to a Modern Myth.* New York: Palgrave Macmillan, 2020.

Kaufman, Peter Iver. “Augustine, Evil and Donatism: Sin and Sanctity before the Pelagian Controversy.” *Theological Studies* 51, no. 1 (1990): 115–26.

Kaufman, Peter Iver. *Incorrectly Political. Augustine and Thomas More.* Notre Dame: University of Notre Dame Press, 2007.

Kelly-Woessner, April. “The New Left and Political Intolerance.” In *The End of the Experiment. The Rise of Cultural Elites and the Decline of America’s Civic Culture*, edited by Stanley Rothman, 187–200. New Brunswick: Transaction Publishers, 2015.

Keys, Mary M. *Pride, Politics, and Humility in Augustine’s City of God.* Cambridge: Cambridge University Press, 2022.

Keys, Mary M., and Colleen E. Mitchell. “Patristic Era. Augustine’s Constitutionalism: Citizenship, Common Good, and Consent.” In *Christianity and Constitutionalism*, edited by Nicholas Aroney and Ian Leigh, 91–107. Oxford: Oxford University Press, 2022.

King, Preston. *Toleration.* 2nd edn. London: Frank Cass, 1998.

Königs, Peter. “The Simplicity of Toleration.” *Critical Review of International Social and Political Philosophy* 24, no. 1 (2021): 5–24.

Kreider, Alan. *The Patient Ferment of the Early Church. The Improbable Rise of Christianity in the Roman Empire.* Grand Rapids: Baker Academic, 2016.

Kries, Douglas. “Rousseau and the Problem of Religious Toleration.” In *Piety and Humanity. Essays on Religion and Early Modern Political Philosophy*, edited by Douglas Kries, 259–86. Lanham, MD: Rowman & Littlefield Publishers, 1997.

Krom, Michael P. "Modern Liberalism and Pride. An Augustinian Perspective." *Journal of Religious Ethics* 35, no. 3 (2007): 453–77.

Kukathas, Chandran. *Tolerating the Intolerable*. No. 33. Papers on Parliament. Parliament of Australia, 1999.

Kukathas, Chandran. *The Liberal Archipelago. A Theory of Diversity and Freedom*. Oxford: Oxford University Press, 2003.

Kundera, Milan. *A Kidnapped West. The Tragedy of Central Europe*. Translated by Linda Asher and Edmund White. London: Faber, 2023.

Kymlicka, Will. "Two Models of Pluralism and Tolerance." *Analyse & Kritik* 14, no. 1 (1992): 33–56.

Laborde, Cécile. *Liberalism's Religion*. Cambridge, MA: Harvard University Press, 2017.

Laegaard, Sune. "State Toleration, Religious Recognition and Equality." In *Tolerance, Intolerance and Respect. Hard to Accept?*, edited by Tariq Modood and Jan Dobbernack, 52–76. Basingstoke: Palgrave Macmillan, 2013.

Lamb, Michael. *A Commonwealth of Hope. Augustine's Political Thought*. Princeton: Princeton University Press, 2022.

Lamirande, Emilien. *Church, State and Toleration. An Intriguing Change of Mind in Augustine*. The Saint Augustine Lecture 1974. Villanova: Villanova University Press, 1975.

Lasch, Christopher. *Haven in a Heartless World. The Family Besieged*. New York: Basic Books, 1979.

Lasch, Christopher. *The True and Only Heaven. Progress and Its Critics*. New York and London: W. W. Norton, 1991.

Leader, Sheldon. "Three Faces of Toleration in a Democracy." *The Journal of Political Philosophy* 4, no. 1 (1996): 45–67.

Leiter, Brian. *Why Tolerate Religion?* Princeton and Oxford: Princeton University Press, 2013.

Levine, Alan. "Introduction: The Prehistory of Toleration and Varieties of Skepticism." In *Early Modern Skepticism and the Origins of Toleration*, edited by Alan Levine, 1–20. Lanham: Lexington Books, 1999.

Levy, Jacob T. *Rationalism, Pluralism, and Freedom*. Oxford: Oxford University Press, 2014.

Lilla, Mark. *The Stillborn God: Religion, Politics, and the Modern West*. New York: Knopf, 2008.

Lim, Paul C.-H. "Owen the Polemicist." In *T&T Clark Handbook of John Owen*, edited by Crawford Gribben and John W. Tweeddale, 197–222. London and New York: T&T Clark, 2022.

Limborch, Philip van. *History of the Inquisition*. London: Simpkin and Marshall, 1816.

Locke, John. "A Second Letter Concerning Toleration." In *Works in Ten Volumes*, vol.6. Londres: W. Otridge et al., 1812.

Locke, John. *Epistola de Tolerantia/A Letter on Toleration*. Edited by Raymond Klibansky. Translated by J.W. Gough. Oxford: Oxford University Press, 1968.

Locke, John. *An Essay Concerning Human Understanding*. Edited by P. H. Nidditch. Oxford: Clarendon Press, 1975.

Locke, John. *The Correspondence of John Locke*. Edited by E.S. de Beer. 8 vols. Oxford: Oxford University Press, 1976.

Locke, John. *Political Essays*. Edited by Mark Goldie. Cambridge: Cambridge University Press, 1997.

Locke, John. "Critical Notes upon Edward Stillingfleet's Mischief and Unreasonableness of Separation." In *John Locke: Writings on Religion*, edited by Victor Nuovo, 73–79. Oxford: Oxford University Press, 2002.

Locke, John. *An Essay Concerning Toleration: And Other Writings on Law and Politics, 1667–1683*. Edited by J.R. Milton and Philip Milton. Oxford: Oxford University Press, 2006.

Lombardini, John. "Stoicism and the Virtue of Toleration." *History of Political Thought* 36, no. 4 (2015): 643–69.
Lucca, Ptolemy of (with portions attributed to Thomas Aquinas). *On the Government of Rulers/De Regimine Principum*. Translated by James M. Blythe. Philadelphia: University of Pennsylvania Press, 1997.
Macedo, Stephen. "Transformative Constitutionalism and the Case of Religion: Defending the Moderate Hegemony of Liberalism." *Political Theory* 26, no. 1 (1998): 56–80.
MacIntyre, Alasdair. *Ethics and Politics. Selected Essays, Volume 2*. Cambridge: Cambridge University Press, 2006.
Mann, Thomas. *Der Zauberberg*. Stockholm: S. Fischer Verlag, 1954.
Manning, Jason, and Bradley Campbell. *The Rise of Victimhood Culture: Microaggressions, Safe Spaces, and the New Culture Wars*. New York: Palgrave Macmillan, 2018.
Mansuy, Daniel, and Manfred Svensson. "Tolerance." In *The Oxford Guide to the Historical Reception of Augustine*, vol. 3, edited by Karla Pollmann and Willemien Otten, 1815–18. Oxford: Oxford University Press, 2013.
Mara, Gerald M. "Socrates and Liberal Toleration." *Political Theory* 16, no. 3 (1988): 468–95.
Marcel, Gabriel. *Creative Fidelity*. New York: Fordham University Press, 2002.
Marcus Aurelius. *Meditations, Books 1–6*. Translated by Christopher Gill. Clarendon Later Ancient Philosophers. Oxford: Oxford University Press, 2013.
Marcuse, Herbert. "Repressive Tolerance." In *A Critique of Pure Tolerance*, edited by Robert Paul Wolff, Barrington Moore, and Herbert Marcuse. Boston: Beacon Press, 1965.
Maritain, Jacques. *Man and the State*. Washington, DC: The Catholic University of America Press, 1998.
Markus, Robert. *Saeculum: History and Society in the Age of St. Augustine*. Cambridge: Cambridge University Press, 1970.
Markus, Robert A. *Christianity and the Secular*. Notre Dame: University of Notre Dame Press, 2006.
Marshall, John. *John Locke: Resistance, Religion and Responsibility*. Cambridge: Cambridge University Press, 1994.
Marshall, John. "Locke, Socinianism, 'Socinianism', Unitarianism." In *English Philosophy in the Age of Locke*, edited by M.A. Stewart, 111–82. Oxford: Clarendon Press, 2000.
Mathewes, Charles. *Evil and the Augustinian Tradition*. Cambridge: Cambridge University Press, 2001.
Mathewes, Charles. *The Republic of Grace: Augustinian Thoughts for Dark Times*. Grand Rapids: Eerdmans, 2010.
Mathewes, Charles. *Understanding Religious Ethics*. Oxford: Wiley-Blackwell, 2010.
Mattison, William. "Jesus' Prohibition of Anger (Mt 5:22): The Person/Sin Distinction from Augustine to Aquinas." *Theological Studies* 68, no. 4 (2007): 839–64.
McConnell, Michael W. "Edmund Burke's Tolerant Establishment." In *Religious Liberty in Western Thought*, edited by Noel B. Reynolds and W. Cole Durham, 203–44. Grand Rapids: Eerdmans, 1996.
Mendus, Susan. *Toleration and the Limits of Liberalism*. London: Macmillan, 1989.
Merleau-Ponty, Maurice. *Humanism and Terror*. Translated by John O'Neill. New York: Routledge, 2023.
Michéa, Jean-Claude. *The Realm of Lesser Evil*. Cambridge: Polity, 2009.
Milbank, John. "Darkness and Silence: Evil and the Western Legacy." In *Evil in Contemporary Political Theory*, edited by Peter Sutch, Peri Roberts, and Bruce Haddock, 10–43. Edinburgh: Edinburgh University Press, 2011.

Miles, Richard, ed. *The Donatist Schism: Controversy and Contexts*. Liverpool: Liverpool University Press, 2016.

Mill, John Stuart. "On Liberty." In *Essays on Politics and Society*, 18: 213–310. The Collected Works of John Stuart Mill. Toronto and Buffalo: University of Toronto Press, 1977.

Mitchell, Joshua. *American Awakening: Identity Politics and Other Afflictions of Our Time*. New York and London: Encounter Books, 2020.

Montesquieu, Charles de Secondat. *The Spirit of the Laws*. Cambridge: Cambridge University Press, 1989.

Mouffe, Chantal. *The Democratic Paradox*. London and New York: Verso, 2000.

Murphy, Andrew R. "Tolerance, Toleration, and the Liberal Tradition." *Polity* 29, no. 4 (1997): 593–623.

Murphy, Andrew R. *Conscience and Community: Revisiting Toleration and Religious Dissent in Early Modern England and America*. University Park: Pennsylvania State University Press, 2001.

Nagel, Thomas. "Moral Conflict and Political Legitimacy." *Philosophy and Public Affairs* 16, no. 3 (1987): 215–40.

Nederman, Cary. *Worlds of Difference: European Discourses of Toleration c. 1100–c. 1550*. University Park, PA: The Pennsylvania State University Press, 2000.

Nederman, Cary. "Toleration in a New Key: Historical and Global Perspectives." *Critical Review of International Social and Political Philosophy* 14, no. 3 (2011): 349–61.

Nederman, Cary, and John Christian Laursen, eds. *Difference and Dissent: Theories of Toleration in Medieval and Early Modern Europe*. Lanham, MD: Rowman & Littlefield, 1996.

Newey, Glen. "Toleration, Politics, and the Role of Murality." In *Toleration and Its Limits*, edited by Melissa Williams and Jeremy Waldron, 360–91. NOMOS, XLVIII. New York and London: New York University Press, 2008.

Newey, Glen. *Toleration in Political Conflict*. Cambridge: Cambridge University Press, 2013.

Niebuhr, Gustav. *Beyond Tolerance. How People Across America Are Building Bridges Between Faiths*. New York: Penguin Books, 2008.

Niebuhr, Reinhold. "The Relevance of Christian Realism: An Orientation." In *Reinhold Niebuhr on Politics*, edited by Harry Davis and Robert Good, 64–69. New York: Scribner's, 1960.

Nietzsche, Friedrich. *Antichrist*. Munich: DTV, 1888.

Nietzsche, Friedrich. *Nachgelassene Fragmente 1880–1882*. Munich: DTV, 1988.

Nietzsche, Friedrich. *Nachgelassene Fragmente 1885–1887*. Munich: DTV, 1988.

Nietzsche, Friedrich. *On the Genealogy of Morals*. Oxford: Oxford University Press, 1996.

Noce, Augusto del. *The Crisis of Modernity*. Translated by Carlo Lancellotti. Montreal & Kingston: McGill-Queen's University Press, 2014.

Nussbaum, Martha. *Liberty of Conscience: In Defense of America's Tradition of Religious Equality*. New York: Basic Books, 2008.

O'Donovan, Oliver. "Reflections on Pluralism." *The Princeton Seminary Bulletin* 29 (2008): 54–66.

O'Donovan, Oliver. "Book 2. Augustine on Religion without Morality." In *The Cambridge Companion to Augustine's City of God*, edited by David Vincent Meconi, 39–52. Cambridge: Cambridge University Press, 2021.

Owen, John. *The Works of John Owen*, edited by William H. Goold. Edinburgh: T&T Clark, 1850–1862.

Paine, Thomas. *Rights of Man, Common Sense, and Other Political Writings*. Oxford: Oxford University Press, 2008.

Pannenberg, Wolfhart. *Grundlagen der Ethik. Philosophisch-theologische Perspektiven.* Göttingen: Vandenhoeck & Ruprecht, 1996.

Passerin d'Entrèves, Maurizio. "Communitarianism and the Question of Tolerance." *Journal of Social Philosophy* 21, no. 1 (1990): 77–91.

Paul, Darel E. *From Tolerance to Equality. How Elites Brought America to Same-Sex Marriage.* Waco: Baylor University Press, 2018.

Pelikan, Jaroslav. "An Augustinian Dilemma: Augustine's Doctrine of Grace versus Augustine's Doctrine of the Church?" *Augustinian Studies* 18 (1987): 1–29.

Perry, John. "Locke's Accidental Church: The Letter Concerning Toleration and the Christian Witness to the State." *Journal of Church and State* 47, no. 2 (2005): 269–88.

Perry, John. *The Pretenses of Loyalty: Locke, Liberal Theory, and American Political Theology.* Oxford: Oxford University Press, 2011.

Pianalto, Matthew. *On Patience. Reclaiming a Foundational Virtue.* Lanham, MD: Lexington Books, 2016.

Pinkoski, Nathan. "Why Alasdair MacIntyre Is Not a Conservative Post-Liberal." *The Political Science Reviewer* 43, no. 2 (2019): 531–63.

Plato. *Gorgias.* Translated by Robin Waterfield. Oxford: Oxford University Press, 1994.

Popper, Karl. *The Open Society and Its Enemies.* Princeton: Princeton University Press, 2013.

Rather, Dan. "America Is Stuck in the Purgatory of Tolerance." *Time*, November 7, 2017.

Ratzinger, Joseph. *Truth and Tolerance. Christian Belief and World Religions.* Translated by Henry Taylor. San Francisco: Ignatius Press, 2004.

Rawls, John. *A Theory of Justice. Revised Edition.* Cambridge, MA: Belknap Press of Harvard University Press, 1999.

Ricoeur, Paul. "The Erosion of Tolerance and the Resistance of the Intolerable." *Diogenes* 44, no. 176 (1996): 189–201.

Rist, John. "Can the *City of God* Help Us Deconstruct Multiculturalism?" In *Kampf oder Dialog? Begegnung von Kulturen im Horizont von Agustins De ciuitate Dei*, edited by Christof Müller, 17–40. Würzburg: Echter, 2015.

Roberts Ogle, Veronica. *Politics and the Earthly City in Augustine's City of God.* Cambridge: Cambridge University Press, 2021.

Robinson, J.H. *Readings in European History. Vol. 2.* Boston: Ginn, 1906.

Roecklein, Robert J. *Machiavelli and Epicureanism: An Investigation into the Origins of Early Modern Political Thought.* Lanham: Lexington Books, 2012.

Rousseau, Jean-Jacques. *Politics and the Arts. Letter to d'Alambert on the Theatre.* Edited by Allan Bloom. Ithaca, NY: Cornell University Press, 1968.

Rousseau, Jean-Jacques. *The Social Contract and Other Late Political Writings.* Edited by Victor Gourevitch. Cambridge: Cambridge University Press, 1997.

Rousseau, Jean-Jacques. *The Reveries of the Solitary Walker, Botanical Writings, and Letter to Franquières.* Edited by Christopher Kelly. Translated by Charles E. Butterworth, Alexandra Cook, and Terence E. Marshall. The Collected Writings of Rousseau 8. Hanover and London: University Press of New England, 2000.

Russell, Frederick. "'Only Something Good Can Be Evil': The Genesis of Augustine's Secular Ambivalence." *Theological Studies* 51, no. 4 (1990): 698–716.

Ryrie, Alec. *The Age of Hitler and How We Will Survive It.* Londres: Reaktion Books, 2025.

Sabl, Andrew. "'Virtuous to Himself': Pluralistic Democracy and the Toleration of Tolerations." In *Toleration and Its Limits*, edited by Melissa Williams and Jeremy Waldron, 220–42. NOMOS, XLVIII. New York and London: New York University Press, 2008.

Sandel, Michael J. *Democracy's Discontent: America in Search of a Public Philosophy.* Cambridge, MA: Harvard University Press, 1996.

Sandel, Michael J. "Judgemental Toleration." In *Natural Law, Liberalism, and Morality. Contemporary Essays*, edited by Robert P. George, 106–112. Oxford: Clarendon Press, 1996.

Scanlon, T.M. *The Difficulty of Tolerance. Essays in Political Philosophy*. Cambridge: Cambridge University Press, 2003.

Schreiner, Klaus. "'Duldsamkeit' (tolerantia) oder 'Schrecken' (terror).' Reaktionsformen auf Abweichungen von der religiösen Norm, am Beispiel des augustinischen Toleranz- und Gewaltkonzeptes und dessen Rezeption im Mittelalter und in der frühen Neuzeit." In *Religiöse Devianz. Untersuchungen zu sozialen, rechtlichen und theologischen Reaktionen auf religiöse Abweichungen im westlichen und östlichen Mittelalter*, edited by Dieter Simon, 159–210. Frankfurt: Klostermann, 1990.

Schuld, J. Joyce. *Foucault and Augustine. Reconsidering Power and Love*. Notre Dame: University of Notre Dame Press, 2003.

Siep, Ludwig. "Toleranz und Anerkennung bei Kant und im Deutschen Idealismus." In *Toleranz als Ordnungsprinzip? Die moderne Bürgergesellschaft zwischen Offenheit und Selbstaufgabe*, edited by Michael Kahlo and Christoph Enders, 177–93. Paderborn: Mentis, 2007.

Solari, Enzo. "De pace fidei: de la libertad a la tolerancia." *Teología y vida* 53, no. 4 (2012): 439–73.

Solari, Enzo. "Contra la ilusión religiosa fanática y la furia de la destrucción: tolerancia, respeto y reconocimiento en Kant y Hegel." *Tópicos, Revista de Filosofía* 62, no. 1 (2022): 121–64.

Spaemann, Robert. "Postsekuläre Gesellschaft." In *Postsekuläre Gesellschaft. Perspektiven Interdisziplinärer Forschung*, edited by Walter Schweidler, 65–75. Freiburg/München: Verlag Karl Alber, 2007.

Spanneut, Michel. "Le stoïcisme dans l'histoire de la patience chrétienne." *Mélanges de science religieuse* 39, no. 3 (1982): 101–30.

Stegmaier, Werner. "Nietzsches Kritik der Toleranz." In *Toleranz als Ordnungsprinzip? Die moderne Bürgergesellschaft zwischen Offenheit und Selbstaufgabe*, edited by Christoph Enders and Michael Kahlo, 195–206. Paderborn: Mentis, 2007.

Strand, Daniel. "Augustine's Privation, Arendt's Banality." In *Augustine in a Time of Crisis*, edited by Boeslaw Z. Kabala, Ashleen Menchaca-Bagnulo, and Nathan Pinkoski, 409–26. Palgrave Macmillan, 2021.

Strauss, Leo. *Jewish Philosophy and the Crisis of Modernity*. Albany, NY: State University of New York Press, 1997.

Stroumsa, Guy G. "Tertullian on Idolatry and the Limits of Tolerance." In *Tolerance and Intolerance in Early Judaism and Christianity*, edited by Guy G. Stroumsa, 173–84. Cambridge: Cambridge University Press, 1998.

Svensson, Manfred. "A Defensible Conception of Toleration in Aquinas?" *The Thomist* 75, no. 2 (2011): 291–308.

Svensson, Manfred. "John Locke, Liberal Theology, and Toleration." In *Liberale Theologie Heute—Liberal Theology Today*, edited by Jörg Lauster, Ulrich Schmiedel, and Peter Schüz, 99–109. Tübingen: Mohr Siebeck, 2019.

Svensson, Manfred. "A Dirty Word? The Christian Development of the Traditional Conception of Toleration in Augustine, Aquinas, and John Owen." In *Secularization, Desecularization, and Toleration. Cross-Disciplinary Challenges to a Modern Myth*, edited by Manfred Svensson and Vyacheslav Karpov, 43–60. Basingstoke: Palgrave Macmillan, 2020.

Svensson, Manfred. "Beyond Dogmatomachy: Eric Voegelin's Bodinian Understanding of Toleration and Symbolization." *The European Legacy* 26, no. 6 (2021): 587–602.

Svensson, Manfred. "Crucis Tolerantia: John Calvin's Theology and Ethics of Toleration." *Political Theology* 24, no. 2 (2023): 183–99.

Taylor, Charles. *Philosophical Papers: Volume 1, Human Agency and Language*. Cambridge: Cambridge University Press, 1985.

Taylor, Charles. "The Politics of Recognition." In *Multiculturalism: Examining the Politics of Recognition*, edited by Amy Gutmann, 25–73. Princeton: Princeton University Press, 1992.

Tinder, Glenn. *Tolerance: Toward a New Civility*. Amherst: University of Massachusetts Press, 1976.

Tocqueville, Alexis de. *Letters from America*. Translated by Frederick Brown. New York and London: Yale University Press, 2010.

Tollefsen, Christopher. "Institutional Conscience, Corporate Persons, and Hobby Lobby." In *Christianity and the Laws of Conscience. An Introduction*, edited by Helen M. Alvaré and Jeffrey B. Hammond, 395–413. Cambridge: Cambridge University Press, 2021.

Tuckness, Alex. "Rethinking the Intolerant Locke." *American Journal of Political Science* 46, no. 2 (2002): 288–98.

Vaughan, Frederick. *The Tradition of Political Hedonism. From Hobbes to J.S. Mill*. New York: Fordham University Press, 1982.

Verkuyten, Maykel, Kumar Yogeeswaran, and Levi Adelman. "The Negative Implications of Being Tolerated: Tolerance from the Target's Perspective." *Perspectives on Psychological Science* 15, no. 3 (2020): 544–61.

Verkuyten, Maykel, Levi Adelman, Sara Cvetkovska, and Rusi Jaspal. "Coping with Being Tolerated: Trans Experiences." *Psychology of Sexual Orientation and Gender Diversity* 11, no. 1 (2024): 31–41.

Vigo, Alejandro. "Liberalismo, tolerancia y bien." *Anuario de Filosofía Jurídica y Social* 17 (1999): 357–65.

Vinet, Alexander. *Outlines of Philosophy and Literature*. London: Daldy, Isbister & Co., 1877.

Virgil. *Aeneid*. Revised edition. Translated by H. R. Fairclough. Loeb Classical Library. Cambridge, MA: Harvard University Press, 1999.

Voltaire. *Toleration and Other Essays*. Translated by Joseph McCabe. New York and London: G. P. Putnam's Sons, 1912.

Voltaire, M. de. *A Philosophical Dictionary*, 6. London: John and Henry L. Hunt, 1824.

Vos, Pieter. *Longing for the Good Life: Virtue Ethics after Protestantism*. London: T&T Clark, 2020.

Waldron, Jeremy. *God, Locke, and Equality: Christian Foundations in Locke's Political Thought*. Cambridge: Cambridge University Press, 2002.

Waldron, Jeremy. "Toleration and Reasonableness." In *The Culture of Toleration in Diverse Societies. Reasonable Tolerance*, edited by Catriona McKinnon and Dario Castiglione, 13–37. Manchester and New York: Manchester University Press, 2003.

Walsham, Alexandra. *Charitable Hatred. Tolerance and Intolerance in England 1500-1700*. Manchester: Manchester University Press, 2006.

Walzer, Michael. *Thick and Thin. Moral Argument at Home and Abroad*. Notre Dame: University of Notre Dame Press, 1994.

Walzer, Michael. *On Toleration*. New York and London: Yale University Press, 1999.

Washington, George. "Letter to Moses Seixas." In *Sourcebook and Index: Documents That Shaped the American Nation*, edited by Joy Hakim, 92–93. Oxford: Oxford University Press, 2002.

Watson, Thomas. *Discourses on Important and Interesting Subjects, Being the Select Works of the Rev. Thomas Watson. Vol. 1*. Glasgow: Blackie, Fullarton, & Co., 1829.

Webber, Jeremy. "The Generosity of Toleration." In *Recognition versus Self-Determination. Dilemmas of Emancipatory Politics*, edited by Avigail Eisenberg, Andrée Boisselle, and Jeremy Webber, 269–92. Vancouver and Toronto: UBC Press, 2014.

Weithman, Paul. "Toward an Augustinian Liberalism." *Faith and Philosophy* 8, no. 4 (1991): 461–80.

Westerholm, Martin. "On the Structure and Significance of Augustine's Moral Grammar." *Journal of Religious Ethics* 49, no. 4 (2021): 715–38.

Wetzel, James. "Introduction." In *Augustine's City of God: A Critical Guide*, edited by James Wetzel, 1–13. Cambridge: Cambridge University Press, 2012.

Wheeler, Sir Mortimer. *The Virtue of Intolerance*. Lincoln and London: Printed for Birckbeck College by J.W. Ruddock and Sons Ltd, 1957.

Wilken, Robert L. "Religious Pluralism and Early Christian Theology." *Interpretation: A Journal of Bible and Theology* 40, no. 4 (1986): 379–91.

Williams, Bernard. "Toleration: An Impossible Virtue?" In *Toleration: An Elusive Virtue*, edited by David Heyd, 18–27. Princeton: Princeton University Press, 1998.

Williams, Bernard. "Tolerating the Intolerable." In *The Politics of Toleration in Modern Life*, edited by Susan Mendus, 65–76. Edinburgh: Edinburgh University Press, 1999.

Williams, Rowan. "Politics and the Soul: A Reading of the City of God." *Milltown Studies* 19/ 20 (1987): 55–72.

Wolfson, Adam. "What Remains of Toleration." In *The Liberal Tradition in Focus: Problems and New Perspectives*, edited by João Carlos Espada, Marc F. Plattner, and Adam Wolfson, 27–38. New York and Oxford: Lexington Books, 2000.

Wolterstorff, Nicholas. *Justice. Rights and Wrongs*. Princeton and Oxford: Princeton University Press, 2008.

Worden, Blair. "Toleration and the Cromwellian Protectorate." In *Persecution and Toleration*, edited by W.J. Sheils, 199–233. Studies in Church History 21. Oxford: Blackwell, 1984.

Wright, N. T. *After You Believe: Why Christian Character Matters*. New York: HarperOne, 2012.

Zimmermann, Harald, and Alexander Patschovsky, eds. *Toleranz im Mittelalter*. Sigmaringen: J. Thorbecke, 1998.

Žižek, Slavoj. "A Plea for Leninist Intolerance." *Critical Inquiry* 28, no. 2 (2002): 542–66.

Žižek, Slavoj. "Tolerance as an Ideological Category." *Critical Inquiry* 34, no. 4 (2008): 660–82.

Index

For the benefit of digital users, indexed terms that span two pages (e.g., 52–53) may, on occasion, appear on only one of those pages.

Index Locorum

For the benefit of digital users, indexed terms that span two pages (e.g., 52–53) may, on occasion, appear on only one of those pages.

The manufacturer's authorised representative in the EU for product safety is Oxford University Press España S.A. of El Parque Empresarial San Fernando de Henares, Avenida de Castilla, 2 - 28830 Madrid (www.oup.es/en or product.safety@oup.com). OUP España S.A. also acts as importer into Spain of products made by the manufacturer.
Printed and bound by CPI Group (UK) Ltd, Croydon, CR0 4YY
18/09/2026
02219030-0001